HER LADYSHIP'S GIRL

Anwyn Moyle was born in 1918 in a poor Welsh mining village. At the age of sixteen she was sent to London to work as a scullery maid. Her long days of domestic service began at 5 a.m., cleaning grates and lighting fires, then she would scrub floors and polish the house – all for two shillings a week. Things improved when Anwyn secured the position of lady's maid in Belgravia and learned to negotiate the social mores of the privileged classes and keep quiet about her mistress's affairs. She went on to be a proficient cook, keeping a detailed diary of the fine foods that were served 'upstairs'.

HER LADYSHIP'S GIRL

HER LADYSHIP'S GIRL

by

Anwyn Moyle
with John McDonald

Magna Large Print Books
Long Preston, North Yorkshire,
BD23 4ND, England.

British Library Cataloguing in Publication Data.

Moyle, Anwyn
    Her ladyship's girl.

    A catalogue record of this book is
    available from the British Library

    ISBN   978-0-7505-4227-2

First published in Great Britain by
Simon & Schuster UK Ltd., 2014

Published in Large Print 2016 by arrangement with
Simon & Schuster UK Ltd.

Magna Large Print is an imprint of Library Magna Books Ltd.

Printed and bound in Great Britain by
T.J. (International) Ltd., Cornwall, PL28 8RW

Contents

Contents

Chapter One

The big copper in the scullery was bubbling and boiling and steam-hot water was spilling out all over the floor. To make matters worse, the coalman had just delivered a couple of hundredweight of anthracite to the cellar and then gone and trod humpbacked through the overspill with dust-black boots and big size-twelve footprints into the kitchen for a thick slice of bread-and-dripping fresh from the frying pan.

'Oh, God help us!'

It was my first whole day as a scullery maid and I'd only gone and filled the copper up too far. Cook was shrieking with a face like a screaming hyena and I thought she was going to throw me into the big vat, along with the washing and boil me alive. I was only sixteen and had never seen a copper before until yesterday and now it had turned on me like the wicked monster it was. Luckily for me, the London season, such as it was, had started and there was a dinner party upstairs that evening. Food and other flavoury stuff was arriving by bread-van and bicycle and dray-horse and handcart, so Cook didn't have the time to nail me to the scullery door.

'Get that water wiped up!'

I turned off the copper and got down on my hands and knees to clean the water and the coal smears from the floor. People were fussing and flustering all round me, tutting as they wiped their boots and shoes – and I listened to all the voices floating above me. They hummed and buzzed around my head and flew into my ears and out again. Words twanged from the mouths of beefy men all a-bustle and fish-eyed boys fetching in meat and game and grayling – bakers with big hats and long loaves and round sodabreads and trifles and tipsy cakes; grocers with green vegetables and potatoes and fruit and fermented peel; milkmen rattling bottles; victuallers with port and brandy and liqueurs, and the butler bringing wines of different flush and blush up from the cellar, to let them breathe. The kitchen maids were here, there and everywhere and Cook had another part-time helper in from the outside world so she could get everything ready on time. The atmosphere in the kitchen was like bath night in Bedlam.

Upstairs was just as jumpy – all a beehive of bluster, with parlourmaids dusting and polishing and the head butler barking orders and the smell of lavender drifting down and mingling with the odours of cooking and carbolic. Anyone would think it was 1834, not 1934 – apart from the fact that London was a much more modern place these days.

But when I arrived yesterday afternoon, I never knew what I was letting myself in for. The slowness and small-village saunterings of home seemed another lifetime away now, even though only one day had passed. The dark sheep and smiling hills and gentle rain and narrow, winding days ... I wanted to go back – to run back. But I couldn't. My mother told me it would be like this in the beginning that it would seem endless and heartbreaking and full of strangers shouting and clocks ticking and I'd want to cry. But she said I was a strong girl and well able to face the world and make it back down from its bullying. So I put away my silly self-pity and rolled up my sleeves and got on with it.

I knew nothing about London or its society soirees. Food was short in the valleys, what with all the unemployment, and this kind of extravagance seemed sinful to me. They would start with soup of some kind and go on to souffles and then fish and then meat with potatoes and vegetables and then pudding and then savouries like stuffed eggs and oysters and shrimps and sweetbreads and last of all the cheese and coffee. Then the men would go away for port and cigars and some serious conversation, while the women waffled on about what they were reading or the latest production in the West End or whatever scandal was doing the rounds of their social circles.

After the disaster with the washing copper, I had to help the kitchen maids setting out the stuff Cook needed for the dinner party – sieves and spoons and forks and flour and salt and seasoning saucepans and silver dishes and chopping boards and mixing bowls. When it was all set out on the big kitchen table, I mucked in with the maids and peeled potatoes and chopped carrots and washed the utensils as they were used and put them back in place to be used again, then washed them again and replaced them again, until it was all done and time to send the great guzzle of food upstairs to the waiting bigwigs and their wives.

Anything perishable that was left over was put in the refrigerator, which was one of the new-fangled inventions that were available in London to those who could afford them. I wasn't allowed a look upstairs to see the latest styles of the guests, although I would have loved to. I had to wash up the plates and pots that came back down from the banquet, some of it hardly touched after all the work that went into it.

Cook put a lot of what came back into a bag to take home with her, but I managed to stuff a few delicacies into my mouth when she wasn't looking. It was late when all the activity slowed down and the guests sloped off back to wherever they came from and the street outside fell silent – holding its breath.

To say I was exhausted would be like calling the devil a dirty rascal.

A few weeks earlier, after working in a hat shop in Maesteg for a year and walking my legs off to get there and back for ls/6d a week wages, I decided I'd had enough of Wales and wearing out my shoes. I was sixteen and, after working in a few jobs since leaving school at fourteen, I felt all grown up like a woman of the world and not the gormless girl I really was. I'd heard stories about the bright lights of London from people who'd been down there and they told me about the West End and the East End and the North and South Ends too – and wondered which End would suit a *merch gweitio* like me the most. I wouldn't leave off about it until a friend of the family got me the job as a scullery maid, even though I didn't know what a scullery maid was, and I couldn't wait to get there and step out onto the Strand or the Piccadilly Circus or the Soho or the Serpentine. I could see myself shimmying through Berkeley Square with a slicked-back sweetheart on each arm and wearing an haute couture from Coco Chanel, or a cardigan jacket from Elsa Schiaparelli and a French beret by Madame Vionnet on top of my permanent wave – styles I'd only seen in magazines on the occasional table in the Maesteg

13

hat shop. And I knew I'd blend right in with the snazziness of it all.

It was a long trip by train from Wales down to Paddington Station, and I had a set of written instructions how to get myself from there over to Hampstead in the high end of the city. When I emerged from the station, I was nearly knocked over by the size of everything – the sights and sounds and smells and the noise of the traffic and the thickness of the air and the movement coming from all quarters. I'd never seen anything like this before and I was all excited. There were street traders peddling fruit and vegetables and roasted chestnuts and baked potatoes and barrow boys and horse-drawn drays with barrels of beer and newspaper boys calling from street corners and trams and trolleys and big red buses and traffic tooting and people with banners and others with billboards all shouting about something or other.

It was a new world, full of energy and colour and sunny skies and shop windows and nervousness and I thought it would swallow me up – that I'd sink down into the soft wonder of it and never be seen again.

When I got my breath back, I found a red double-decker bus that took me through places with London-sounding names, like Marylebone and Maida Vale, and I got off at Hampstead and followed the written directions to a big house near the huge heath. It was a quiet street, after the madness of the earlier city, and I walked up and knocked on the front door. A snooty-looking man wearing a dark suit answered it.

'Yes?'

'I'm Anwyn, the new scullery maid.'

'Downstairs.'

Then he slammed the door in my face. I looked around and saw a flight of stone steps behind some black railings, leading down to a basement at the side of the house. I hesitated at the top, looking into the lowness of it, after all the earlier expectation. Then I set my foot on the first step and went down. It was half past three in the afternoon and I was ready for a cup of tea and a little lie-down and a chance to catch my breath. But who did I think I was, the Queen of Caerphilly?

A maid in an apron answered the basement door and took me through to the kitchen to see the cook. She grunted some kind of greeting and I was put to work without even having a chance to get my coat off – immediately elbows-deep in a big sink full to overflowing with pots and pans and skillets and stewbowls. They must have been there waiting for me for a week or more because the crud was crusted to them and the water was barely lukewarm. Cook gave me a steel wool pad with some kind of soap inside and

I had to scrub like a sailor to get all the utensils clean. My hands weren't used to this kind of work and they were soon red raw. It was after seven when I finished and in all that time not a single person spoke a civil word to me. The cook came back in while I was sitting at the table and she sprawled herself across the chair opposite. She was a big, burly woman and her face looked like a well-slapped baboon's behind.

'Right! Now you've had an easy start, let's get your work sorted out so you know what's expected.'

She gave me a uniform to wear – not a full uniform, just a grey dress and a white apron and lace cap to cover my hair – and a spare one of each.

'You'll have to wash them every other night to have them ready for the next day.'

She then recited the litany of my duties as a scullery maid – cleaning the stove and raking the grates and doing the washing and helping in the kitchen and scrubbing floors and polishing the steps and beating the carpets. My head was going as numb as a mangle in a frozen field – where did she think we were, Bleak House? Didn't she know those days were over? I stopped listening, because my eyes were closing in my head from the tiredness and I wondered if anyone else was expected to do any work in this place besides me. She gave me some bread and cheese and a cup of milk and then I was allowed to go to my bed. I would have preferred a cup of tea like a civilised person and the cheese and bread tasted like leftovers and I wondered if that's all I'd ever be given to eat – like a lost dog.

'Could I not have a cup of tea?'

'Tea?'

Her face looked even more baboon-like than before and she turned into Mister Bumble the Beadle from the orphanage in *Oliver Twist*.

'What sort of an impudent girl are you?'

'I'm not a girl, I'm nearly seventeen.'

Apparently, scullery maids were normally no older than fourteen when they started and I was long-in-the-tooth at sixteen. But I was still a skivvy.

'And don't you forget it!'

I could tell we weren't going to get along.

When I finally got to my room, which was up four flights of back stairs, right at the top of the house, I found out I was sharing with an Irish colleen called Kathleen. Like me, she was nearly seventeen and had been there for two years and it was her job I was taking over, on account of her being made up to be a parlourmaid. She was a pleasant enough girl and made me feel as welcome as was possible in the little room with two single beds and no heating. The mattresses were thin and thrown on top of iron-sprung beds and we were covered over with two blankets apiece. I couldn't keep my eyes open to chat with Kathleen and find out more about the Bumble Beadle like I wanted to – and soon the soft little paws of sleep came creeping.

I'd only been asleep for five minutes when I was woken again by a tap-tapping on the door. I got out of the thin bed and rubbed the sleep into my eyes and yawned so wide I nearly got lockjaw. There was a young lad of about my age outside and he said his name was Bart, which was short for Bartholomew – but everybody called him Brat. Kathleen was still asleep in the other bed and curled up like a child.

'What time is it, Brat?'

'Five o'clock.'

'Is it that late?'

'In the morning.'

'Lord save us, it's the middle of the night.'

'You don't want to be late on your first day. It's going to be a very busy one.'

An early sun struck the windowpane a glancing blow and poured a gentle glow into the room through a gap in the curtains. It melted over the walls and crept like velvet-silk across the floor. I rinsed my face and under my arms in tepid water in the small washroom on our floor, got into one of the skivvy uniforms that Cook had given me, and made my way down the back stairs, the same way as I came up the night before. The

18

basement was big, with rooms to the left and right of a long hall – the kitchen and the scullery and storerooms for food and coal and a cellar for wine. The gardener went home every day like Cook and none of the live-in maids were yet stirring. I was trying to remember what I was supposed to do first, because there was no one else up to ask and Brat had disappeared somewhere into thin air, like Ariel.

All right, I said to myself, first rake out the range and light the fire ready for Cook. Put the kettle on and get the big copper going. That was a task in itself! I made myself a cup of tea when the water boiled and then went for a mooch around while everyone else was still snoring. There wasn't much to see in the basement, so I sneaked upstairs. Mirrors and paintings lined the walls and there was a chandelier, the likes of which I'd never seen before, in the hallway. There were rooms here and there and everywhere and, I thought, surely they couldn't fit so many into the one house? It didn't look that big from the outside. I didn't know what they were all used for, or why they were needed for only four people.

The floors were covered with thick rich carpets and the windows hung with velvet curtains and the furniture looked like it had come from a prince's palace. There were enough books to fill fifty libraries. I was fond of reading when I was at school – I liked Alexander Carmichael and D. H. Lawrence and the Brothers Grimm and Shakespeare – but I'd never seen as many books as this. I wondered if they'd all been read, or if they were just on the shelves for show.

It was summertime, so they didn't have that many fires burning in the house, but I came across Kathleen raking out and lighting a fire to take the morning chill off for the family when they got out of their beds.

'Morning, Kathleen.'

'Anwyn, what are you doing up here?'

'Mooching around.'

'You better get back down before Cook catches you.'

When I went back, the kitchen maids were there and I helped them with the breakfasts. I had a toasted bun and another cup of tea before Cook arrived – I didn't dare ask her for anything again, in case the Beadle marched me off to the oakum room with a bowl of fly-infested gruel. She came in at about half past eight and soon had me on my knees scrubbing the floors and brushing the stairs and, despite her dour disposition, I stayed cheerful and the morning moved along before I had time to feel sorry for myself. I was in the scullery seeing if the copper was working and starting the wash, when Cook came and called me out in an angry voice. I'd only forgotten to red-polish the front steps and she gave me a shrieking that the whole house must have heard because there would be a lot of guests coming later that day and it wouldn't do at all for the steps to be scruffy.

'See to it straight away!'

So I did.

That's when I went back downstairs and found the copper boiling over and I've already told you about the rest of that day.

Next morning, Bart the Brat woke me at five o'clock again and got me out of the bed where I'd been so safe and sound. I didn't see much of the other servants during that first day, because everything was so manic and full of mayhem. I didn't know who was who or what they did, except for Irish Kathleen. Bart said it would be quieter today after having been thrown in at the deep end yesterday, and I'd be able to get my bearings a bit better and settle in to service as a skivvy. He called me the same as Cook did, but I don't think he meant any insult by it like she did – it was what scullery maids were known as.

The rest of the day passed without a boiling-over or a bungle on my part and I was starving half to death by dinner-time, which was at seven o'clock in the evening for us servants. Cook was gone home from half past six and it was the first chance I had to get to know the other inmates – that's

21

how it seemed to me, like we were prisoners in a private workhouse.

Bart was a trainee gardener. He was seventeen and from Leeds and a likely looker. Then there was Kathleen the parlourmaid, who I already knew – she was a shy type and only said a few words. Mona was a lady's maid and spent most of her time upstairs; she was twenty-one and snooty as a sow's ear. Lilly, the nanny, was about thirty-five; she was a teacher-type and plain in comparison to Mona. She ate with the two children of the house: Lucinda aged seven and Jonathan aged five. I didn't see much of her the whole time I was there because she was always with the kids. The two kitchen maids were Nora, who was nineteen, and Biddy, who was eighteen, and you could tell they liked to have a bit of fun with the boys. There was another upstairs parlourmaid called Fanny, short for Frances, who was in her late twenties and might have been married. She went home in the evenings as well. There was the gardener and general handyman, who was Bart's boss, but over it all was the head butler, who opened the front door to me that first day, then slammed it in my face. His name was Mr Ayres and he looked like Uriah Heep from *David Copperfield*. He always wore an impeccably pressed dark suit, with a white shirt and black tie. He was clean-shaven and spoke like he had a hot potato in his mouth. Mr Ayres was the king of this castle and a man who was not to be messed about with.

We sat talking. Most of the other girls were human enough and I asked if there was any chicken left over from earlier in the day.

'You don't want to touch that.'

'Why not?'

The kitchen maids smirked and said they saw Cook put the arse-end of the chicken over a mantel and let the gas go inside like stuffing. Then she lit it and it flared up like a firework and after that she washed and cooked it. I didn't know what they were talking about and I thought that must be how the London entrepreneurial classes liked to have their poultry prepared.

'It was smelly and slimy.'

'That's why she filled it with gas.'

'To get rid of the pong.'

Which struck me as strange, but I didn't want to show my ignorance by asking stupid questions. So I just took their advice and stayed away from the chicken.

It was pleasant enough having a bit of a chinwag with the other maids and they all mucked in to help me finish my jobs so we could go to bed at the same time. It was gone half past eight when my head hit the pillow and I was spark out for the counting.

The Brat woke me at five every morning. I wasn't sure if he lived in like us maids, or went home every evening with the others. I heard his tap-tapping on the door, like a little bubble of morning memory that rose up and burst on the roof of my brain.

'It's Bart, Anwyn.'

'I know who it is.'

I was so tired and stiff from the few days before that I could hardly move. I washed in tepid water again and went downstairs to start the new day. I was hungry after cleaning and lighting the stove, so I pinched an egg and boiled it and ate it with a cup of tea, before anyone else got out of bed. After doing all the early routine jobs and not seeing a soul, I came back down to the kitchen to help with the breakfasts and I could hear Cook questioning the two kitchen maids about the missing egg. I just kept my head down and stayed out of the way until the dragon went to her lair.

'What's all the fuss about, Nora?'

'She's missing an egg.'

'What? All that *trafferthu* [toil] over an egg?'

'It's one less she'll be able to steal.'

Nora told me that Cook had a coat with deep inside pockets on both sides and every evening she stuffed them with food before going home. She said Cook came from a dodgy London family who were mixed up with toughs and criminal types and it would be dangerous for anyone to dob her in.

After breakfast, I made sure I red-polished

the front step before scrubbing the hall floor – it was long and wide and tiled black and white and, while I was doing it, I noticed someone standing over me. I looked up and saw this well-dressed woman of about thirty-five or so. She was small and nervous-looking and wearing clothes that I'd only seen in magazines.

'And what's your name?'

'Anwyn, Madam.'

She gave me a funny kind of look, like she wasn't sure if I was really a girl, or some nanny goat that had wandered in from the garden. Then she nodded and walked away.

I got on with my scrubbing.

Back downstairs, I put the copper on and made sure not to overfill it this time. Biddy came over to me.

'Listen, anything you want to half-inch, do it before Cook makes her count.'

'When does she do that?'

'Just before she goes home.'

I had my toast and another cup of tea before tackling the rest of the day. There seemed to be even more washing today than yesterday and, even with the wooden dolly, my hands were hurting from the hot steam. Cook came over to me with a frown on her face like a wet Sunday in Llandudno.

'When you're asked, your name is Moyle, not Anwyn.'

'Why?'

'Because skivvies like you don't have first names.'

I was going to tell her I was just as good as she was but then, I was in a strange city, and she might get her dodgy relations to come round and garrotte me with piano wire in the middle of the dark and desperate night.

I decided to keep my eye out for Cook and keep out of her way as much as possible for as long as I was to be the lowest of the lowly in that house.

Later in the day I noticed she was soaking a big boiling ham in vinegar, so I asked Nora what she was up to.

'Apart from when there's a party, she buys meat that's on the turn cheap in the market, then she washes it in vinegar to take the smell out.'

'Why don't she buy fresh meat?'

'God, you are naive, aren't you, Annie!'

Nora laughed. I'd have to be careful what I ate – if the others didn't touch it, then neither would I. I was skinny enough as it was, but I thought to myself I'd fade away to a farthing here. But I didn't want to get sick because I'd been sick before and it wasn't something I wanted to go through again and, as much as I hated the job, I didn't want to be sacked and sent back home, humiliated. I was surprised them upstairs didn't all die from galloping gut-rot, but maybe the rich had better constitutions than the poor.

Cook had all sorts of tricks for fiddling the people she worked for, but it was none of my business and I'd only get shot by a soldier of Diamond Jack Sloane or some other gangster if I didn't keep my nose out. So I did.

Once the washing was on, I helped prepare the vegetables and then it was on to the ironing. My mother's iron at home had to be heated on the fire and it had to be just right – if it was too hot, it would burn through the covering cloth and if it wasn't hot enough, it wouldn't get the wrinkles out. But the one I used here was the latest in electric flat-irons and much easier to use, though it took me a while to get used to it. I saw Bart in the yard later, when I was hanging out the washing.

'Where's your room, Bart?'

'In the basement.'

'And you come all the way up to the top to wake me at five?'

He gave me a wink and I wondered what that meant. You see, despite the fact that I thought of myself as an intellectual, I was really just a wet-behind-the-ears Welsh valley girl with a hankering for fine clothes and didn't know the difference between a nod and a wink. But I soon would.

Other than finding out I didn't have a Christian name any more, the rest of the day went well enough and I now had four friends. I asked the kitchen girls if we could go out for a walk after we finished in the evening.

'If you have the strength left for it, Annie.'

That's what they called me, short for Anwyn. When the day's work was finally done and Cook was gone off home with her coat full of cheese and crusty bread, I was sitting in the kitchen having a little chat with the others. I noticed the Brat paying a lot of attention to Biddy and I knew she had a room close to mine and Kathleen's on the top floor. Nora showed me a hiding place where she and Biddy stored food before Cook did her count. There was bread and eggs and cheese and meat and cake and biscuits – and we could help ourselves if we got peckish before breakfast-time came round in the morning. She put a finger up to her lips and I thought, there's some good people in this place after all.

Like I said, I didn't see much of Lilly the nanny or Mona the lady's maid. Lilly was a jolly kind of woman but Mona was the toffee-nosed type and suited her nickname –Mona the moaner. She called me 'Moyle' like she was the lady of the house and knew I had no Christian name, even though she was a servant, just like me. She wore fashionable clothes and I wondered how she came by that job and I thought it was something I might like to be some day. But there was a long way to go before I got that far above my station.

Kathleen and Nora were right: I was too

tired after the long hard day to go walking and all I wanted to do was fall flat into my little thin bed. On the way there, I noticed Bart slipping into Nora's room and the penny dropped – he paid attention to Biddy in the kitchen so nobody would make the connection between him and Nora. He was only a young dog, but already a sly one. Kathleen was in the room when I got there.

'Listen, Annie, I should tell you ... you'll have to watch out for Mr Harding.'

Harding was the name of the family who owned the house and Mr Harding was the head of that family. I'd not seen him so far.

'Why?'

'He has no respect for women.'

I wondered what she meant by that, but I didn't worry too much about it because I was already asleep before my head even hit the pillow.

I didn't want to get up the next morning; my body felt like it had been beaten with a blackthorn bush. I was in pain from the bun on the top of my head to the nails on the toes of my feet. As time went on, Cook put more and more work my way and I came to realise that she was right: a scullery maid's life was the lowest of the low. I had many bosses, not just the tyrant cook, and all the hardest and dirtiest jobs going – and only two shillings a week in wages, one of which I had to send home for the family. I was working sometimes sixteen hours a day and I only got one afternoon off, on a Sunday. If my mother could've seen me she'd have tut-tutted and rolled her eyes and bit her nails to know what I'd become.

At sixteen, I was still the youngest member of staff and that meant doing what I was told, no matter who was doing the telling. The only good thing about it was that new-fangled, labour-saving devices were coming out all the time and the Harding household was forward-looking enough to try them – things like a washer/wringer and the electric flat-iron and refrigerator and an Electrolux vacuum cleaner. But there was still a lot of scrubbing and scraping and beating carpets over a line and polishing steps and, if anything went wrong, I got the blame and blather – whether it was my fault or not.

Like when Lucinda spilled her watercolour on the stairs – it was supposed to be watercolour but I don't know what else was in it, because it just wouldn't come out. And I had to wet it and dry it and wet it and dry it until the stain was the same colour as the rest of the rug. It took me ages and I got behind with my other jobs and had Cook on my back the whole live-long day after that. It wasn't my fault in the first place, but I got the blunt and badger of it. That kind of thing happened a lot in the house and being called nasty names by some of the staff made me feel bad.

Many's the time I wanted to run out the door and find my way back to my family in Wales. Many's the time I would've cried into my pillow at night if I hadn't been too tired for tears. But I decided not to let it drive me down into the dust, and I knew who I was to myself – even if I was only a skivvy to everyone else.

Chapter Two

Long before I became a skivvy, I was born in Llangynwyd, a mining village in the Llynfi Valley and part of the medieval *cymwd of Tir Iarll* [Earl's Land]. Back in those olden times, the basic unit of land was a *tref* and a *cymwd* was about thirty or forty *trefs*. Even as a young child, I was always interested in the old ways and I read what little I could find about the things people believed in before the Christians came. My grandmother on my father's side knew a lot of stuff that she learned from the elders when she was a young girl. She told me stories from the *Mabinogion* and the *Dynion Mwyn* [The Fair Men] and the *Cymry Gwyddoniad* [spiritual path of the 'cunning ones' of Wales], and I always felt I had more in common with those old legends than I had with the chapel-goers.

I was given the name Anwyn, which means 'very fair' – Annwn, with a double n and without the y was also the name for the Otherworld in Welsh mythology. It was a world of eternal youth with no disease and an abundance of everything and a far cry from little skinny-legged, black-faced me. The year was 1918, and more people were employed in the coal industry in Wales than ever before or since. We lived in a valley with hills and mountains all around and a tributary of the Nant y Gadlys running through a forest close by. Although the river wasn't very big, it was sometimes fast-flowing as it hurried on its way to meet the Afon Llynfi. We climbed the mountains to get away from the choking coal dust and jumped the rocks in the river like gadding goats, and fell in more times than we got safely across. It was all a part of growing up in the dull, starless streets and the breath-taking highness of the hills.

Llangynwyd was a small village back then and the only work was down the mines – everybody depended on 'the coal' for their bread and butter and beans and there were five or six working pits dotted around the area, all connected by a little railway. You could see the steam engines chuffing around the hillsides and the smell of slack and steam hung in the air and the dust covered the houses and the lower slopes. At the pithead, coal was brought up to the surface and loaded into drams. The drams were coupled together like big buckets on wheels and pulled steeply up along a ramp that eventually tipped them into the waiting railway trucks, to be taken away to keep the fires of industry burning around the whole of the United Kingdom and maybe further afield as well.

All the miners were allotted a free allowance of coal and this was issued by the ton and dumped by a lorry outside the houses. Everyone in the street would come out with their buckets and tin baths and shovels and brooms and make short work of shifting the lot through the house and into the *cwch* at the back. Our house was small, with the barest bits of furniture and a lavatory down the end of the garden where the spiders wore striped jerseys. Water came from a tap on the side of the house and the cooking was done on an open fire that was part of the range. We had gaslight downstairs and candlelight upstairs and it was a place that some city people might call picturesque – but not them that had to live there.

Sheep wandered anywhere they liked and did their droppings everywhere they liked and everyone knew everyone else's business. There was no cinema or anything like that to entertain us kids, and television hadn't been invented – at least not in Wales. So we amused ourselves with our own version of knockdown-ginger, where we tied a thin string at night to one door knocker and the other end to a knocker across the street. Then we'd knock on one of them and, when the person in the house opened the door, they'd pull the string which would raise the knocker on the other side and, when they closed the door, the knocker would fall and knock that door. The other house would then open the door and you can see what happened. Us kids would be hunkered down and hooting until the people realised what was happening and came chasing us down the dark road. Other games were bobby-kick-a-tin and skipping and us girls would knit squares to make blankets out of and the crocheted shawls of many colours that all the women wore. We'd go up the river to find birds' nests and snakes and try to catch trout by tickling them under their bellies – but I never could get the hang of that and the coughing from the coal dust always frightened the fish away.

The coughing was caused by what we called 'black lung' and it was dangerous if it developed into emphysema or bronchitis, which it often did. But I was lucky because my little lungs were healthy enough to cough up the coal dust and I left the village before something more serious than coughing took hold of me. I survived, which was more than many other tumble-headed little smowt did back then.

I was the first-born of four children – Walter came after me in 1920 and Gwyneth in 1922 and Bronwyn in 1924. Some people asked who made my mother pregnant with me, considering my father was a soldier at the time. But she said it was when he was home on leave and he was happy with that explanation – at least, he seemed to be. Whether he actually was on leave at the time or not, I'll never know. My father's name was Hugh and he was gassed during the Great War, but he never knew how bad it affected him until later, after he came home. He married my mother, Katherine, and went down the mines with the rest of the men, hewing coal in the dark and dangerous world underground. He'd come home covered in black dust from the pit and wash it all off in a big wooden bath in front of the fire – that was before he developed the broncho-pneumonia.

It was when Katherine was having her fourth baby that he had the first attack. He said it was caused by the coal, but the bosses said it was caused by the gas he inhaled during the war. After that, he couldn't work anymore, so my mother had to do it all instead – she did the washing for people who could afford it and painted their walls with distemper, and she had so much mother's milk on Bronwyn that she breastfed babies for drier women and they paid her a few pennies for the protein. Us kids would fill old sacks with coal we found lying around and collect sheep dung from the roads and sell it for a ha'penny a bucket. People soaked it in water then poured the slurry over their vegetable plots – or they dried it out and burned it on the fires to make the coal go further. It was a hard enough life, but most were in the same boat and no doors were ever locked and neighbours would pop in and out during the daffodil days for a cuppa and a mouthful of Welshcake that some called bake-stones and others called griddle scones.

As well as all the work she did, my mother would traipse into Maesteg once a week to get her 'Lloyd George'– which was the benefit of those days, brought into being in 1911 by David Lloyd George, who was Chancellor of the Exchequer at the time. It gave workers the first contributory system of insurance against illness and unemployment and took away the need for the stigmatised social welfare provided under the Poor Law. All workers who earned under £160 a year had to pay 4d a week into the scheme; the employers paid 3d and the government paid 2d – Lloyd George called it the 'ninepence for fourpence'. Workers were paid ten shillings a week for the first thirteen weeks of sick leave and five shillings for the next thirteen weeks and they were also given free treatment for tuberculosis. My mother took me and my brother and sisters with her sometimes to collect the Lloyd George and do her shopping in Maesteg and we stayed close to her all the way through the dingles and dells, which were full of *afancs* [monsters that live in lakes and marshes] and *gwyllions* [ghosts, spirits or night-wanderers] and *llamhigyn y dwrs*, [the water leaper] waiting to leap out at us children and drag us away to *diawl* [hell].

And in winter, just after Christmas, the Mari Lwyd, or Grey Mare, would come trotting down the Street with its 'Ostler' and Merryman and Sergeant and with Punch and Siwan dressed in tattered clothes with blackened faces. Its bony mare's skull would be bleached white and have green fire inside its eyes and its jaws would snap and frighten the living daylights out of the women as well as the children.

This darkest time of year was traditionally believed to be the time when the veil between the upper world and the underworld was thinnest and creatures could cross from one to the other. The tradition of Mari Lwyd was a calendar custom that went all the way back into ancient times and the festivities would go on for a week or two and was supposed to bring good luck.

A mare's skull was fixed to the end of a wooden pole, with a white sheet fastened to the back of the skull, hiding the pole and the man underneath carrying it. Black cloth ears were sewn onto the sheet, along with ribbons and bells, and the eyes were made of green glass. The jaws could open and snap shut again at passers-by and people in the houses where it would stop. The Mari Lwyd was led by the Ostler with his whip or stick and the Merryman played music and the others sang songs as they wassailed along the way. Punch carried a long iron poker and Siwan swept the road before them with a besom broom.

The skull was carried through the streets of the village and they stood outside the doors of the houses and pubs, banging to be let in. They'd sing a verse and my father would try to sing a verse back at them from behind the closed door. They'd start off with something the likes of–

Wel, dyma ni'n diwad
Gyfeillion diniwad
I ofyn cawn gennad – i ganu

And my father would cough –

Os na chawn ni genad
Rhowch glywed ar ganiad
Pa fodd mae'r madawiad nos heno

And they'd come back at him with another verse and he'd answer them and Punch would rap on the door with his poker and Siwan would beat her broom against the windows and it would go back and forth until the coughing got the better of my father and he couldn't answer any more. Then we'd have to let them in. Us children would cower in the corner because, once they got inside, the Mari would run around the house neighing and snapping its bony jaws and it would chase us into the arms of Punch, who would try to kiss the girls and be beaten over the head by Siwan. My father would offer them food and drink and eventually they'd move on to the next house, after bringing good luck for the coming year and frightening away the bad luck of the previous year, and everything would quieten back down into the dark dull wintertime, while we waited for the spring.

As I got older, the fire-and-brimstone-breathing chapel preachers tried to stop the Mari Lwyd, because it had a bad reputation for drunkenness and rowdiness as it roamed round the village. They preached from the pulpits about unholy pagan practices and we should be doing something more saintly instead, like taking part in *eisteddfodau* [Welsh festival of literature, music and performance]. They hated the Mari Lwyd and the tradition died out over the years of breast-beating and crippling Christianity. I hear there's a revival under way by folk groups and traditional types – although it'll never be as hair-on-end as in the old days.

As far back as I remember, I went to chapel every Sunday with the rest of the family. The whole village would be there and the preacher, who was called 'Eyebrows' Evans, would tell us about Christian Socialism and how Christ was in the coalmines with us – although nobody ever saw him swinging a pick nor wielding a shovel. I'm sure his intentions were good, but that's all they were. We continued to live in poverty, despite the Lord and the Congregationalists, with their choirs and eisteddfodau and festivals and processions. And even though they made the pubs close on Sundays, the shadows could still be seen inside the back rooms where the police came to play a few hands of poker with the priests.

By 1925, coal production in the valleys had crashed from its all-time high a few years earlier. It affected everybody, because the price of coal fell with the decline in production. The mine owners didn't want to cut their profits, so they cut wages instead, and a general strike in defence of miners' wages broke out in 1926. But the blacklegs and the scabs and the fascists joined forces with the government and the strike failed – and us children of the South Wales valleys descended into even more appalling poverty, which had been our playmate since long before I came into the coal-black world. I can still hear them, even now, the voices of the mongrel children in the hunched-down doorways, with dysentery and impetigo and hepatitis taking their toll – along with rashes and breaks and burns and stillbirths and infant mortality and malnutrition. I can still see them, even now, the spectres running in the smoky streets – playing hide-and-seek amongst the houses. I can feel the small ghostly hands touching me with cold fingers, faces wide-eyed and white in the morning light. I can smell the disappointment in the faraway and forgotten little lives and I sometimes say a prayer for them – with them.

Mother Earth be always there
And keep me safe within your care.
Lord of night please dance and sing
And happy dreams to me please bring.
And when I wake to greet the day
Brother Sun please light my way.

The dust-strewn streets and the black hills in the distance, which we had to climb for a long way to reach the green of the grass, grew even dustier and blacker. The narrow houses and grey men and shoeless children – the slag-heaps and smoking chimneys and the politicians with a different smile on either side of their faces remained, along with the never-ending hopelessness that spread itself like a slate blanket over our lives.

Though life was grim, grimmer than anyone who didn't experience it could imagine, grimmer than any generation since could imagine, we simply didn't know any better and so accepted our lot, and the Christians consoled themselves with songs and saints. The church in Llangynwyd was dedicated to Saint Cynwyd, the sixth-century son of Cynfelyn the Chief. And the old village of Top Llan was the home of the legendary Maid of Cefn Ydfa, whose name was Ann Thomas and who inspired the song 'Bugeilio'r Gwenith Gwyn'. The story goes that Ann was forced to marry against her wishes and died pining for her true love. The man she had to marry had money, but she loved a penniless poet. The poet left the village, but she pined and pined and pined so much for him that he had to come back, just in time for her to die in his arms. The poet wrote the song – it means 'Watching the White Wheat', but it wasn't the wheat he was watching, it was Ann. When I was a young girl I couldn't understand why any woman would want to pine herself to death over a man – and when I grew up and got married myself, I couldn't understand why every woman didn't want to kill her husband. Maybe that was the way with Ann Thomas, maybe she wanted to kill the wealthy bugger she was married to – and that would've been better than pining herself to death over some penniless poet who would probably have turned out to be a big disappointment in any case.

Like I said, we lived in a two-up-two-down terraced house with an outside toilet. The back garden was fifty foot long and rose up into the hill at the back of the street. It was a black hill, like all the rest, and it was a constant struggle to make anything grow in that garden – even the grass. But my mother tried, to her credit. She was sometimes able to grow hardy vegetables like cabbage and mustard greens and turnips and radishes and English peas and Irish potatoes. She also had a little herb patch of sage and wintergreen and fennel and holy thistle and house-leek and stinging nettle that she kept under a sheet of glass to keep the coal dust and ashflakes off and we used it as medicine for all sorts of ailments. If the summer was good, she used to grow a species of night-shade that tasted like tobacco when it was dried and she sold it to the locals for their pipes at sixpence an ounce.

Electricity came to the valley in 1926, after the general strike had succeeded in making things worse for miners and their families. Not that it was the fault of the strikers, but the coal bosses refused to take back many of the men who went on strike and that made the unemployment even worse. So, maybe the government felt guilty for the way it put the boot into us poor people and thought it would make things a little easier. No one could afford to pay for the new electricity, of course, but where there's a will there's a way – as they say. The men of the South Wales valleys were nothing if not versatile and they soon worked out how the power ran along the wires and how to stop it and how to start it. And, when the power company came every month to check the meters, they saw that nothing had been used – officially. As soon as they knocked on the door of the first terraced house in the street, the people would bang on the wall with a secret knock code and the second house would bang on the wall of the third and so on up the whole street. And all the illegal wires that were being used to bypass the meters would be pulled out and we'd all smile at the power company men with innocent faces.

In autumn, us kids went fruit – and berry – picking across the undulating countryside, miles and miles from the ash and dust and slag, to help our mother out. Sometimes it took hours to get there and the farmers didn't like us scrumping their orchards and they fired at us with buckshot from their guns. But we were always too far away for them to do any damage and we could run like the wind, despite the coughing and crouping. Mother made pies from the gatherings we brought back and sold any surplus to other families whose kids were too lazy or too laid-up to go scrumping for themselves – or families whose kids had died from one disease or the other. And so, between this and that, we scraped an existence out of the way we lived and, like I said, we knew no better and accepted it all in our stride. Until, of course, I was fourteen and could leave school and go to work.

I mostly got part-time jobs to begin with, like cleaning the lavatories and collecting glasses in the local pub. Then milking cows on a farm. And finally working in the hat shop in Maesteg – where I read the magazines on the occasional table and saw the styles of the ladies who came in for a straw cloche or a wool beret or a felt satin bow or a Henry Pollak or a topper with a feather flower. Then I realised there was more to life than drudgery and more to the world than Wales.

Chapter Three

So, that's how I ended up as a scullery maid and, as time went by, I was getting used to the life of a skivvy over in Hampstead. For the first few weeks, I rarely got to go outside, except when I was hanging out the washing or beating the ugly rugs and, on Sunday afternoons, everyone did what they were accustomed to doing and I was left alone. I was apprehensive about going out on my own because of the tales of murder and mayhem in the big city – what if I got lost and couldn't find my way back before dark? I might be molested or ransacked by Cook's relations. So I stayed in the room and wrote long letters to my mother. I never said how sad and lonely I was, because that would only have made her feel bad as well, so I said I was doing fine and had made a few friends and was looking forward to seeing everyone at some time or other in the future.

Jobs finished at one in the afternoon on a Sunday and Kathleen was in the room when I got up there on this particular day.

'Fancy going out, Annie?

'Oh, yes!'

It was a nice day and I was glad of her offer,

so we went to the park and saw Lilly there with the children. She never spoke to us and neither did the kids and we didn't try to speak to them, in case it went against some outdated social etiquette or other. So I just enjoyed the sun and the light and the sounds all around me of people laughing and playing and the smell of grass and the taste of the air. It reminded me a bit of home – just a bit, mind you, and I wanted to sit there forever, amongst the sounds of the afternoon. And I realised for the first time that humanity could only really be understood at arm's length – like a painting on a wall – up close it was a mass of random patterns and abstracts and waves and from a distance it blended into the bigger surroundings and was no longer separate from them.

But it was soon time to go back and, on the way, our path was impeded by a march coming down Haverstock Hill towards the West End. I think it was the Socialist Youth or the Young Communists, I can't be sure now, but there were lots of banners and loud voices chanting against the rising un-employment of the time and the police were keeping a close eye on things. I didn't know too much about politics back then, but I'd seen what unemployment did in the valleys of South Wales, and I felt an affinity with the marchers and a yen to be stepping alongside them. Wasn't that strange? Here was I, working for the rich, yet wanting to walk with the poor. The parade soon passed and we went on home and I had myself a cup of tea and a jam sandwich that Cook hadn't made, so I knew it was safe to eat. I washed and ironed my uniform and then I went to bed, exhausted by the good feeling the trip to the park had given me.

Monday morning I was awake before Bart tapped on the door, just lying there in bed thinking about things. I wondered what would become of me and where I'd be in a year's time and five years' time and ten years' time – when I'd be twenty-six. I didn't have a clue, so I gave up the wondering and got out of bed and washed as usual in lukewarm water and went downstairs. Later that day, I saw the lady of the house again.

'Hello, Anwyn.'

At least she knew I had a Christian name, even if Cook didn't. I hadn't seen her husband yet and I was thinking about what Kathleen told me. There were plenty of men who had no respect for women, so how was he any different?

It was a new week. Down in the kitchen, I was thinking about my tasks and using my loaf to make life easier for myself. I got piping-hot water from the copper to wash up with and I'd figured out how to make a lot of the other jobs lighter as well – like wrapping a wet cloth round the broom to mop the floors standing up instead of kneeling down and making the coalman take off his boots before traipsing in for his fried bread. I was getting things done in half the time and I wondered why I didn't work all this out much sooner. Out hanging the washing, I saw Bart. He gave me another wink and this time I winked back, as much as to say his secret was safe with me.

When I went back to the kitchen to do the vegetables, I saw that Cook was baking bread. Bread! That was another thing I wouldn't be able to eat any more. She told me to wash down the shelves. I carefully took down the china dishes and washed every-thing and was putting the cups and saucers back when the dragon knocked over a plate and it smashed on the floor in smithereens. She ran straight over and walloped me round the head and sent me flying across the kitchen floor.

'Clumsy girl!'

Nora came in to see what the ruckus was about.

'She broke a plate!'

Nora looked at me and she knew the truth, but neither of us said anything. I wanted to wallop her back, and I would have, but for fear of being beaten to death by one of her kinfolk out on the street. After the clout, my head was hammering and I felt sick as a spaniel, but I had to carry on with my jobs and there was a load of ironing to do. I was still feeling sick that evening after Cook went home and I didn't want anything to eat. Nora and Biddy washed up and cleared away for me and I went to my room and sat on the bed. My head was still pounding when Kathleen came in with some hot tea and a plate of buttermilk biscuits.

'I don't want them.'

'You have to eat, Annie.'

'I saw Cook baking today.'

'Not these biscuits; Brat got them from the shop for you.'

So I ate them and drank the tea. Kathleen told me that Bart had got some eggs from chickens a friend of his kept on an allotment near Highgate and passed them on to Nora for me. They were in the secret hiding place with the rest of our stash and there was no fear of getting into trouble for pinching them. I lay down and tried to get some sleep. I thought about what it must have been like for the skivvies back in times gone by if Cook could clout me like that and get away with it, what must those poor girls have had to put up with? I thought about making a complaint to Mrs Harding about it, but if she took Cook's side, it would make things even worse for me. I decided to wait and see if it happened again.

And so the weeks wore on – weeks of fireplace-raking and floor-mopping and step-polishing and potato-peeling and dishwashing – drudgery and dogsbodying and donkeywork and all kinds of daily grinding, despite the labour-saving devices. I had to scrub down the kitchen table once a day, clean the cupboards and dressers inside-out, wash down the shelves once a week, along with all the plates and platters and bowls and biscuit tins and sauce boats and soup tureens. But lighting the range every morning became the bane of my life. It was a big, black surly monster and it ran on solid fuel, not gas nor electric, and fired up inside with rolled paper and kindling first, then coal and more coal, until it glowed like a blacksmith's forge. The washing copper also growled at me and threatened to overflow if I didn't treat it with the respect it demanded. All the jobs had to be done in the proper order – my days were timed according to my many duties and I worked in terms of rotas and routines and regimens and never-ending rituals.

It was inevitable, I suppose, that I would eventually run into Mr Harding, the owner of the house. I was in the kitchen one day on my own, Cook had gone to the shops to buy some meat and Nora and Biddy were on their break. He was a tall man of about thirty-five, with dark hair and a handsome face. He looked a bit like the actor William Powell and he was wearing a double-breasted grey flannel suit, with a buff-coloured shirt and a silk tie. I'd heard bits and pieces of conversations about him having interests in South African gold mines and that was how he managed to avoid the effects of the Great Slump that had brought other rich people to grief. I remembered Kathleen's words and wondered why a man who looked so bright and shiny was one to be wary of.

'Have you seen Ayres?'

I didn't know whether I should bow or curtsey, so I kind of genuflected like when I was in church.

'No, Sir.'

'And you are?'

'Anwyn, Sir. No, sorry, Moyle, Sir.'

'Which is it, Anwyn or Moyle?'

'Both, Sir.'

He shot a hint of a smile in my direction and walked over very close to me. He looked down and I looked up and the room seemed to become enveloped in a sensual shade of purple and a strange and scandalous thrill tingled through my body. Then the girls came back from their break and the spell was broken. He turned and walked away.

'If you see Ayres, tell him to come and find me.'

'Yes, Sir.'

Nora and Biddy giggled to themselves, as if they were sharing a joke that I was excluded from. I didn't ask them what they were sniggering at because I was behind with my work and wanted to get on with it before Cook came back and tried to belt me round the lughole again. So I put my head down and got on with what I was doing, but the sense of danger stayed with me for the rest of the day – the perception of menace that wasn't altogether unpleasant and tingled inside my stomach like a buzzing bee.

It was part of my job to make sure everything in the basement was cleaned regularly and I don't suppose the family even noticed because they rarely came down there. But Cook did. She was a stickler for what she called 'hygiene' and I thought that was rich, considering what she did with the cheap meat she bought. Nobody said it, but I got the impression she pocketed the money she saved by buying this dodgy food. So, she must have been on a budget of some sorts and I wondered if Mr Ayres was in on the fiddle too? Or was he above and oblivious to this kind of crookery? It seemed ironic to me, because the rich people who lived in those big houses were particular about who they hired. They didn't trot down to the labour exchange to hire staff; you had to be recommended and have a reference – even a lowly skivvy like me, and they wouldn't have taken me on if the friend of the family hadn't vouched for me. They'd be afraid I might make off with the silver or slit their throats in the middle of the night.

I wondered who'd vouched for Cook?

As the year wore on, and I was gradually getting on top of the routine of my working day, different seasons brought different duties for me to perform. The game bird season got pheasants and partridges and plovers and red-legged grouse sent down specially from the country to grace the tables of Hampstead and Hendon and Harrow, and the Harding household got its share. Although they weren't aristocrats from a titled family or anything, I think they liked to pretend this was the case when they were entertaining, and they liked to show off what their new money could buy. It couldn't buy them a way into the very top circles of society, but the professional people were establishing their own propriety and weren't all that bothered about the declining nobility. Anyway, it was my job to gut and pluck the birds that came into the kitchen.

Now, I'm sure everybody knows that game should be well hung – sometimes for weeks, until the meat is almost rotten. By then, these birds were infested with maggots and gutting them was disgusting, even to a hardy Welsh girl like me who'd seen many disgusting things in her short life to date. The birds were kept in a small room well away from everything else and the smell in there was overwhelming and made me retch in the beginning. Biddy, the kitchen maid, gave me a piece of cloth tinted with rose water and told me to tie it over my nose. It didn't make a lot of difference, but just enough to stop me from being sick and it helped me long enough to get used to the stink and the texture of guts and putrid gore between my fingers. Then, just when I was beginning to breathe normally again, the game bird season was over and we were back to bacon and beef and black pudding.

By the time my first Christmas as a skivvy came round, I was well used to the hard work and hassle and was starting to take it all in my stride. I missed my family back in Wales though and wondered when I'd ever get to see them again. For once, Cook spared no expense and the Christmas dinner was a joy to behold. An enormous goose was cooked, along with a matching turkey stuffed with chestnuts and apricots and mushrooms and onion and herbs. The aroma was mouth-watering and could have been bottled and sold to starving children as dream-mist. The goose was stuffed with small potatoes in their jackets, along with apples and parsley and cloves and prunes. The golden birds went upstairs with roast potatoes and parsnips and sprouts and mashed swede – accompanied by dishes of apple sauce and bread sauce and cranberry sauce and sausages wrapped in streaky bacon. The family and guests up there in the big dining room were treated to smoked salmon pâté starters and canapés and stuffed mushrooms before the main course, then Christmas cake and mince pies and plum duff served with brandy and eggnog and sloe gin for afters.

As with all the upstairs soirées, a lot of the food was left untouched and it came back down to us. We were allowed to feast on what was left after Mr Ayres and Mona and Lilly had their fill – and Cook loaded up her bag to take some home to her villains and vandals. Once she was gone home and the staying guests had retired to their rooms, the rest of us pulled home-made crackers and drank home-made ale and sang home-made songs and danced in a little home-made circle. The men chased the girls with mistletoe and the kitchen was alive with laughter – until the tiredness took hold of me and I headed off to dream of Christmases to come.

Next morning was Boxing Day and my head was killing me from the glasses of strong ale I'd drunk the night before. I still had my duties to perform, but Nora cheered me up and gave me something to look forward to.

'There's a dance down Cricklewood tonight.'

'A dance?'

'You know … with boys, Annie.'

I blushed a little, remembering the encounter with Mr Harding all those months ago.

'You coming?'

'Can I?'

'If you want to.'

'What about my work?'

'It's Christmas, Annie, forget about work for once.'

I had a bit of money put away from my shilling a week that I wasn't able to spend because I never went anywhere, so I thought, 'Why not!'

The other girls helped me finish my work early and as soon as Cook went home we were free. The Harding family had left to visit relatives for a few days and this gave Mona and Lilly an opportunity to take a little holiday and be with their families for a while. Mr Ayres had no family to go home to, so he stayed to look after the house. I often wondered about him, alone in his room, trapped between two worlds – not one of them and refusing to be one of us. I wondered what he thought about at night, what he dreamed about when he slept, if he'd ever been in love, what he wanted to be when he was a boy. I couldn't believe that any boy would want to be a butler – maybe a fireman or a soldier or a miner or a farmer, but never a butler. But, back then, people went into service because it ran in the family. If someone's mother was a cook, they might follow in her footsteps. Or if their father was a butler, they might take the mantle from his shoulders when he had no forelock left to tug. Like I said, the rich liked to know who was living in their houses, and what better way than to have the servants bred specially for the role.

Anyway, we escaped from the house that had seemed to be my shroud for the past seven months – me and Nora and Biddy and Kathleen and Bart the Brat. The dance-hall was Irish and Kathleen felt immediately at home. There was a lot of tough-looking builder types drinking and trying to throw their legs in the air to a hornpipe or a reel or a double-jig – I couldn't tell the difference. There was also a lot of other servants from the big houses to the east of Cricklewood. Gossip was rife and some of it was about Mr Harding. Apparently, he had a reputation with a lot of the high-class ladies of London – and some low-class ones as well. But I put all that out of my mind as I was grabbed by a young Irishman and dragged out into the whirling mass of bodies moving round in a mad circle. His name was Jack and he was from a place called Athlone and that's all I could hear above the noise and knockabout of the melee.

But the Irish boys, in their best brogues and shirt studs and hair slicked down in some places but sticking up in others, were paying a lot of attention to Nora, and Bart didn't like it.

'She's a handsome little colleen, ain't she, boys?'

'Leave her alone!'

'And who would you be?'

'I'm her boyfriend.'

They all laughed and formed a circle round Bart, pushing him from one to the other and asking him what he was going to do about it. Me and Biddy and Kathleen were dancing and didn't notice what was going on, because the music was loud and we were in a crowd and it was like nothing I'd ever experienced before – all the swinging and flinging and jigging and whirly-gigging. Until Nora came bursting in on our shrieking and hoolying.

'Bart's in lumber.'

'How so?'

'It's my fault.'

She pointed across to where the circle of Irish boys were ragging Bart and it was getting a bit too rough for comfort. But what could we do? We were four young girls in amongst a mass of strangers who might turn on us at any minute and then we'd be in real trouble.

'Leave this to me!'

Kathleen took out to stride across the dance floor and pushed her way into the threatening circle and stood there, hands on her intimidating hips. The Irish boys stopped passing Bart around like a parcel and studied her up and down.

'And who might this be?'

Kathleen fixed a fierce eye on the ringleader and he took a step away from her baleful frown. Now, like I said before, all the time she was my roommate I'd always seen Kathleen as a shy, quiet little mouse of a girl, with nothing to say for herself. But now she was showing another side that we didn't know was there.

'You boys should be ashamed of yourselves.'

'Should we now?'

'Behaving like bullies and making a holy show of us good Irish people.'

Some of the younger lads started to look a bit shamed round their red faces and their heads sank. But the ringleader was a brash fella of about eighteen and he stepped forward again after getting over the initial surprise of being challenged by a slip of a girl.

'Don't tell us what we should and shouldn't be ashamed of.'

'Your mammy should have smacked your arse when you were a babby!'

Everybody laughed. The bully looked round for support, but his mates had deserted him. He was embarrassed, and that made him even more dangerous. No one likes to be laughed at in front of their friends. He had a point to prove and he raised his fist. We all screamed – but before he could swing it, the punch was grabbed from behind by a big man wearing a grey tweed suit and a flat cap. He was the bouncer. And before the bully could say another word, he was caught by the scruff of the neck and the seat of his trousers and slung out into the street. The big bouncer came back, smacking his hands together as if he was cleaning some dirt off them.

But the incident had a sobering effect on us and we couldn't settle after that. We were worried that the bully might be waiting outside for us when we left. But he wasn't. We peered out the door and up and down the street, then made a run for it to catch the last bus back to Hampstead. When we were safely on board, we lightened up and laughed about the adventure and chattered and chirruped in an excited manner, the way people do when their nerves are a bit on edge and they don't want to show it. But Kathleen's display of courage was to influence me and stand me in good stead as an example to follow when I was later threatened by men.

I was tired that night by the time I got to the top of the house. Kathleen fell asleep in the other bed and never mentioned the confrontation in the dancehall. It was an incident that broke into the monotony of daily life in the house and it reminded me that there was a big world out there, full of all sorts, and that one day I'd be out there too, not stuck in a scullery skivvying.

Chapter Four

You have to understand that I wasn't an ignorant girl – not by any manner or means. I started school on All Hallows' Eve. I should've started in September with all the other kids, but I was ill with whooping cough, a disorder that caused me to make a sound like a constipated owl when I was rasping and rattling. My mother made me drink a mixture of pine-needle tea with cherry bark and honey and that finally cured the coughing. I wondered if the date was significant in some way – Halloween, the old-time festival of Samhain, when spiritual journeys could be made – and my spiritual journey was to school.

The sky was lead-grey and winter was well on the way, with its ice and snow and snivelling and snotting. My mother took me there on that first morning. It was still dark and our words floated in front of our faces in the silver moonlight. The moonlight was cold, even though my mother's hand was warm, as she held on to mine to stop me from being spirited away by the *Coblynau* [Gnome-like creatures said to haunt the mines and quarries of Wales]. Morning was just emerging from behind the mountains. It moved in slow motion and enveloped the land and made it come alive. The silveryness gradually grew more gilded as the sun came up and drove all the demons away.

The schoolhouse was big and looked down on little me with a frown and I didn't want to stay there when my mother left me. I wanted to run after her and tell her to take me home because I was afraid of all the words I didn't understand and everything was a jumble – a stumbling fumbling bumble in my brain. The other kids laughed at my apprehension and I had no older sisters or brothers to keep them at bay. But once I got used to it and the bullies found more frightened kids to pick on, I actually liked school – particularly reading. Which seems strange, considering there wasn't much to read in our house at any time. But I took the books home whenever I could and I went from looking at the pictures to being able to understand the printed words and I read them in the gaslight downstairs and the candlelight upstairs and later by the light of the stolen electricity, until I was as good with the English language as anyone in the village.

I was six and going to school for a while when my sister Bronwyn was born and my mother sold her milk to make ends meet. Gwyneth and Walter were already in the world, and, as we got older, we climbed up the black hills and down the deep glyns and in between the coeden in the wild ffridds [part of the classic Welsh landscape arising from hill farming], calling to one another so as not to get lost and eaten by the *Dreigiau* [Dragons].

Maesteg was a big town to us, with lots of shops, and we'd go there to spend some of the money we made from selling the sheep-droppings. We bought hardboiled sweets and fudge and humbugs and marzipan and butterwelsh, even though we were told not to. And the young years were all much alike, in the shadow of the slag heaps and the steeply sloping streets and the small, back-to-back terraced houses and the occasional patch of blue in an otherwise slate-grey sky. And the low mumble of adult voices of an evening in their lilting, swaying accents, as if they were going to break into a song at any second. And the pale sun in summer and the pale snow in winter and the shortness of the seasons in between.

All the days rolled away from us children – some took a long time to go and others disappeared in seconds. They looked back at us before dissolving into the coal-dust sky and shook their heads, as if to say a time will come when you'll regret the wishing of us away. School holidays were the favourites of most of the village children and they'd gad about like spring lambs, so happy to be free from the restriction of the stone school-walls. But sometimes they made me sad – they were too long if I was working to help bring in some money for my poor mother and too short if I was reading the books the school allowed me to take home with me. The last page always came long before the holidays were over and I'd read them again – and again. Dickens, with his eccentric characters with equally eccentric names, and Emily Brontë with her dark-hearted, handsome hero, and Barrie with his enchanted children, and Thomas Hardy's Tess who reminded me of myself and Alice's wonderfully satirical adventures – and many, many more. They took me to other worlds, where I could be someone else, not Anwyn Moyle, the winsome waif of South Wales.

At chapel on Sundays, the preacher led us all in prayer and hymns and warned us about the practice of witchcraft that was widespread in Cymru and that we should always be on our guard against it. I thought he was talking about the Mari Lwyd and I wondered why he wasn't able to stop the grey mare from coming round every January and causing chaos. The witches, he said, could use spells and the evil eye to seduce us children away from our god-fearing parents and I would imagine the glass-green eyes in the white skull as it hacked around the houses.

The minister's voice fell to a whisper when he told us the witches would make puppets in our images and stick needles into their hearts to harm us and then we'd be doomed for all eternity. The adults hung horseshoe amulets outside the houses to ward off such evil, but they didn't stop the Mari Lwyd or the Merryman or Punch and Siwan, and maybe it's just as well. Personally, I preferred what my grandmother told me about – the old collaboration between a female god and a male one, who both followed the natural seasons and celebrated them – to a vengeful Christian god who killed and burned and tortured to have his way. But I was only very young, so what did I know about anything?

Worse than any witch were the feral cats that plagued the village. They brought them to the mines to kill rats to begin with, but the buggers bred and bred and bred and there were hundreds of them all over the place. They'd kill everything in sight, birds and bees and rabbits and fleas, and my father would try to shoot them through his coughing convulsions if they came into our garden. Us children would chase them with sticks and stones and catapults and snowballs in winter and chestnuts in autumn, but they were clever, with springs for legs and rubbery bodies that could fall backwards from a twenty-foot wall and still land on their feet. They spat and snarled at us and threatened us with unsheathed claws and even the dogs wouldn't go too near them, for fear of losing an eye or suffering a split nose.

And it was such a long time ago, as I remember, that time when there were witches in Wales and I was so young, like a little coal-smeared bird that flew across the corrugated hills. And I sang this song to myself sometimes –

> *Mi sydd fachgen ieuanc ffôl.*
> *Yn byw yn ôl fy ffansi*
> *Myfi'n bugeilio'r gwenith gwyn,*
> *Ac arall yn ei fedi.*
> *Pam na ddeui ar fy ôl,*
> *Rhyw ddydd ar ôl, ei gilydd?*
> *Gwaith'rwyn dy weld, y feinir fach,*
> *Yn lanach, lanach beunydd!*

> *I am a young and foolish lad*
> *Who lives as I please*
> *I lovingly tend the ripening wheat*
> *And another reaps it.*
> *Why not follow me*
> *Some day after another?*
> *Because I see you little lass,*
> *Purer and purer each day!*

– in memory of the Maid of Cefn Ydfa. And

67

we played hide-and-seek under the dese-
crated slopes and waited out the young
years until some of us decided to leave – to
get away from the smell of scarcity and the
soul-destroying days of unemployment that
were to come and drive us all down into the
coal dust. And we scavenged for lumps of
coal with chapped red fingers in the wintertime, in the wheel-rutted snow, amongst the
ghosts of previous generations who did the
same and died of malnutrition and tuberculosis. Their cold voices called to me from
the fading distance as I trudged uphill to my
house, a hessian sack across my shoulders
and my younger sisters and brother trudging behind.

At night the haunted streets stood still,
like the inside of dark train tunnels and I
was often afraid to look out my bedroom
window, in case a grinning witch with an
Anwyn puppet and a pin might be looking
back at me. The wind through the trees
made noises like a wheezing banshee that
whispered to the trolls that lived in secluded
places and around street corners. I said my
prayers to my Druid gods and asked them
to keep me safe from the Christian god and
the mine-owning speculators and to deliver
me from all evil.

Amen.

Because my father couldn't work, my
mother had to. No one in the village had

much money to spend, so sometimes she worked for food – a few vegetables if the growing in the garden wasn't good, or a scrawny chicken or a leg of mutton or a brace of rabbits or a poached duck. She would distemper people's walls and they always used dark colours so the dirt and coal-dust wouldn't show. As the eldest, I used to help her when I wasn't at school or reading, and at twelve I got my own cleaning job for which I was paid a little pocket money. I gave it all to my mother, to help ease the burden of her heavy life. She also took in washing and I helped her hang and fold for them who were too feeble or too foolish to do it for themselves. So, it was no easy life, but us children didn't complain too much, because we thought everyone else was in the same boat – we didn't know until later, when we grew a little older, that there were other children who had everything they wanted – and the reason they had everything they wanted and didn't have to do anything to get it was because they were riding on our scrawny backs.

When I finally turned fourteen, I was able to leave school, even though I was sad to do so. I missed the books and the learning, and my grandmother had died, so there were no more stories about Rhiannon and Pryderi, or Gronw and Blodeuwedd, or Culhwch and Olwen. After working part-time in the pub and on the cow farm, I got a job in Maesteg as a dogsbody in a hat shop. I wasn't allowed to serve the customers or anything like that. I had to stack and sweep and make tea for the saleswomen and run errands to other shops and milliners and people who mended and repaired the feather pillboxes and wide-brimmed wools and felt skulls with Bakelite badges and cherry-black straws and brimmed flappers.

Maesteg was two and a half miles from Llangynwyd and I had to walk it every day in hail, rain or snow – and all for 1s/6d. But they had a long low table in the shop for the ladies who were waiting to be fitted and the gentlemen who were waiting for the ladies who were waiting to be fitted. And the table was always stacked with the latest magazines. *Vogue* and *Women's Sphere* and *Le Petit Echo de la Mode* and *Harper's Bazaar* and *Marie Claire* and *Collier's* and *La Femme Chez Elle* and *Hemmets* and *Life*.

And the hat-buying ladies would shimmy in looking like Jean Harlow or Greta Garbo in bias-cut slip dresses and cap sleeves and ruffles and maxi lengths and crêpe silks and shoulder pads. I studied the magazines every chance I got and could soon identify Grecian styles and bolero jackets and high-fronts and low-backs and I soaked it all up and wished that someday I, too, would wear a Schiaparelli or a Maggy Rouff or a Lucien Lelong or a Robert Piguet. But how would that ever happen for a rag-tailed girl from the valleys who liked to read books and dream the impossible?

And that brings me to the Henry Pollak, which was a green wool supra felt hat with a wide ribbon and an artificial beige spray. I found it in a fitting room I was cleaning out one day. I knew it wasn't one of the shop's hats, because we didn't sell that particular design. I took it to the shop manageress and she remembered the woman who came in wearing it.

'That's Mrs Reynolds's hat.'

Mrs Reynolds was the wife of Arthur Reynolds, a very rich man who made his money exporting coal to America. The manageress fished out Mrs Reynolds's address and handed the hat back to me.

'You better run it round to her, Moyle.'

She said that as if it was just round the corner. So off I went on my tired feet, traipsing all the way out to the financially correct side of the suburbs. The address was a big two-storeyed house out in Mount Pleasant, with six red-brick steps leading up to the large green front door that had an arched fanlight and a gold knocker. The outside walls were also red brick with a frontal arch supported by four Corinthian columns. The roof was gabled and hipped and two prominent exterior chimneys stood either end, framing tall casement windows

71

with green shutters. I'd seen houses like that before – in the magazines.

I was half afraid to trudge up the gravelled driveway, for fear I might be taken for a tramp and the dogs set upon me. But I had no choice. I knocked as softly as I could and waited for the barking – but there wasn't any. So I knocked again, harder this time. Still no answer. I didn't want to have to come all the way out here again, so I left the hat in a bag by the front door. I was halfway down the steps when the door opened. A woman of about forty stood there with the reddest hair I'd ever seen and a figure that rivalled Mae West's and a set of pearly white, smiling teeth. She was wearing a dress I recognised from *Vogue* as a Madeleine Vionnet and she was smoking a cigarette in a long, black holder.

'What's up, honey?'

Her accent was American and friendly. I took the hat from its bag and held it out to her.

'You left this in the shop.'

She laughed.

'Oh, that old thing! Don't tell me you came all the way out here to bring it back?'

'Yes, Madam.'

'Why, you must be exhausted. Come in.'

She opened the door wider and I didn't know whether to go inside or make a run for it. She smiled her American smile again.

'Come on, honey, I won't bite.'

I shuffled my way past her and into a big reception room. She closed the door and walked ahead of me into what looked like the National Library of Wales. I'd never seen so many books in one place. She saw my surprise and was amused by my awe.

'You like books?'

'I love books!'

'Have one.'

I thought she said 'Have one', but that couldn't be right. I must have misheard.

'Have two ... or three. We got plenty.'

I didn't know what to say. I'd never met anyone like her before.

'Oh no, Madam, I couldn't...'

'Why not? Nobody in this goddamn house reads them, they're just for show.'

I tentatively approached the shelves and looked along them, running my fingers across the spines. They felt so exotic – so seductive.

'Go ahead, honey, pick three or four.'

Row upon row, title after title – some of the authors I'd heard of before and some I hadn't. I stopped at *Mathilda* by Mary Shelley and she urged me to pick some more. I ended up with *Self-Made Woman* by Faith Baldwin and a translation of The *Songs of Bilitis* by Pierre Louÿs.

She was drinking something from a stemmed glass that had a green berry on a stick floating in it.

'You want a cocktail? No, I guess you're too young. What about a soda?'

I didn't know what a soda was, so I thought I'd better not accept her offer in case it was something I didn't like.

'No thank you, Madam. I'd better get back.'

She looked at the hat as if it was something nasty that had blown in on the wind.

'I left the hat there deliberately. It's out of fashion. I thought you'd just throw it in the trash.'

I started to move towards the door, in case she changed her mind and took the books back.

'I'll bring the books back when...'

'Nah, you keep them, honey.'

She reached for her handbag.

'Hey, let me give you a tip.'

'Oh no, Madam, I'm not allowed to take money from customers. I'd lose my job.'

'I got to give you something for coming way out here on a wild goose chase.'

I told her the books were enough and I was ever so grateful to her for her kindness and kept edging closer and closer to the door.

'OK, look, take the hat. You want the hat?'

Of course I wanted the hat. I loved the hat and would never be able to afford one like it. I put up my hands in false protest, but she threw it to me and I caught it.

'I'll never wear it again.'

'Thank you. Thank you, Madam.'

I replaced the hat in the shop bag and was bowing and trying to curtsey in gratefulness, as if I was in the presence of a duchess or a dame.

'I didn't get your name, honey?'

'Anwyn Moyle, Madam.'

'Nice. Well, so long, Anwyn Moyle.'

She smiled that big smile of hers and I left her standing by the front door, watching me hurry down the gravel drive. She was smoking another cigarette from the long, black holder and looking like she'd just stepped off a Hollywood movie set. And how I wanted to look like her – when I grew to be a woman.

I knew the manageress wouldn't believe that Mrs Reynolds gave me the hat and books, so I had to hide them somewhere before I went back to the shop. I thought of secreting them in a storeroom round the back, where we kept cardboard boxes and wrapping and other stuff like that, but if they caught me leaving with them, I'd be accused of stealing and probably arrested. There was nowhere else around where I could leave such valuable items and be sure they'd still be there when I came to collect them after work. There was only one thing for it – I ran the two-and-a-half miles home and hid the hat and books in my bedroom. Then I ran the two-and-a-half miles back to the shop. The manageress wasn't too pleased when I came panting in.

'And what kept you, Moyle?'

'Sorry, miss, I lost my way.'

'You lost your way?'

'Yes, miss.'

'A likely story, Moyle.'

She was convinced I went skiving off round the shops or met some friends or larked about in the park for a while before coming back.

'I'm sorry, miss.'

'Sorry isn't good enough, Moyle. I'm going to have to let you go.'

I'd been there nearly a year and I was fed up with wearing out my shoes for ls/6d a week anyway. I was also coming up to sixteen and Mrs Jones the school janitor said she could get me a job in service through an agency she once worked for when she was younger. And so I said goodbye to Maesteg and the hat shop and, a few weeks later, I was on a train, skimming past towns like Swindon and Reading and Slough – all the way to Paddington in the fabulous city of London.

And when I went, I took the green hat with me.

Chapter Five

But that was back then, before I knew anything about being a skivvy, when I saw London through a glass darkly and imagined a life of glamour and glitz awaiting me in the big city. The reality of it broke the spell and I saw things as they really were – face to face. I'd been at the Hampstead house for nearly a year now and had turned seventeen. Nobody celebrated my birthday and I felt something sad – a loss, like something had died. Maybe it was my innocence and maybe it was just my optimism. Mind you, I looked older than my years and could pass for twenty on a good day. But most of my time was spent scrubbing and shining and I usually looked like something the cat dragged through a hedge backwards.

The big sink was always full of greasy pots and saucepans that the dishwasher couldn't handle, and the steps always needed redpolishing and the letterbox brassing and the drawers dusting and the daily grind constantly threatened to swallow me up – to overpower me until I wouldn't be able to breathe and I'd expire there on the cold scullery floor.

The routine of the work was worst – the same thing every day. Mrs Harding liked to have the latest gadgets in her house but, even with all these, it was still the same thing over and over and over again. I could do the jobs with my eyes closed by now and I longed for something new and challenging, so I watched Cook and picked up some culinary techniques, although the Beadle was hardly the best mentor in the world. But I learned how to make a soufflé and a variety of sauces and bake a partridge pie and a loaf of soda bread.

I watched and learned how to stuff a quail and quenelle a rabbit and croquette a pheasant. I also followed Mona around whenever I could, seeing the things she did as she went about her lady's maid duties, until she saw me and shooed me away – and I wondered if all these dormant talents would ever come in useful as I made my way through the windswept world. Sometimes I thought about Mrs Reynolds, who gave me the green hat, and her wide, American smile, and I wondered what it felt like to be her – with nothing to do all day but drink from a stemmed glass with a green berry on a stick floating in it and smoke cigarettes from a long, black holder and look beautiful.

I hadn't seen much of Mr Harding since that day in the kitchen, when he came looking for Mr Ayres and found me instead. I just caught fleeting glimpses of him every now and then, here and there in the distance, like an abstraction – a figment of my adolescent imagination. He never seemed to notice me, but I remembered him – his presence and the closeness of him to me; the scent of sage and cedarwood and the taste of his breath on the side of my face, almost overpowering me. Then, one day, Mr Ayres sent me to clean a stain from one of the bookcases in the library. I took my cleaning cloths and my vinegar and polish and proceeded to the big room. I always loved being in the library, even though I rarely had occasion to go inside, because the parlourmaids were responsible for cleaning in there. It was every bit as big as the library in Mrs Reynolds's house on the outskirts of Maesteg, only I got the feeling that these books were not just for show – they were read.

I ran my fingers across the leather bindings and looked at the titles – there were books on history and politics and more on exotic places around the world – and philosophy and gold-mining and memoirs and encyclopaedias and poetry and novels. I liked the novels best. I loved to read translations of folklore stories, like *East of the Sun and West of the Moon* and wild romances like that of Heathcliff and Catherine Earnshaw and women's writing like *Orlando* by Virginia Woolf and *The Visioning* by Susan Glaspell.

They were all here, in this library in Hampstead and I was in love with the room.

But daydreaming over the books wasn't getting the work done, so I started gingerly applying the vinegar solution to the stain, making sure I didn't discolour the wood. The stain was dark and reddish, almost blood-like, and I wondered what had made it. It was an irregular shape, like a splash, and I supposed it could have been port wine or claret. But, if something like port or claret splashed on the bookcase, wouldn't there be some on the floor as well? It was none of my business what the stain was – it could have been anything. And who did I think I was, Miss Marple?

As I worked, I started to hum a tune I'd heard the other girls singing. It was 'Two Cigarettes in the Dark' by Bing Crosby. Then I started singing the words – softly – to myself.

Two, two cigarettes in the dark
He strikes a match 'til the
Spark clearly traces
One face is my sweetheart

It was then I sensed I wasn't alone in the library. I looked towards a high-backed, studded leather chair that was facing away from me, just as a match struck and nearly made me jump out of my uniform. Mr Harding stood up, holding two cigarettes and a lighted match. He started to sing – softly – to me.

> Two, two silhouettes in a room
> Almost obscured by the gloom
> We were so close yet so far apart
> It happened that I stumbled in
> Upon their rendezvous

Then the match burned his fingers.

'Ouch!'

He started to laugh. I laughed with him, even though that probably went against some other outdated etiquette.

'I'm sorry, Sir. I didn't know anyone was in here.'

'Don't be sorry. It's Moyle, isn't it? Or is it Anwyn?'

'Both, Sir.'

He came closer, still holding the two cigarettes, until I could feel his breath on my face, smell the scent of sage and cedar-wood. Again.

'Would you like a cigarette, Anwyn?'

'I don't smoke, Sir.'

'Of course you don't. Well then, I won't either.'

He replaced the two cigarettes in a silver case, then moved past me to the library door. I thought he was going to leave and let me get on with my work, but he didn't. He stood inside the door and looked back at me.

'Should I lock the door, Anwyn?'

'What for, Sir?'

'Why, in case someone should come in, of course.'

I may have been naive, but I wasn't totally stupid, and I knew what he meant. Kathleen's words came back to me and he must have tried it on with the other girls too. But I was strangely flattered – that a man like this would find me attractive. A sophisticated man with soft hands and straight teeth and a seductive scent and words that weren't spoken – that were blown at me like kisses.

My legs felt weak, like they wouldn't be able to support me for much longer, and I must have looked like a fawn that had been caught in the headlights of a car. He didn't wait for my reply, but turned the key in the lock and slipped it into his waistcoat pocket. Then he came back across the room – slowly, deliberately – smiling with the same set of teeth Mrs Reynolds used to smile at me, all that time ago. And I didn't feel like Anwyn Moyle any more, I felt like her. I was beautiful and glamorous and drinking from a stemmed glass with a green berry and smoking a cigarette from a long, black holder. Maybe that's why I didn't call out – or maybe it was because, if I did and somebody came, it would be his word against mine and who would believe me? In any case, I didn't want to call out. I was seduced by the situation – entranced by the man's aura – overcome by his all-pervading presence. He wasn't Mr Harding – he was Heathcliff, or maybe Paris, or Mr Darcy, or Edmond Dantès – or all of them rolled into one.

Up close, his skin looked tanned and seemed to glow, or maybe it was the light in the library. He had a thin moustache that was impeccably groomed and his hair was brushed back in a wave. Almost without me knowing, his hands were cupping my face, but his touch was gentle, more a caress than a clasp. His eyes were green like the Mari Lwyd's and they looked deep into mine, through me and into my soul. He was looking for a word that didn't come to my lips – a word that said either 'yes' or 'no'. But nothing came – no word came up from my heart and into my mouth. Not a syllable. So he assumed the positive rather than the negative. His lips were as gentle as his fingers, barely touching mine, brushing mine, while his right hand moved slowly down my body to my breast and there it stayed, waiting to see if I objected. His left hand moved to the nape of my neck and then down along my spine to my waist. He whispered something. but I didn't understand the words and had no need to – little indistinguishable sounds that meant the same thing in any language.

I wasn't afraid in the room; in the gloom.

I knew Mr Harding was a formidable man, but I wasn't fearful of him. I had the reckless courage of my youth – of who I believed I was – and what I believed I would become. I didn't want to go back downstairs to the kitchen, to the skivvy I was down there. Here in the library I was Mrs Reynolds and I wanted this man to know me, who I could be – better than all the others. He was making me feel emotions I'd never experienced before and, for the first time since I came to this place, I felt alive – really alive, not just going through the motions. I felt eternal – part of everything, like the lady of Llyn y Fan Fach [Lady of the Lake] or Gwenhwyfar [Guinevere], here in the library with him. And the books were symbolic, all around us, looking on at us making our own legend. I was soaring in the sky and I knew who I really was.

For the very first time.

He spoke again, close to my ear. His voice was soft and sensuous and his words floated around my head like little stars. He was more than a man to me at that moment in time and I knew he could teach me things – how to live. How to love. How to listen – and laugh. And then he'd teach me how to cry. And maybe that was something I had to learn in order to become a real woman. Not a fake, sterile shadow of something I might become someday. Not Cook, or my mother, or Mona or Lilly, but a woman with a deeper light – a more profound identity, with a soul that any man could float away on. A woman who needed no man to make her whole, but who could accommodate men if she felt like it – if it was something she wanted. Would Mr Harding make me that kind of woman, or would he break me and throw me away like a twig?

But there was something about him, not just the charisma or style or charm or the scent of sage and cedarwood – something else. I couldn't put my finger on what it was exactly but he had it and I wanted it. Or maybe it was just my fantasy and there really was nothing for him to give – nothing *of* him to give. Just a figment of my adolescent imagination, what I wanted him to be. He was something and I was nothing – what could there be between us, apart from a cheap thrill? I tried to tell myself that, not to be stupid, to push him away and threaten to call out. But I couldn't. I wanted to be here with him because there was nowhere else worth being right then. I knew his reputation – the rumours. But there had to be more to the man than his reputation – maybe he didn't even know it himself. And that didn't make it any less there; the thing about him.

But for now I was just in the moment and it was good to be beside Mr Harding, to feel his body close to mine. My breath came faster as he moved his left hand inside my blouse and across my bare back. I closed my eyes. He kept speaking all the time as if to reassure me and his voice was like velvet as he lowered me down to the carpeted floor. A strange apprehension that wasn't fear nor fretfulness came over me, until it felt like I was drowning in expectation, and my breath came in short gasps and my voice sounded like a distant animal – not really a voice, but a feral whispering. It was growing dark in the library as the evening closed in and Mr Harding was unbuttoning my blouse and I was unbuttoning his shirt. Outside the locked door, I could hear the faint sounds of my little world and I wondered why nobody had come looking for me yet. Then I remembered it was Mr Ayres who'd sent me up here and I couldn't help feeling it was all arranged and everybody knew where I was – lying on the floor in the library with Mr Harding.

I didn't care. His hands were making patterns on my soul, and his body seemed to know mine so well, even though they'd never met before. All thoughts of who we were and our polarised stations in life flowed away on the tide of passion and pleasure that was starting to wash over me. Until a rattling of the handle, followed by a loud knocking on the library door, brought me back to rude reality.

'William! William, are you in there?'

He stopped and moved himself away from me, with a shushing finger up to his lips. Then he quickly adjusted his clothes and went to the door. I lay motionless, afraid to move on the floor. Mr Harding turned the key in the lock, and I heard the sound of his wife's anxious voice.

'It's dark in there, William. What were you doing?'

'Reading. I fell asleep.'

He eased her away from the entrance to the library and closed the door gently behind him. I jumped to my feet and pulled my uniform back into place. I cautiously checked the hallway outside, before running back downstairs – forgetting completely about the dark reddish stain on the bookcase.

Next day, I was getting funny looks from the other girls and it seemed to me that the whole house knew about the encounter in the library – except for Mrs Harding. And maybe she did too, for all I knew. Then I remembered the cleaning cloths and vinegar and polish, and I ran up there to retrieve them, but they were gone. And so was the stain. I concluded, in the cold light of day, that it was lucky for me we were interrupted before any real damage was done, before I lost my maidenhead or even became pregnant. What a lucky escape! I saw Mr Ayres later in the day, but he said nothing. It was as if there never was a stain on the bookcase and I never went up there to clean it and never met with Mr Harding. As the days passed, I began to think I'd dreamt it all and it was just wishful thinking on my part – just my vivid imagination from reading too many romantic novels. Life returned to the drudgery of the scullery and the never-ending scrubbing and scouring.

When domestic servants are portrayed in dramas and books, it's always about the butler and the cooks and the housemaids and the groundsmen and affairs between the handsome gardener and the lady of the manor – like in D. H. Lawrence's *Lady Chatterley's Lover*, or *Jane Eyre*, where the lord of the manor falls in love with his governess. But there's never been any books or dramas about a seventeen-year-old scullery maid and the thirty-five-year-old master of the house. It would be a scandal, not a romance, especially in 1935. All right, things were changing in the external world around the house in Hampstead – the Communist Party was demonstrating in Trafalgar Square and the Greenshirts were marching and throwing green-painted bricks through windows in Downing Street. But things inside the big houses changed more slowly, and the people who lived behind those impervious walls would have been affronted, whether trade or thoroughbred. Appalled. Outraged. So no novels were written about us poor skivvies, even though we had feelings like everybody else. We were the lowest of the low – ignored, stepped over, trodden on and abused.

So what was I thinking of!

Anyway, I put the incident behind me and resolved never to be so foolish again. A few weeks later I was up early as usual and trying to light the monster of a stove. It was a temperamental beast and you had to treat it with respect or you'd get nowhere fast with it. Little balls of rolled-up newspaper and then just the right amount of kindling and the ritual of drawing, to fetch enough draught for it all to catch light. Once it had a good flame to it, I'd put on a few heavier logs and then some coal to redden it up and keep it going. I'd just finished and was about to put the kettle on so Cook and the kitchen maids could have their cup of tea when I heard someone behind me. I thought it was Nora or Biddy down early, but when I turned I saw it was him – Mr Harding – standing there looking a bit sorry for himself.

The early morning kitchen didn't have the same ambience as the dimly lit library and I was dirty and busy and I knew Cook would be like a demon if she didn't have her tea handed to her as soon as she came through the door. So I wasn't going to fall under his spell this time, and I resolved to clout him across the forehead with the poker if he tried it on – no matter what the consequences. But he didn't come closer, just stood in the doorway and looked at me all doe-eyed.

'Sorry, Anwyn.'

That's all he said. I was going to ask what for, but I decided not to say anything in case I inadvertently encouraged him. We stood there, looking at each other in silence for what seemed like a long time.

'Sorry.'

He said it a second time and then he was gone, disappeared from the doorway as quickly as he'd appeared. Like a ghost.

Later that day I was summoned to Mr. Ayres's office and he told me they were letting me go. I asked why and he said Mrs Harding wasn't happy with my work.

Chapter Six

They were gracious enough to give me a week's notice – which I had to work out, of course. All the girls were sympathetic and told me it wasn't fair and even Cook had a consoling word for me. Mr Ayres said he'd give me a written reference, and, although it was a catastrophe for me, I was also relieved. No matter what happened, it would bring a change – and change was what I needed right then. Kathleen found a week-old page of classified ads from *The Times* and she told me to look through it for a scullery maid vacancy. There weren't any in there, but I did find one or two for live-in barmaids and I thought I might give that a try instead. But most of them wanted experience and I had none, except for cleaning lavatories and collecting glasses. I was just about to resign myself to going back to Wales when I saw this –

WANTED: lady's maid who is modest in person and manner and maintains the strictest sense of honour. Trust is a must. She will read and speak pleasantly; and have neat, legible handwriting. Preferably skilled in plain work [darning stockings, mending linen]. Fastidious and discreet, the ideal candidate will have the ability to plait muslin in addition to performing daily duties in a timely manner. Experience desirable. References essential.

The address was a private house in Belgravia and not an agency, so I thought I'd give it a try. Anything moaning Mona could do, I could do – I was sure of that. And it couldn't possibly be as hard as skivvying. I had nothing to lose. All they could say was no and, if they did, I'd go back to Wales.

I wrote a letter of application in my best handwriting and literary style –

91

To whom it may concern,
*I would like, herewith, to apply for the position
of lady's maid, as recently advertised in* The
Times. *I am eighteen years old, of modest disposition and manner and with the strictest sense
of honour. I am very well-read and you may
judge my handwriting from this application. I
am skilled in many aspects of plain work, as well
as being fastidious and discreet. I have some
experience and can provide references.*

Yours faithfully,
Anwyn Moyle (Miss)

I received a reply on the last Friday of my
notice week in Hampstead, just when I was
giving up hope. I was invited for interview
on the following Monday at 1:00 p.m. precisely. And so I worked through the weekend, counting the hours until I would have
to go along to Belgravia and back up my
lies. Though I didn't consider them to be
great lies – not huge, black lies. No, they
were more the product of invention than
deliberate deception, and displayed a talent
for creative thinking. At least, that's what I
told myself at the time.

Monday morning came and I collected my
final week's wages and added it to the few
shillings I had saved. The servant girls all had
tears in their eyes, but had to get on with
their work and weren't given much time to

say goodbye. Kathleen hugged me and Biddy kissed me and Nora shook my hand. Cook gave me some food wrapped in a piece of muslin cloth and Mr Ayres gave me a typed-out reference. I didn't see Mona or Lilly and I didn't want to, because they'd only have sneered and said it served me right. But Bart the Brat was waiting outside and he carried my bag down the street for me and kissed me goodbye on the cheek at the bus stop. It was early in the morning, before the rush and crush started, and I waited for a long time, thinking about how I'd got myself to here and how this day might shape my future for some time to come.

Kathleen gave me directions and told me the right routes to take and it all seemed a big adventure at my young age of seventeen – all part of the life I was going through. So I waited to see where the wind of change would blow me. I had to take the trolleybus through Chalk Farm and Primrose Hill, then a number fifteen tram down past Regent's Park and Hyde Park and another past Buckingham Palace to Pimlico. The last bus dropped me on the King's Road and I had to walk the rest of the way. But I was far too early for my appointment, so I sauntered into a tea room on the corner of Symons Street and Sloane Square. I was lugging my case and looking for a table in amongst the breakfast crowd of people making their way to work and a young nippy in her black-and-white uniform came over to help me. Tea shop waitresses were known as 'nippies' because of the speed at which they nipped between the tables when serving customers.

'Take this table here, love.'

'Thank you.'

She looked at my case.

'Just arrived?'

'Yes ... no, not in London. I'm going for a job.'

'Is that right. Whereabouts?'

'Chester Square.'

'Very posh. You want a cuppa?'

'Yes please.'

She returned with the tea things on a tray. I asked her how much and she said to pay her when I was ready to leave – just in case I wanted to order anything else. I took my time with the tea because it was only eight o'clock and I had another five hours to go before my appointment. The rush hour passed and things quietened down in the tea shop and the nippy came back over to my table. The pot was empty now, so she brought another and joined me on her break. She lit a cigarette and asked me if I wanted one.

'No thanks, I don't smoke.'

'What job you going for?'

'Lady's maid.'

'What, in one of them big houses?'

'I suppose so.'

She looked me up and down and I could see her thinking I was a bit young to be a lady's maid – and if I couldn't fool her, how was I going to fool the toffs?

'How old are you?'

'Eighteen.'

'Is that right?'

She was about seventeen herself and I could tell she was a kindly sort, even if she was savvy with it. I told her I couldn't pay for too much tea and she said not to worry about it – it was on the house.

'What time's your interview?'

'One o'clock.'

'It's only half ten.'

'I know.'

'Let's me and you go stretch our legs.'

She had a half-hour break before the mid-morning crowd came in. She put my case behind the counter for safety and we set off up Eaton Square, where the houses were white and snobbily superior and bigger even than the one in Hampstead. They were mostly four storeys high, with attics and steps leading down to the basements and they all had columns and balustrades that leaned imposingly out over the main road. We turned right into Elizabeth Street and then left into Chester Square. The houses there were almost as impressive as the ones in Eaton Square, but with black railings and balconies, and the street was less ostentatious and more serene.

We found number twenty-four, where I was due at 1:00 p.m., and we stood on the opposite side and looked over at it. There was no sign of life and I was afraid someone might be peering out through a window and spot me staring and recognise me when I came calling later in the day. They'd probably think I wasn't the full shilling, so I said we should move on.

We walked up to Eccleston Street then turned into the other end of Eaton Square and headed back down towards the tea shop. The nippy told me her name was Lucy and I said I was Anwyn and she asked what would I do if I didn't get the job.

'Go back to Wales, I suppose.'

'And do you want to?'

'Not really.'

She said I should come back to the tea shop if my interview was unsuccessful. They were looking for a girl and I seemed like the type who would fit in well.

'But, Lucy, I have nowhere to live.'

She lived with her family down in Bermondsey and travelled up here on the tram every day to work. I could share her room with her and we'd be company for each other on the way. I was slightly sorry I'd applied for the lady's maid job now, because the tea shop seemed like more fun. But if I hadn't gone for it in the first place, I wouldn't be here now – kismet? Or *wyrd*, to put it the old Welsh way. And there was little chance of me being taken on, so I thought I might as well keep the appointment – for the experience.

Lucy said I could leave my case in the tea shop and, at 12:30 p.m., I made my way back up to 24 Chester Square. I gave myself half-an-hour for the five minute walk, so I'd be nice and early and make a good impression. I didn't know what sort of formalities I'd have to go through but, even if I wasn't going to get the job, I wanted to let them see I was a real person and not some stereotype to be snorted through their noses at. So I got out the green hat Mrs Reynolds gave me and wore my best few stitches of clothes and Lucy helped me with some lipstick and make-up and I thought I looked the bee's knees and it made me feel confident.

'Good luck, Anwyn.'

'Thanks, Lucy.'

When I got to the house, I didn't know whether to knock on the front door or go down the steps to the basement, like I had to at Hampstead. But I thought, I'm here for the job of lady's maid, not skivvy, so the front door it was. It was a big black door, heavy and intimidating. The single step was polished and the brass handles and knocker were gleaming, and I thought some poor scullery maid was probably out doing that work at the crack of dawn this morning. It was a while before the door opened. I didn't want to knock again and seem impatient and impertinent. When it did, a thin man in a tailcoat stood there, looking down his long beak of a nose at me.

'Yes?'

'I'm Anwyn Moyle.'

'Yes?'

'I've come for an interview.'

I could see him looking me up and down and I thought he'd seen through me already and would send me packing with a flea in my counterfeit ear. But he held the door open and I walked through into a spacious hallway. The thin man in the tailcoat led the way to a waiting room, where two other women were already seated. The merest hint of a smile ran across their faces when I came in, as much as to say, not much competition there.

Other women joined us in the waiting room as the minutes ticked slowly past and it ended up with eight of us altogether. They were all older than me and looked so sure of themselves that I was going to get up and leave, as it was obvious I'd never get the job and I was a fool for applying in the first place. But I started to read the fashion magazines that were strewn on a well-polished walnut occasional table in front of us. None of the others read, just sat primly perched on their chairs as if they knew they were being observed through some secret spyhole in the wall – while I slouched back in my seat and crossed my legs like a layabout and looked through all the magazines.

On the stroke of 1:00 p.m., the thin man in the tailcoat began calling us out of the room, one by one. There seemed to be no order to his selection and women who'd arrived after me were being called before me. Eventually I was the only one left in the waiting room and it was 6:00 p.m. and I'd read all the magazines from cover to cover and I was starving. I wished I'd brought Cook's little muslin parcel of food so I could have a chew on something, but I'd left it in the case, back at the tea shop. Finally, beak-nose came and called me.

'Anwyn Moyle.'

'That's me.'

'Come.'

I followed him up a flight of stairs and then down a long corridor to a kind of anteroom with a frosted glass partition. I could hear voices coming from the other side when tail-coat went through and announced me.

'Anwyn Moyle.'

'Show her in please, Jacob.'

He stood in the entrance and beckoned me to step through.

The room was large and luxuriously fur-nished, with big casement windows looking out onto the square below. A shiny, black grand piano stood silent in one corner and there was a large mahogany desk in the middle of the room, with two people sat behind it – a middle-aged man who looked like a solicitor or an accountant, and a stylishly dressed woman of about thirty. There was another person some distance away in a secluded corner and it was difficult to make out whether it was a man or a woman.

'Sit ... please.'

The man behind the desk stood up and pointed to a chair placed several feet back from the other side. His voice was pleasant enough and I seated myself as comfortably as I could, under the inquisitional circumstances.

'I'm Mr Peacock, advisor to the household, and this is Mrs Staines, the outgoing lady's maid.'

I nodded to them and handed over my reference. The woman behind the desk smiled and inclined her head slightly to one side. Mr Peacock didn't introduce the person in the gloom at the other end of the room, who was preoccupied with reading a book.

Mrs Staines spoke and her voice was soft and accent-free. She looked directly at me and her eyes were a pale-blue colour and they seemed to pierce my very soul.

'How old are you, Miss Moyle?'

'Eighteen, Madam.'

They glanced at each other for a brief moment, Mr Peacock and Mrs Staines, but didn't pursue the age question any further and seemed to accept that I was a year older than my birth certificate would have confirmed. Peacock began the interview.

'Your letter of application is certainly impressive, Miss Moyle ... good handwriting and a nice turn of phrase. Short and to the point.'

'Thank you, Sir.'

'And what have you read?'

I recited a litany of the books I'd read over the years and he seemed impressed. Mrs Staines was more pragmatic, while Mr Peacock perused my reference.

'Tell me, Miss Moyle, what experience do you have?'

'I was a scullery maid for a while, Madam, as well as a kitchen maid, so I can clean and cook and sew and mend and–'

'I was referring to lady's maid experience, my dear.'

'Well, your advertisement said experience desirable, not essential.'

'And your application said you had some.'

She'd called my bluff. I had no experience as a lady's maid – I didn't even know what the job entailed, apart from the bits and pieces I'd seen Mona doing up in Hampstead. I'd been found out, exposed for what I was – a fraud. Mr Peacock chirped in, to save my guilty blushes.

'It's a good reference.'

'Thank you, Sir.'

'But it's from the butler, not from the lady of the house.'

'No, Sir.'

That was it, I was finished. This would be the shortest of all the interviews. I expected they were tired after the long afternoon and wanted to get away to their tea or dinner or whatever it was they would be getting away to. Then the figure in the corner moved out of the shadows and I could see it was a woman of about twenty-six or -seven. She put down the book and spoke for the first time.

'You worked for the Hardings, didn't you?'

'Yes, Madam.'

'That explains why you didn't get a reference from the lady of the house.'

She came closer and I could see she was quite beautiful, in a wild sort of way, with jet-black hair and dark eyes. She was slightly shorter than me, but her figure was statuesque and her demeanour was somewhat imperious.

'Can you think for yourself, Anwyn Moyle?'

I didn't understand the question.

'In what way, Madam?'

'There is only one way a woman can think for herself.'

'If you mean, do I respect myself as a woman, then I most definitely do, Madam.'

She turned away and picked up the book again. It was obvious she knew all about me and I hadn't given her the answer she wanted. Mr Peacock stood up and rang a little bell.

'We'll let you know, Miss Moyle. Where shall we send our decision?'

'I beg your pardon, Sir?'

The woman with the book spoke again. This time she didn't look at me, but addressed the page she was reading, or pretended to be reading.

'The Hardings let you go, didn't they?'

'Yes, Madam.'

Peacock smiled condescendingly and spoke again.

'So, where should we send our decision?'

I couldn't tell them to send it to Wales, and there was nowhere else – except the tea shop.

'To the Sussex Rose Tea Rooms ... in Sloane Square.'

'I know it.'

Beak-nose appeared like a spectre in his tailcoat. Peacock handed me back my reference.

'Good evening then, Miss Moyle.'

I was on my way to the door when the woman with the book called after me.

'That hat ... where did you get it?'

'It was a gift, Madam.'

'What design is it?'

'It's a Henry Pollak, Madam.'

And that was it. I was outside on the step with the cool evening breeze blowing on my face and the whole interview seemed bizarre, like a chapter out of one of Mrs Beeton's books.

I went back to the tea shop and Lucy was waiting for me after finishing her shift. I opened my case and devoured the food Cook had given me, along with a pot of tea. Lucy was anxiously waiting for me to stop stuffing my face and tell her what had happened, but I was famished and couldn't talk until I'd eaten everything in the piece of cloth.

'You were gone so long, Anwyn.'

'I was the last one to be seen.'

'That's a good sign.'

'Is it?'

Lucy had been to many interviews and she told me they normally keep the most likely candidate till last. But I didn't believe that applied in this case. I said they knew who I was and that I'd been sacked and I wasn't eighteen and had no experience – so why would they give me the job?

'Why did they ask you for interview in the first place, if they already knew all that?'

It was a question I couldn't answer. A total mystery. And it didn't solve my immediate problem – I was jobless and homeless. Lucy said I could come back to Bermondsey with her that night and we'd sort everything out the following day.

Chapter Seven

Bermondsey was a slum area of London in the 1930s and Lucy's father was a docker who worked on the wharfs along the Thames and Surrey docks, which was a centre of the timber trade and barge-building and rope-making. Food factories flooded the area, with Crosse & Blackwell in Crimscott Street and Lipton's on Rouel Road and Pearce Duff on the Spa Road and Peek Frean's by the St Saviours dock – and Courage had a brewery near to Tower Bridge. Most of the work in these places was casual and wages were low and the area was deprived and poverty-stricken. Housing conditions were bad, with overcrowding and poor sanitation and absentee landlords nor caring if their tenants had to live like rats. The industrial activity contributed to poor air quality and endemic health problems – and I'd thought life was tough in the coal-mining villages of South Wales. When I got down to Bermondsey in 1935, things were beginning to improve. Slums were being demolished and streets cleaned up and communal laundries opened. What couldn't be cleaned was radiated in a purpose-built solarium and tuberculosis dispensaries and foot and dental clinics were being set up.

But conditions were still very bad.

Although Lucy's family had a two-bed-roomed house, she had three sisters, and they shared a toilet with another family from next door. There was clearly no room for me, even though they made me feel as welcome as they could. Her mother said she shouldn't have let me think she had her own room and was sorry that I'd been deceived so. Lucy said she just wanted a friend that she could travel back and forth from work with and I had no place else to go and I could sleep with her in her bed and have half her food. But it wasn't right. I just couldn't put upon poor people like that. So, when we went back to the tea shop in Belgravia the next day, I took my case with me. Lucy was a bit upset and said I didn't have to leave – but I knew I couldn't stay.

The tea shop was run by a woman called Hannah who said she'd give me a week's trial as a nippy starting on the Wednesday, but it got very busy and I'd have to be on my toes. There was a little room with a bunk and a sink at the back of the shop and I could sleep there until I found something better. But once the shop shut in the evening, I'd be locked in and couldn't leave until it opened again at 7:30 in the morning. I said I didn't mind and at least I'd have some time to myself in the evening to read. I went to the local public lending library and took out some books and magazines and other stuff, and while I was there I came across a manual about how to be a lady's maid and I thought I'd have a flick through it, just to see what I was going to be missing when they didn't give me the job.

That night was lonely in the bleak little back room with the late London noises all around me but strangely separated from me. I heard a mouse scrabbling somewhere and then I fell asleep reading an edition of *The House of Dreams* by Katharine Tynan.

My first day in the tea shop was disastrous. I was all the time depending on Lucy and the other nippies to tell me this and that and what a masala chai or an oolong or a lapsang souchong was. Don't forget, the shop was in a high-class area and the clientele liked to show off their aesthetic knowledge by ordering the most obscure beverages they could think of. This was no bacon buttie place and there was a bewildering assortment of cakes and tarts and scones and croissants and strudels and bizcochos and eclairs and pains and sandwiches and shortbreads to choose from. They had a specialist Chinese tea-brewer in the kitchen and a patissier for anything that wasn't à la carte and it was total confusion in the busy periods.

At the end of that first day, my feet were

nearly crippled from running between the tables in the block-heeled strap-boots they gave me as part of the black-and-white uniform, and I was glad when it was all over and they locked me into the little back room to rest and recuperate.

That night, instead of studying the menus, like Hannah told me to, to better accustom myself with the tea shop's cuisine, I picked up the lady's maid manual and thought to myself that I was a bit premature in not caring whether I got the job or not. I read that a lady's maid had to be a combination of seamstress and hairdresser and beautician and masseuse and secretary. They reported directly to the lady of the house, rather than the housekeeper or head butler. Their duties could range from bringing the mistress breakfast in bed to selecting her wardrobe and jewellery and styling her hair. A good lady's maid could make a plain woman look beautiful and more recherché than she really was, and often it was the lady's maid's taste that was behind the outward show of her mistress. She would supply the glamour and sophistication required to maintain these upper-class women in high society and the skills of the lady's maid could mean the difference between triumph and disaster.

The lady's maid needed to be aware of the latest fashions and choose perfumes and ball gowns and perform manicures and pedicures and facials. She should know about etiquette and local customs and cultures and formalities, so the mistress didn't put her foot in it with dignitaries. She'd be responsible for the upkeep of the lady's wardrobe and would be skilled in the care and cleaning of valuable clothing.

And I thought to myself, maybe it's just as well I didn't get the job, as I didn't have a clue about most of that stuff. All right, I'd seen moaning Mona perform some of her duties at the Hardings', but our paths didn't cross that often and she wasn't one for fraternising with scullery maids.

Thursday in the tea shop was just as frantic, with Hannah frowning at me for not doing what she told me and studying the menus and the methods of serving and satisfying the delicate Belgravian palates. I was slower than the day before because my feet were killing me from long hours in the boots and I knew I wasn't going to make it as a nippy and would be on my way back to Wales at the end of the week's trial. By Friday, though, things were starting to get a little bit better. I was getting used to the work and the customers and the cuisine and the different types of tea. But Hannah was making grumpy noises about the back room and if the owners found out I was living there she'd get it in the neck and I knew she wanted me out. I was thinking, if I could just get somewhere to live, then this job might not be so bad after all. I made up my mind to go searching on Sunday for a room or a boarding house somewhere, but it would mean being locked out of the shop from Saturday night until it opened again on Monday morning.

Then an embossed envelope was delivered by hand to the tea shop. It was blazoned with a lion couchant and it was addressed to me. I opened it, expecting to be told I hadn't got the job as a lady's maid.

Dear Miss Moyle,
Thank you for attending for interview on Monday. We would be grateful if you could return for a further, informal consultation on Sunday next at 11:00 a.m.
Thanking you in anticipation,
Yours sincerely,
Walter Peacock ACCA

I showed the letter to Lucy and she was convinced they were going to give me the job after all.

'Surely not?'

'Why would they ask you back, then?'

'Maybe I'm not the only one?'

So, Saturday after work in the tea shop, I collected my wages of half-a-crown and lugged my case back down to Bermondsey to spend one more night with Lucy and her lovely family. I gave her mother a shilling for my bed and board and she didn't want to take my money, but I made her.

Sunday morning I was up early and washed and dressed in my best and Lucy did my make-up and I set off for Belgravia, again in my green hat. I arrived at Chester Square at 10:45 a.m. and the tailcoat opened the door and showed me into the waiting room. I was the only one there and I waited for the others to arrive – but nobody did. At 11:00 a.m. precisely, tailcoat came back and called me from the room. I followed him up the stairs again and along the corridor, but this time he showed me into a smaller room, with a fire burning in the grate and a table set for tea and *petits fours*. He took my hat and coat and motioned for me to sit at the table, then he left. I waited for about five minutes before the book-reading woman I met at the first interview came into the room and sat opposite me.

'It's always best to allow the tea to draw for a few minutes, don't you think? Shall I be mother?'

Before I could answer, she poured two cups of tea and shoved the plate of little biscuits my way.

'It's only Darjeeling, probably not what you're used to at the Sussex Rose Rooms, but I'm sure it will suffice.'

'I'm sure it will, Madam.'

We sipped the tea in silence for a while, with her looking at me and me looking away from her, so as not to upset social niceties and catch her eye. Eventually she spoke.

'Why did you apply for this job, Anwyn Moyle?'

I didn't answer immediately. It needed a bit of quick thinking.

'Because I know I can be a good lady's maid, Madam.'

'And how do you know that?'

How indeed? My brain was racing round the room, trying to find an answer that wouldn't sound completely ridiculous. And I got the feeling if I didn't find a good one, I'd be shown the door again. She was testing me, I knew that – to see what I was made of.

'Because I can think for myself, Madam.'

She smiled. Not a broad smile – more with her eyes than her mouth. I took a petit four from the plate and nibbled at it delicately.

'Wait here.'

She rose without saying another word and left the room. I thought I was being clever, but maybe I was being conceited. I should have said, 'Because I can clean and sew and I know something about fashion and I'm young and can learn and my mind is open.' But it was too late now; tailcoat would be coming any minute to throw me out.

After about quarter of an hour, Mr Peacock came in and sat at the table opposite me. He had a couple of documents in his hand.

'I'm pleased to inform you, Miss Moyle, that, should you still be interested in the position of lady's maid, we are prepared to offer it to you on a month's trial basis.'

'I'm still interested.'

I said this too quickly. Too eagerly. His left eye twitched slightly as he looked at me.

'If Mrs Bouchard is happy with your work after that period of time, the position will be offered on a permanent basis.'

'Thank you, Sir.'

Mrs Bouchard. It was the first time I'd heard her name mentioned – the woman I'd be working for. It sounded French, but she didn't speak with a French accent. Peacock placed the documents on the table in front of me, along with a pen.

'A contract of employment and a confidentiality agreement.'

I didn't know what a confidentiality agreement was, but I signed both documents just the same.

'The wages'll be five shillings per week for the trial period, rising to eight shillings if you are deemed suitable and then to ten shillings after a year. Is this acceptable, Miss Moyle?'

'Eminently.'

He smiled covertly at my sauciness. But he didn't shake my hand, and it seemed to me he wasn't completely happy with my appointment.

'When can you start?'

'Tomorrow?'

'Tomorrow would be capital, Miss Moyle. Shall we say seven o'clock? In the a.m. of course.'

'Of course.'

Jacob the beak-nosed butler showed me out again. A timid, early spring sun was shining in Chester Square as I skipped my way down the street. I'd be sad to leave Lucy; she'd been so good to me when I needed a friend. But the tea shop was only five minutes away and I was sure we'd be able to meet up quite often and carry on our friendship into the future. I hurried back to Bermondsey to tell her the news and we all celebrated that night in her family's humble home and drank dandelion and burdock and ate friendship fruit cake and had a little sing-song till it was time to go to bed. Everyone had to be up very early in the morning.

I couldn't sleep and I wrote a letter to my mother in Wales, telling her about my good fortune. I was all excited and happy and thinking about what I could do with eight shillings a week. I'd send half home to my mother and I'd be able to go dancing and dining and delighting myself with the rest. Then the doubts crept in and they kept me awake more than the excitement. How would I be able to cope with this job? What would they expect of me? They'd find me out for a fraud after the first day and then I'd be disgraced – have to crawl back to the tea shop with my pretentious tail between my legs. Have to scuttle back to Wales and arrive at the same time as this letter, promising my mother half-a-crown a week for the trial period. I tossed and turned and turned and tossed in the bed beside Lucy. I counted sheep until I could've collected ten buckets of droppings and sold them for fire-fuel. The next I knew was Lucy shaking me by the shoulder.

'Anwyn, get up! It's half-past-five.'

I jumped out of the bed and took my turn in the shared toilet to have a wash. Then I dressed and had a cup of tea and a bit of leftover bun from the night before. Lucy did my make-up as usual and I lugged my case down to the number thirty-six tram stop at a quarter-past six. I was standing on the step outside 24 Chester Square at ten minutes to seven. Tailcoat took my case and put it some-where, then he introduced himself as Jacob, the first footman, even though there were no other footmen in the household. He took me through and introduced me to the cook, whose name was Mrs Jackson – she was a jolly sort of woman in her mid-forties and not at all like the Beadle of Hampstead. She had two kitchen maids under her, Esther and Annie, and she said they'd call me Miss Moyle so nobody would be confused. I don't know if she meant that as a joke and they all knew I was just a jumped-up scullery maid, or if she was being sincere. The scullery maid was Josie and she genuflected when I shook her hand, even though I was only a few years older than her. Tom, the chauffeur, was having his breakfast and he was an ex-army man and asked 'How are you, young lady?' I told him I was well and he said he was glad to hear it.

We then went upstairs and Jacob introduced me to the two parlourmaids, Heather and Beatrice, both of whom were about eighteen, the age I was pretending to be. They giggled when I shook their hands, as if they were party to a joke and I wasn't. There were no children in the house and no nanny and, finally, I was shown into the housekeeper's drawing room to meet Miss Mason, the head housemaid, who was responsible for catering and linen and the supervision of the other female servants. She was a severe-looking woman of about thirty-five, dressed all in black and buttoned up to the neck in a figure-hugging frock. Her face was pale and thin and her features were sharp and her hair was pulled back in a severe braided bun. She barely touched my hand when I offered it to her, as if she might catch something unpleasant from it. Then she sniffed and waved to Jacob and I was taken away. The footman then took me to my room, saying I'd meet

Mr Biggs the butler and Mrs Hathaway the housekeeper later in the day. My case had already been delivered to the room and he left me and closed the door behind him, not mentioning what I was expected to do or what my duties were or what would happen next.

The room was spacious enough, bigger than anything I'd ever been used to, at least. There was a fair-sized sprung bed with a thick mattress and a matching set of walnut bedroom furniture, consisting of a bedside cabinet and a mirrored dressing table and a big wardrobe. The room was carpeted in brown and beige, and matching floor-length curtains covered the window that looked out over the manicured back of the house. I unpacked my case and put my stuff away in the drawers but, when I opened the wardrobe, I found there was already an assortment of clothes hanging there – dresses and coats and jackets and cardigans and rayon stockings and five or six pairs of shoes on the floor. So I left my own couple of dresses in the case, thinking these clothes belonged to Mrs Staines the previous lady's maid, and she'd be sure to be coming back for them. There was a crystal jug with water and a set of crystal glasses on a table close to the window, so I poured some and had a drink to quench my thirst and sat on the bed and waited. It was only about half-past eight in the morning.

I didn't have to wait long. A few minutes later I heard a knock on the door.

'Come in.'

It was Heather, one of the young house-maids.

'Would you like breakfast in your room, Miss Moyle?'

'As opposed to...?'

She didn't seem to understand my question for a moment, then she giggled and put her hand up to her mouth.

'Oh, sorry ... or with Miss Mason in Mrs Hathaway's parlour.'

'I'll have it here, thanks.'

I couldn't tell if it was a giggle or a snigger, but she left the room with her hand still up to her mouth and, ten minutes later, came back with a pot of tea and a fried breakfast of bacon, sausage, eggs and toasted bread. My eyes lit up and I started tucking in straight away because I was famished. Heather watched me for a moment, as if I was behaving exactly as she supposed I would.

'Bon appetit.'

She said it in a fake French accent and I thought it must be some kind of sarcasm that fitted the context of Mrs Bouchard's name.

I waited again after breakfast, but still nobody came to tell me what my duties would be or when I should start them or what I should be doing now that I was here. At

11:00 a.m., I could stand the prevarication no longer, so I decided to venture out of my room and take a look around, not knowing what parts of the house might be off limits to a lady's maid in waiting.

My room was on the second floor, as were three other private bedrooms, all much bigger than mine and one with a separate dressing room. There were two bathrooms, one en suite to the master bedroom, which I presumed was Mr and Mrs Bouchard's, while the other bathroom was smaller and I expected it was for use by the rest of the family. The first floor consisted of a large, opulently furnished drawing room, a music room, which housed the piano, and a tea room, where I'd been the day before. The ground floor housed the large entrance hall, another drawing room, smaller than the one on the first floor, and a library, similar in size to the one at Hampstead, and a room which I could only assume was Mrs Hathaway's parlour. The basement of the house accommodated the kitchen and scullery, of course, and the male servants' quarters, while the top, or attic, floor housed the female servants' rooms. There was also a third floor which seemed to be unused at the moment, but which might be utilised from time to time as guest rooms, when the house hosted parties or soirées.

It was midday by the time I finished my

little tour and, while I was mooching about, I saw no one, except for a brief glimpse of Beatrice the housemaid in one of the drawing rooms, and the cook and her kitchen maids in the basement. At one o'clock lunch was served and this time I was summoned to the housekeeper's parlour. Jacob showed me in and I was confronted by Miss Mason, all buttoned up in her black and still sporting her stern face, and a middle-aged woman with dark eyes and dressed in a tweed two-piece. She was of stout stature with a pleasant face and her greying hair was done up in a loose sock bun on top of her head.

'I'm Mrs Hathaway, the housekeeper. Please, sit down.'

We sat and the maids served us with a lunch of tomato and cheddar soup, followed by pork cutlets dressed with fennel, dill and cucumber and accompanied with a spoonful or two of diced potatoes, along with yellow watermelon for pudding. Not much was said during lunch and I found I wasn't all that hungry after the big fried breakfast – I wasn't used to eating like this and my stomach would take time adjusting to it. But I did my best, as I was always taught to waste not and, consequently, to want not, and I believed that lie. The two other women settled back with cups of tea when the dishes were cleared away.

Mrs Hathaway was just about to say something to me, when the door opened and a tall man came into the parlour. He was about forty-five or fifty, dressed in a tailcoat and striped trousers like Jacob's. He wore a white shirt and black tie under his waistcoat and his hair was blackish grey and sleeked back by a pomade, which was an emulsion of water and mineral oil and stabilised with beeswax. He looked a bit like Bela Lugosi and Miss Mason almost swooned when he came in. She and Mrs Hathaway rose from their seats to greet him.

'Mr Biggs... we weren't expecting you till later. We've already had lunch.'

'Not to worry, Mrs Hathaway, I've already dined.'

He looked down at me with an ominous glare. I thought I'd better stand too, so I did.

'This is Miss Moyle, the new lady's maid.'

He looked me up and down for a moment, as if he was judging a heifer at a cattle fair.

'How old are you, my dear?'

'I'm eighteen.'

'Rather young...'

He mumbled this last remark to himself and shot a raised-eyebrow glance at the other women. Mr Biggs then poured himself a cup of tea and we all sat down again.

The other three spoke amongst themselves about household matters and largely ignored me for a while, until I eventually interrupted them.

'Excuse me...'

They all stopped talking and turned to look at me.

'What am I supposed to be doing?'

Mrs Hathaway spoke first, in an offhand, sarcastic way.

'Don't you know?'

'Not really ... I mean, I know what my duties will be, but I expected some sort of agenda...'

Mr Biggs swallowed the last of his tea and stood up.

'Mrs Bouchard is away today, so you should take the opportunity to settle in. I'm sure she will instruct you tomorrow.'

The others stood too and it looked like lunchtime was over. I returned to my room and read for the rest of the day, interrupted only by Heather bringing me a supper of mackerel fillets with lemon and coriander, a mixture of mashed carrot and potato and some roast figs with honey – along with another pot of tea. I left most of it and fell into a fretful sleep later in the evening, when it was dark and forsaken outside in the groomed garden below my window.

Chapter Eight

I was already up and dressed when Heather brought my breakfast at 8:00 a.m. next morning. She was more subdued today, and there was no sniggering behind her hand. At about 8:30 a.m., Jacob came and knocked on the door.

'Madam Bouchard will see you in half an hour.'

He was about to leave, but I jumped up and grabbed his arm. He looked startled, like he'd just been bitten by an uncivilised dog and he pulled himself away from me.

'Jacob, please ... wait.'

'What is it?'

'I want to know about Mrs Bouchard.'

'Then you should ask her.'

'I'm asking you. Please, Jacob...'

My big eyes and girlish guile must have softened his heart. He came back into the room and closed the door.

'You mustn't say I said anything.'

'Upon my apostate soul.'

His voice was a low whisper, as if someone might be listening, and he told me what he knew about Madam Bouchard, as he called her. Her maiden name was Brandon and she held the title of 'Lady'. Her family went all the way back to Charles Brandon, Duke of Suffolk, who married Mary Tudor, one of the daughters of Henry VII. They had several children, one of whom, called Frances, married Henry Grey, who was also Duke of Suffolk, and their daughter was Jane Grey, who was queen of England for nine days, before being executed by Bloody Mary when she was sixteen. But Madam Bouchard's ancestors were from the more obscure branch of the family tree of one of Charles Brandon's illegitimate children and couldn't claim any entitlement to the throne. The Madam herself had a younger brother who would inherit her father's title and also the country estate in Warwickshire. He had a separate house in London and he rarely visited Chester Square.

Jacob didn't want to go on, but I knew there was more to it and I stood inside the door and wouldn't move out of his way until he told me. More recently, Mr Brandon senior was involved in military intelligence during the Great War. He was attached to MI3d, which apparently handled Scandinavia. Mr Brandon junior was too young to be involved in the war, and he didn't really do anything these days, but follow his adventurer father round the world on his trips to out of the way places. The Brandons kept their cards close to their chests and that's all

Jacob knew about them. Madam Brandon, as he called her, was the black sheep of the family. She'd married an Algerian called Emile Bouchard against her family's wishes and they disowned her for that and she went to live in the city of Oran with her husband.

Bouchard was of French ancestry, even though he was born in North Africa. He was killed in a bar-brawl with some Algerian nationals two years earlier. Madam Bouchard's family relented after this and allowed the prodigal daughter to return home and bought her the house in Chester Square and gave her access to society again. She had no children and was the only one living here, apart from the servants and occasional guests.

'That's all I can tell you, Miss Moyle. Now can you please get out of my way.'

'Of course. Thank you, Jacob.'

He hurried out the door and, half an hour later, came back again and escorted me along the corridor to the master bedroom. He knocked on the door.

'Come in.'

Jacob indicated for me to enter the room, which I did. Mrs Bouchard was sitting up in bed, eating breakfast from a tray that was set on a little trestle across her lap. Jacob didn't come into the room, but closed the door behind me. Mrs Bouchard pointed to a chair beside the bed, but didn't speak until she'd swallowed what was in her mouth.

'So sorry I wasn't here yesterday, Anwyn. Shall I call you Anwyn? I think so, don't you?'

'Yes, of course, Madam.'

'And you must call me Miranda.'

I didn't think I'd be able to call her that. Nobody ever called the toffs by their Christian names, or any other name except their title.

'Are you sure, Madam?'

'Of course. You do know who Miranda was, don't you?'

'From Shakespeare's *The Tempest*, I think.'

'Yes, the motherless magician's daughter. Quite analogous to myself, really.'

She finished eating and indicated for me to remove the trestle, which I did and just stood there holding it, not knowing what to do next.

'Just put it on that table.'

She reached for a packet of cigarettes and lit one. I placed an ashtray close to her on the bed.

'You're a very literate young lady, Anwyn. Do you know what the name Bouchard means?'

'No, Madam ... sorry Miranda.'

'It means big mouth. So, let's talk, shall we?'

Over the next hour or so, Miranda Bouchard smoked half a dozen cigarettes and outlined what my duties would be. I'd have to help her dress and undress, although she said she was no invalid and wouldn't require to be treated as one. I wouldn't need to bring her breakfast, as one of the parlourmaids would do that, but she wanted me to eat with her in the dining room for lunch and dinner, except when she was entertaining guests.

I was too inexperienced to select her wardrobe and jewellery, but I knew a fair bit about fashion and she was prepared to listen to my advice, if I wanted to give it. And I'd be expected to learn this aspect of the job, through observation, as I went along. She had a hair stylist who came down from Carlisle Street for the big jobs, but I'd be required to tend to her hair on a day-to-day basis and maybe learn enough to take over from the stylist in time. I'd also be required to apply and remove make-up and perform manicures and pedicures. I'd have to clean and tidy the master bedroom, her dressing room and her bathroom, as these places were where she kept her most intimate possessions and she didn't want the other servants handling them. Well, cleaning and tidying a few rooms would be no bother to someone like me who'd spent the last year or so scrubbing and shining and sprucing.

I wouldn't be required to mend clothes, as that was a specialised job, but I would be required to deliver and collect items to and from a seamstress in St Martin's Lane. Miranda Bouchard didn't usually rise until 9:00 a.m. and I'd have to be ready when she did. She suggested I continue as I did that morning with breakfast being served to me at 8:00 a.m. and for me to come find her when I was finished. She couldn't be as precise when it came to going back to bed in the evening – her hours were erratic and she might want me at any time. On such occasions, if I wasn't accompanying her, I should go to bed when I wanted and she'd wake me or have me woken if she needed me. I'd also have to tend to her if she was ill, administering medicines prescribed by her doctor and, if necessary, sleeping in the master bedroom with her. But probably the most important of my duties would be to circulate with other ladies' maids whenever I came into contact with them and to extract as much information as possible about who would be wearing what and who was having a liaison with whom and all the other little secrets of Mrs Bouchard's social group.

In 1935, the heyday of the socialites was over. Estates were being sold off left, right and centre. I'd heard Mr Harding and Mr Ayres discussing it once at Hampstead and they said that only a third of the families listed in Burke's Peerage actually held land any more. Mr Harding wasn't bothered about that because he was an industrialist, not an aristocrat. With the decline of the aristocracy came the decline of what was called the social calendar. But the London season was still happening, though maybe not in such an extravagant way as before. And the picture of the Mitford sisters in all the papers, posing with the Nazi stormtroopers at that Nuremberg rally, didn't endear the toffs to the ordinary people who were suffering the effects of the Great Slump. It all seemed so objectionable, these people swaggering and flaunting, while the rest of the country were tightening their belts. But the shrunken social scene meant there was even more gossiping and backstabbing than before and everyone wanted to be one step ahead of everyone else.

'It's a very claustrophobic world, Anwyn, but one I have to live in.'

'I understand.'

'Good girl.'

She said I'd also be expected to travel with her. There would be Cheltenham in a few weeks' time, and Ascot and Epsom in June, Henley Regatta in July and Cowes week in August. I'd also be required to accompany her to spas and vapour treatments and restaurants and department stores and cinemas, unless she was accompanied by someone else. There would also be all the London events, like the Chelsea Flower Show, tea parties in May, the Garter Service in June, the Royal Academy Summer Exhibition and the West End theatre scene. There would be the many balls and champagne parties during the summer season – the May Ball at Grosvenor House, the Cavalry and Guards Club Ball and other private soirées, up to the end of the season in September. The house in Chester Square would then be closed up and put into the hands of the caretakers, while we'd all travel up to Warwickshire to spend the winter on the Brandon family's country estate.

There was no 'summoning' bell in my room and I wondered how Mrs Bouchard would call me when she wanted me. She said she'd either come and get me herself or send someone for me.

'There are strict rules of behaviour that we'll have to adhere to, Anwyn.'

'I'm sure there are, Madam.'

'Miranda.'

'Yes, Miranda, sorry.'

I was going to find it difficult to get used to calling her by her Christian name.

'They aren't my rules, please understand that. They're society's rules.'

'I understand.'

'Things are changing. Anwyn, but some of these rules still can't be challenged, especially by a woman.'

'I suppose not.'

By now, the bedroom was full of cigarette

smoke. She pulled back the bed sheets and revealed that she was wearing nothing but her underwear – no nightdress nor robe nor chemise of any kind and I must have appeared a little startled.

'I got used to sleeping naked in Algeria, so now I just can't abide a lot of clothes on me in bed.'

'Quite right.'

'You don't have to agree with everything I say, Anwyn.'

'I know that. But you haven't said anything I disagree with yet.'

She laughed a little and discarded the underwear and walked naked to the bathroom.

'You'll need to draw my bath for me after breakfast. But I'll do it myself today. I like the water to be about thirty degrees ... not too hot. And just clear water, no salts or soap suds of any kind.'

'Very well.'

'You can use the other bathroom, you know where it is?'

'Yes. Thank you.'

I opened the windows to let out the smoke while she was bathing. I stripped the bed of its sheets and found replacements in a linen cupboard in the hall. I also found Beatrice and asked her to bring me some paper and kindling and coal and, while I was waiting, I tidied up the bedroom and selected what was for washing and cleaning and which clothes could be put back into the huge wardrobes. Miranda was in the bathroom for almost an hour and, when she came back out, the bedroom was tidied and the windows closed against the springtime chill and a lively little fire taking hold in the grate.

'You've been busy.'

'Just doing my job.'

'Mrs Staines never lit the fire.'

I wondered about Mrs Staines and why she left. It was none of my business, but I thought I might as well ask, just in case there was something I should know about.

'She got married. The best ladies' maids are single, so they're available all the time and can travel at short notice.'

Mrs Bouchard said she wasn't going out that day and just wanted to read and take care of some household matters with Mrs Hathaway. So I helped her dress in some casual clothes and did her hair for her in a brushed-back tutorial style and, as she didn't want to wear any make-up, she was ready to leave the room. When she did, I cleaned up the bathroom and put everything back in its place. Then I emptied the ashtray and cleaned it and also the hairbrushes and made sure everything on the dressing table was where I thought it should be. I realised that the cigarette smoke in the room would eventually discolour the curtains and bedspreads, as well as the walls and ceilings, and I resolved to talk to Miss Mason about getting them cleaned. By the time I was finished, it was almost midday and I went back to tidy up my own room. I'd only just finished when Jacob knocked on the door again.

'Madam Bouchard requires your company in the dining room.'

I followed him downstairs and he held a chair for me while I sat close to Miranda at a long, highly polished teak dining-table.

The housemaids served us lunch of leek and mustard soup, followed by coronation chicken with sultanas and pineapple and spring onion and a seasonal salad, with home-made vanilla ice cream for pudding. Miranda didn't speak until the ubiquitous tea pot was on the table.

'You think this is decadent, don't you?'

'What is?'

'All these servants for just one woman.'

'It is a bit excessive, I must agree.'

'My family insists, for the sake of appearances.'

One of the strict rules of society she spoke about earlier, no doubt. And I did think it was decadent – all the food that would have fed half the poor in London and the frivolous waste of money that could have paid to improve the lives of working-class families like Lucy's. But I'd learned to 'know my place' to a degree that was mutually acceptable – to me and those I was serving – and I didn't know Miranda Bouchard well enough to expose my inner feelings to her.

'I agree with you, Anwyn. We had no servants in Algeria. The servants in this house make work for themselves. They cook for each other and clean up after each other for the most part. Very little of their time is devoted exclusively to me. In that respect, you're unique amongst them.'

She lit another cigarette and offered me one from the packet. I declined. She sat back puffing it and observing me, as if she was assessing whether she could trust me or not.

'I'm sure you know something of my background, don't you?'

'Not much, Madam ... sorry. I can't get used to Miranda.'

'You mustn't lie to me, Anwyn. Above anything else, I must be able to trust you. You must always be totally honest with me.'

'I know you were married and your husband was killed in Algeria.'

She smiled, inwardly, to herself. It was a smile that was meant for the memory in her head, and nothing else.

'Dear Emile...'

'It's not my business to know...'

'Yes, it is.'

She stood up and walked to the window and looked out over Chester Square – and spoke with her back to me. There was a slight quiver to her voice and I wondered if there was a tear on her cheek.

'I loved him so much. But he died ... got himself killed.'

I said nothing, just listened – giving her time to compose herself. After a moment or two, she returned to the table and lit another cigarette and I realised for the first time how utterly lonely this woman was – how desperately isolated, despite being surrounded by everything. And I also realised she wanted more than a lady's maid – she wasn't all that bothered about the cleaning and the dressing and the hair-doing and the strict rules of society – her society. Above all, she wanted a companion – someone to talk to. Someone who could understand what was in her soul. And I wondered why she had picked me, out of all the women in the waiting room that day. Did she see something in me that was lacking in the others and, if so, what could that something have been?

In the afternoon, Mrs Bouchard disappeared into the library with Mrs Hathaway and I busied myself by doing the washing that I gathered from the bedroom and bathroom that morning, and cleaning out and resetting the fire in the master bedroom. Then I read for a while, until I was summoned to the dining room for dinner at 7:30 p.m. Again, Miranda and I ate alone. The parlourmaids served an appetiser of smoked salmon slices with cream cheese, then roast beef with steamed asparagus and butter dressing, followed by English trifle. This time, instead of tea, they served dinner with a red Bordeaux wine and Miranda insisted that I have a glass, even though I told her I didn't drink much alcohol.

'You'll have to lose that bad habit if you're going to travel with me, Anwyn.'

I let her pour a glass and sipped it slowly through the meal. Again, she didn't try to converse while there was food on the table, and I always thought the toffs prided themselves on their clever dinner conversations. But I was learning that Miranda Bouchard wasn't just any aristocrat. She was very different.

This time I didn't wait for her to speak first.

'I meant to say, there are still some of Mrs Staines's clothes in the wardrobe in my room.'

'They're not Mrs Staines's, they're mine ... yours now.'

'I don't understand.'

'It's a traditional perk of a lady's maid's job, Anwyn, to get the cast-offs of her employer. Unless, of course, you think it's an impertinence on my part?'

'Oh no, not at all.'

'And they're mostly new. I've hardly worn any of them.'

'But...'

'But nothing. You're a big girl for your age and I'm a small-boned woman. They should fit well enough, after some slight alterations.'

'Thank you.'

This was, to be sure, a perk of the job. I was worried about going places with her in the few tattered clothes I'd brought with me from Wales. Now I had a complete new wardrobe and, from what I'd seen of it, it was all very fashionable couture. Miranda finished the bottle of Bordeaux while I was still sipping at my glass. She asked for another one and then dismissed the maids, so that we were alone.

'Have you wondered why I chose you above the other candidates, Anwyn?'

'Yes, I have.'

'It's because all the others were vetted by my family.'

'Vetted? How?'

'Why, through Mr Peacock, of course. He works for my father, not for me.'

I was confused. Mr Peacock had interviewed me as well and he made it clear he knew all about me. She seemed to read my mind.

'Of course, he interviewed you as well, but you have no history like the others.'

'History?'

'Yes, all the others have history, Anwyn. They can be bought or blackmailed.'

'To do what?'

'To spy on me, of course.'

She was well into the second bottle of Bordeaux by now and I imagined this was the drink talking – and the large dining-room was already filling with cigarette smoke.

'Since Algeria, they need to keep me under control, so I don't disgrace them again. Mrs Staines was their spy, handpicked by them, and they wanted to replace her with another of their spies. But you're a virgin ... not in the biblical sense, Anwyn ... what I mean is, you can't be bought or threatened. Peacock didn't want you, but I insisted. He only relented because he thinks you're an ignorant country girl and he can easily manipulate you. But I've got to you first and you must promise never to betray me.'

'I promise.'

'Thank you.'

The maids came back in to clear up at 9:00 p.m. and the second bottle of wine was empty by then. Miranda said she wanted to go to bed, so I helped her upstairs to the master bedroom, undressed her to her underwear, and tucked her into the big bed. I was just about to leave when she turned towards me.

'There is another reason why I took you on.'

'And what was that?'

'William Harding asked me to.'

Chapter Nine

I was a quick learner and Miranda was easy to get along with. I liked being a lady's maid and the duties were a lot easier than the work of a scullery skivvy. I was Mrs Bouchard's companion as well as her maid and some of her sophistication was soon to rub off on me. Being with her took the rough edges off my small-village ways and I began to see things with a broader view – a more open outlook. Even though I wasn't yet eighteen, I was tall for my age and her clothes fitted me well. My hair was shoulder-length and a chestnut colour and my figure was filling out nicely. I wasn't bad-looking either and, with make-up on, I could easily pass for an elegant twenty. We made a very classy couple, lady and lady's maid, and we turned heads wherever we went.

But things were changing in the world around us. Europe was in turmoil, both from the lasting effects of the Great War and the rise of the new, right-wing politics. I didn't pretend to know everything, but I was as aware as anyone in my position could be about what was going on – and more than some. Miranda didn't seem to notice. At least, she gave the impression of not noticing, of ignoring it all. And it was impossible not to notice. Almost every time we went out, the streets would be full of people protesting about one thing or another – marching with banners and bands – Communists and Socialists and Fascists and Blackshirts and Greenshirts and every other colour shirt as well. It was all very noisy and passionate – even threatening sometimes. I loved the urgency of it and it felt to me like I was living through an important period. But it all seemed to just wash over Miranda Bouchard, as if she was in another world and it didn't affect that world – and was never going to.

After I'd been at Chester Square for a few weeks, she told me after lunch that she'd like me to accompany her to a dance club that evening and asked me if I could recommend somewhere. This took me by surprise, because the upper classes had their own private clubs and wouldn't be caught dead in the dives that us service people frequented. It would be social suicide. But Mrs Bouchard didn't seem to care, so I gave her the benefit of my limited experience.

'There's the Hambone in Denman Street, or the Morgue in Smith's Court, or the Shim Sham in Brixton, or the Lex near Oxford Street.'

'Hmmm, I think Brixton is a bit off the

beaten for me, Anwyn. The Lex sounds nice ... is it?'

'It's good. They have proper bands and you can get a drink and something to eat.'

'Excellent! It's the Lex, then.'

We got there at about 8:00 p.m. and Miranda whispered something to the doorman on the way in. She gave me some money and asked me to go to the bar for a couple of soft drinks, while she sat at a secluded table on the raised area away from the dancehall. It was a Wednesday night and not very busy, but the band was half-decent and it wasn't long before my foot was tapping under the table. After about ten minutes, the doorman came with a note and gave it to Mrs Bouchard. She read it and smiled.

'Listen, Anwyn, I have to go.'

'So soon?'

'Something's come up.'

'I'll get our coats.'

'No ... please, you stay here.'

'Oh no...'

'I insist!'

She gave me ten shillings from her purse and told me she'd be about an hour. I should wait until she came back and use the money to buy drinks or food or whatever I wanted. Then she was gone, in a swirl of blue velvet and Vol de Nuit perfume.

I bought myself another lime squash with the ten bob note and sat back down. Then I noticed the piece of paper the doorman had delivered – it was still on the table. I had to have a look, of course.

I have a car outside
Come now!
W

I didn't need to have a degree from Oxford to guess that the 'W' might have been William Harding. He obviously knew Miranda Bouchard very well to be able to get her to hire me as her lady's maid. Did he do it to make up for his wife sacking me? I believed so. And I thought, how romantic! An assignation – a rendezvous – it was the stuff of novels. And I was helping to make it happen. I was a covert chaperone – a silent stand-in to enable the lovers to be together. But then I remembered the library in Hampstead and I wondered if Miranda Bouchard wasn't making a fool of herself – if indeed it was William Harding who had the car outside the dance club that night. I was almost certain it was, but I couldn't be absolutely sure. In any case, it was none of my business and I'd promised Miranda I'd never betray her. It wasn't due to any servile mentality on my part. It was nothing to do with a sense of class or place or obligation – it was just one woman to another. Nothing else.

Being on my own, it wasn't long before I

142

attracted the attention of the likely lads who frequented the Lex. After about twenty minutes there were four of them sitting round my table, all wanting to buy me drinks. I told them I had my own money, thanks very much, but I wouldn't mind a dance or two. They kept me busy, taking it in turns to whisk me round the dance floor with a waltz or a quickstep, and I didn't notice the minutes of the hours rushing by.

'What's your name?'

'Anwyn. What's yours?'

'Mickey.'

'Mickey the mule?'

'I'm no mule.'

'And I'm no fool.'

But they were a good-natured bunch of boys and, as I didn't take any drinks from them, I was under no obligation to take anything else either.

Mrs Bouchard came back at 10:30 p.m., over two hours after she left. Her hair was somewhat tousled and her make-up needed refreshing, but she was in good spirits and even thanked the young men for keeping me company.

'You can go now.'

She waved her hand imperiously and they melted away, bowing awkwardly and tripping over their toes, as if they were in the presence of royalty. I offered her the change from her ten shillings – I'd hardly spent anything from being on the dance floor so much – but she told me to keep it as a thank you for my patience.

'I think we should leave now, Anwyn, don't you?'

'Of course.'

And that was it, the night was over.

Back at Chester Square, she drank some wine and smoked some cigarettes in her room, while I prepared her for bed.

'I hope you didn't mind, Anwyn?'

'Mind what ... Miranda?'

'My leaving you like that.'

'Of course not. I had a great night.'

'Wonderful. We must do it again.'

But we never did. I don't know why.

She didn't mention the note and neither did I. She obviously forgot about it in the heat of the passionate night – and neither of us mentioned where she might have been for the two hours and fifteen minutes of her absence from the Lex Club.

Next day, I had to take some items of clothing over to the menders in St Martin's Lane and I was told to wait and bring them back with me. The seamstress said the work would take about an hour or so and she gave me a cup of tea while I was waiting. I was content enough, reading the magazines that were laid out for the customers, when a group of other maids came into the shop. They were chattering between themselves until they saw me, then they fell silent and started giving me sideways looks. I remembered Mrs Bouchard's instructions, that the most important of my duties would be to circulate with the other ladies' maids whenever I came into contact with them and extract as much information as possible about their upper-class households. So I thought now was as good a time as any to start snooping.

'Hello, girls.'

Nobody answered. They just sat there in silence.

'Nice day out.'

More stony silence. I wondered why they were giving me the cold shoulder. Was it because I was younger than any of them, or was it because I got the job at Chester Square over some of their friends?

Finally, one of them gave me a haughty look and said with a kind of sneer–

'You're Miranda Brandon's girl, aren't you?'

'I'm sure you must mean Mrs Bouchard.'

'Oh yes, Mrs Bouchard.'

She said this with a faux French accent and the others all giggled like epileptic geese.

'And who might your lords and masters be?'

One of them was a lady's maid for a Mrs Heathcote-Forbes of Chelsea and another for a Belgian woman who lived in Mayfair.

There was a parlourmaid from the house of the Dowager Duchess of Glamorgan and a nanny from Mrs Leopold Mercier's house in Belgravia.

'And how is Mrs Bouchard these days?'

'She's in the very pink of her prime, thank you.'

'Is she seeing anybody at all?'

'Seeing? In what way?'

'You know what way.'

I told them Miranda was living her life without the familiar attention of any gentlemen and had been for as long as I was at Chester Square. They didn't believe me and one of them mentioned Mr Harding from Hampstead, with a sly inflection in her voice, as if she knew something no one else did. I told them I'd worked for Mr Harding and he was happily married and a perfect gentleman at all times.

'That's not what his parlourmaids say.'

'Well, I wouldn't believe everything that comes out of a parlourmaid's mouth.'

That upset the parlourmaid in the company and she fell into a sulk. But the others had loosened up a bit now and they gabbled on about the goings-on in their various households. I made mental notes of it all to relate to Mrs Bouchard over dinner that night.

'Well done, Anwyn. Did anyone mention me?'

'Your name came up.'

'In connection with?'

'Nothing specific.'

'Anyone specific?'

'William Harding.'

She smiled in a sultry kind of way, and explained that she and Mr Harding were friends from way back, before either of them got married. She didn't offer any more information on the subject and it wasn't my business to ask.

'And how did you respond, Anwyn?'

'I told them you were totally celibate.'

This made her laugh out loud.

'Good girl.'

I avidly read the newspapers Miranda had delivered each day. Earlier that year, Iceland became the first country to legalise abortion and women were finally allowed to vote in Turkish elections. Amelia Earhart had flown non-stop from Honolulu to California and Karoline Mikkelson was the first woman to set foot on the continent of Antarctica. Women around the world were starting to become independent. Most of the time Miranda didn't even bother to read the papers herself – but I did. Here in London, from a woman's point of view, less spectacular things were happening, but I was happy with my position in life and hopeful for the future. I was also beginning to be accepted by the other servants. I kept Mrs Bouchard happy and, if she was happy, Mr Biggs was happy and, if he was happy, the rest of the staff were happy.

One evening, I was coming back in the dark after visiting a late-night chemist for some painkillers to relieve Miranda's wine headache. It was very foggy, like it could get in London in the mid-thirties. A pea-souper they used to call them, because you could hardly see five feet in front of you. The chemists was located on Pimlico Road and I had to make my way back through Holbein Place and past the old brooding church in Graham Terrace. All the little streets in the area were dimly lit at the best of times, but that night I could barely make out where I was going. I suddenly got the feeling I was being followed, but every time I turned round I couldn't see anyone behind me. Yet, when I walked on, I could hear footsteps again. I quickened my pace, trying to stay in the lamplight as much as I could, keeping out of the shadows and carefully negotiating the corners. Then, suddenly, a huge shape loomed up out of the fog in front of me. I almost ran straight into it. I screamed. It grabbed me by the shoulders.

'Are you all right, Miss?'

Then I saw the uniform – and the helmet. It was a bobby on the beat.

'You gave me a start, officer.'

'I'm sorry, but you shouldn't be wandering about on a night like this ... young girl on her own.'

'I'm almost home.'

I told him I was in service in a house in Chester Square. He offered to escort me to the corner of Gerald Mews and I was grateful for his protective company. Then he continued on his beat down Elizabeth Street. I quickly turned into Chester Place and up to the front of number 24. I was just about to bang on the door for tailcoat Jacob, when I heard a soft voice from somewhere behind me.

'Anwyn...'

I whirled round, but could see very little through the thick fog.

'Who's there?'

'Is that you, Anwyn?'

'Who is it? Who are you?'

A figure approached out of the murk. I was about to scream again, when I recognised a familiar face.

'Bart?'

'It's me, Anwyn.'

'What are you doing here? Have you been following me?'

He said he had, but he wasn't sure if it was me or not in the dark gloominess.

I asked him what he wanted and he said he had a note for me.

'A note? From who?'

'Mr Harding.'

He handed me a sealed envelope with my name on it.

'He made me swear I'd give it to nobody but you.'

'Did he now!'

'What's going on, Anwyn?'

'I don't know.'

His expression told me he suspected the worst. I couldn't believe it.

'Nothing's going on. You don't think...'

'You'll only get yourself hurt, Anwyn.'

'Listen, Bart, I'm not...'

But he was gone, turned back into the foul London pea-souper. I opened the envelope to find another one inside, addressed to Miranda Bouchard. Mr Harding obviously didn't care if people believed he was having some kind of intrigue with me as long as they didn't know he was having a liaison with Mrs Bouchard.

I handed the envelope over to her along with the painkillers, and she smiled and thanked me.

Next time I was over in the seamstress's shop in St Martin's Lane the other maids giggled even more dementedly than before. Bart had obviously told Nora and Nora had obviously told someone else and now the word was out. But it was drawing attention away from Miranda Bouchard and I suppose that was also part of my job – along with everything else. I wondered why two people who seemingly had everything would still want something they couldn't have. I wondered if William Harding loved Miranda Bouchard or if he was a philanderer like everyone said he was and she was just another of his conquests, to be discarded when someone new came along. I wondered if Miranda loved William Harding, or was she just bored and he was something to fill her idle days and nights? I thought of all the poor people like my family and Lucy's family who didn't have the time or energy for such shenanigans. But it wasn't for me to judge. Mrs Bouchard was paying me to do a job and I'd do it to the very best of my ability. And, anyway, I liked her, even if she was rich and spoiled – she had a mind and a will of her own, like Mrs Reynolds, and I admired women like that who weren't afraid to go up against a man's world.

I hoped I could be like them one day – like them, but not like them, if that made any sense. I hoped I would grow up to be a strong, independent woman, with my own income and my own life. I didn't envy Mrs Bouchard either, who was conditioned by her status in society, or Mrs Reynolds, who was the wife of a rich and powerful man and was viewed as an extension of him. I didn't want to be an extension of anyone. I wanted to be my own woman. Big dreams for someone who was merely a maid, you might say, someone's lackey – but dreams were the same as aspirations. And I was sure someone, somewhere, at some time, said that aspirations were the building blocks of achievement.

Chapter Ten

Mr. Peacock came to see me a couple of weeks after I started. He asked to see me alone in the music room.

'How are you settling in, Miss Moyle?'

'Very well, Sir.'

'Excellent. I'm glad to hear it.'

He looked uneasy, calculating what he was going to say. I already knew what that was, as Miranda had briefed me. But he didn't know that and I wasn't going to make it easy for him.

'This is quite delicate. Mrs Bouchard has had, how should I say, quite a colourful past.'

'Really, Sir?'

My innocent expression would have convinced a magistrate.

'Yes, really. Now, I would like you to be on the lookout for ... anything out of the ordinary.'

'Out of the ordinary, Sir?'

'Yes ... rendezvous ... strange men ... assignations, that kind of thing.'

'I'm not sure I know what you mean, Sir.'

He was becoming exasperated with his inability to express himself and he started pacing up and down the room, looking for the right words.

'Look, you're a plain girl, Anwyn, so I'll speak plainly. I want to know if Mrs Bouchard entertains or meets privately with men. I want you to take note and describe them to me.'

'Oh dear, Sir, the lady does nothing of the sort. Why, she barely leaves the house, except to shop and go to the theatre, and I'm always with her when she does.'

'Good. But keep your eyes open. I shall make it worth your while ... for information. Do you understand?'

'Worth my while, Sir?'

He explained that Miranda's family were very well-connected and they considered Miranda to be their most valuable 'asset' – that's how he put it, as if she was a piece of property or a stock option or a racehorse. I couldn't believe it. After all the things that had happened over the past twenty years or so, some of these aristocrats still believed they were living in the eighteenth century. Mr Peacock was an educated man, I wondered if he agreed with this outdated estimation of women, or if he was just obeying orders. But I had to pretend I was going along with him, otherwise they'd get rid of me and replace me with someone else – a woman who would spy on Mrs Bouchard like a snake in the grass.

'Do you understand, Miss Moyle?'

'I understand, Sir.'

That evening at dinner I told Miranda what he said and we laughed and knew we could feed him just whatever we wanted and he'd be none the wiser.

Over the course of the London season, myself and Miranda Bouchard were almost inseparable, apart from the rare occasions when she had guests and other company. Apart from William Harding, there was no one who could remotely be identified as 'a man in her life' of the kind that Mr Peacock was so anxious about. So my occasional reporting to him was mainly truthful and only based on a single lie. I learned the duties of a lady's maid avidly, soaking up everything like a sponge, watching and observing, listening, taking instruction, asking questions, conversing with other ladies' maids at the seamstress's shop or the cleaners or in the places that were set aside for us at events and functions, and finding out what was going on in the circles of high society so I could report it back to Miranda. And I became that rare and curious commodity – a really good lady's maid.

I became more competent as each day passed. I began to understand the intricacies of hairdressing, the craft of dressmaking, how to pack for journeys, how to make arrangements for dinner parties and balls. I acquired 'good taste' and added it to my other attributes. I learned how to take care of Mrs Bouchard's every need. I was honest, trustworthy, quick-witted, eager to learn, impeccably clean, methodical and patient, and I even began to learn French so I could converse with Miranda in front of the other servants and they wouldn't know what we were talking about.

The months were a whirlwind to me and my feet barely touched the ground as I accompanied Mrs Bouchard here, there and everywhere. The first event after I started was the Cheltenham Festival in March – which was happening at the same time as Adolf Hitler was invading the Rhineland, but none of that social circle seemed to care. A car came and collected us at Chester Square and drove us to Lodge Park in the Sherborne Estate, Gloucestershire, which was converted into a dower house for the wife of the 4th Baron Sherborne. I stayed in a room in the rear wing and wasn't introduced to the other guests with Miranda. I spent my time with the other Ladies' maids, gleaning the gossip, when I wasn't attending to Mrs Bouchard, and we travelled over to the Festival by car on

155

the Friday for the Gold Cup, which was won by Golden Miller, a horse that had won the race the last four years in a row and set a record that would never be equalled. Mrs Bouchard's company had a course-facing box with a dining area. I didn't attend her in the box, but waited with the other maids in the paddock area. Afterwards, we returned to Lodge Park and I didn't get to bed till 3:00 a.m. because Miranda drank quite a lot of champagne and I had to ensure her safe transference from the evening's banquet to her bedchamber.

The private parties in London were the same – always late to bed, with Miranda consuming a lot of champagne. But she'd lie in late the next day and I wouldn't be required until the afternoon. This gave me time to study up on etiquette and my French and do any jobs that were out-standing. I wanted to go back down to the tea shop in Sloane Square to see Lucy, but things were so busy in the beginning, with me trying to learn as much as I could about the job as quickly as I could, and the travel-ling about and late nights, I didn't get a chance. I felt guilty and didn't want Lucy to get the idea I thought I was too uppity for her now. She'd been good to me during the short time I knew her and she was my friend when I had no one else.

The weather warmed and in May we attended a tea party at the Chelsea Flower Show on the 11th and Miranda met the King for the first time – while I waited for her in the tea tent. There was a military band that played the national anthem and a big buffet on long tables covered with snow-white tablecloths and enormous quantities of food that could never be eaten by the guests – not in a month of masked balls. I wondered what would be done with it at the end of the day. Would it be thrown away, or given to the poor, starving children of the slums? We left for an after-party at about 6:00 p.m. and I didn't get to bed until two in the morning. After that came the May Ball with all the gowns and grandeur and the dancing and drinking. I observed it all from a balcony and kept an eye out to see if there was any one man paying particular attention to Miranda. But there wasn't. Not that I would have reported it to Mr Peacock if there was, but I was curious to know for myself. I thought it strange that I hadn't seen or heard anything of Mr Harding after that night at the Lex and the subsequent note sent via Bart. And I wondered if something had happened between him and Miranda.

The debutant girls had already been presented at Buckingham Palace in March and the May Ball, or Queen Charlotte's Ball as it was called, was the highlight of the season. It was called Queen Charlotte's Ball because it was first inaugurated by King George III to celebrate his wife's birthday on the 17th of May and it was an event for all the blue-blooded young girls to display themselves after 'coming-of-age'. Grosvenor House in Mayfair used to be the London residence of the Dukes of Westminster, until it was turned into a posh hotel in 1929. It had a separate bathroom and entrance lobby for every bedroom and running iced water in every bathroom. It also had Turkish baths and squash courts and a swimming pool and gymnasium. It was a sickly sweet spectacle of garish ostentation, like a ridiculous cour-tesan in a baroque periwig.

All the debutants arrived in limousines with their fur-wrapped mothers and top-hatted, moustachioed fathers. They came in pure white full-skirted silk dresses and in flowing lace and smothered in mother-of-pearl. There was a giant white cake in the centre of the ballroom and it seemed to me that the debutantes were curtseying to it, but they weren't really, they were curtseying to the assembled high-ranking dignitaries who posed like Louis XIV table-legs. Miranda told me all the girls were trained to make this elaborate genuflection by Madame Vacani, a dancing teacher who held a royal warrant for it. The left knee needed to be locked behind the right, allowing a graceful descent with the head erect and hands down by the sides. A

Vacani curtsey was part of the etiquette of the occasion.

It was really a marriage market, where the girls were displayed to potential suitors who could eye up the young women newly released into society. It was a way of meeting the 'right' people, a system of exclusion, connecting like with like with the sovereign's blessing – a way of centralising wealth and power and influence, and it had been going on for hundreds of years, but was now in decline, like the rest of the upper-class rituals. The white dresses were symbolic of virginity, which was the young debutante's best selling point, apart from her name and the colour of her blood. Underlying it all was a belief in protocol and love and respect for king and country – as well as self-interest.

On the Monday before Royal Ascot, we went to the Garter Service at Windsor and Miranda had lunch in the Waterloo Chamber, while I waited with the spectators. After lunch, the Knights made their way on foot to a service in St George's Chapel, wearing blue velvet mantles and black velvet hats with white plumes. After the service, they all emerged through the Great West Door and returned in carriages and cars to the Upper Ward of Windsor Castle and, in the evening, numerous exclusive parties struck up around the town. And Mrs Bouchard took advantage of the occasion to drown the dark sorrow in her heart that sometimes seemed to stalk her. When we got back from Windsor, Miranda was tired the next day and decided to stay in bed, as she wanted to be fit for Ladies' Day the following Thursday. I took this opportunity to finally get down to the Rose of Sussex Tea Rooms to see Lucy.

She was a bit cool with me at first, because I was dressed in one of the outfits Mrs Bouchard had left in my wardrobe and she probably thought I was flaunting it. I looked like I was twenty-five, not eighteen. Lucy was sarcastic when I came into the tea room during one of their quiet times.

'Yes, Madam, and what would you like today?'

'Lucy, it's me ... Anwyn.'

'I know it's you, you silly mare.'

She showed me to a corner table and Hannah and the other girls all came over and everybody was amazed at the way I looked – so sophisticated and chic.

'You look like a real lady, Anwyn.'

'Thanks, Hannah.'

'You could easily fit in with the customers we get in here.'

'Not that I'd want to.'

'Oh, go on with you, I bet you love it.'

And she was right. I did love it. It was a new world to me – a big wide world that I never knew existed and I was in a whirl and a spin at being part of it, even if I was only observing it from the sidelines and would never really be a part of it. Even if I was cynical and sarcastic about it and considered it to be a crime; when so many people were so poor, it was still something to see and, for a young woman of my impressionable age who'd been brought up in a coal-dusted Welsh mining village, a wonderment to behold. But, at the same time, I was glad it was a world that was in its death-throes and wouldn't be seen again in the same guise, but would have to dress itself in the lie of democracy.

'You want to come dancing down the Palais, Anwyn?'

'I don't know. When?'

'Every weekend ... any weekend. They get Jack Hylton and Joe Loss and even Billy Cotton. You must get a day off, surely?'

And I thought, do I get a day off? It hadn't occurred to me since I started with Mrs Bouchard that I was at her beck and call seven days a week. Not that I minded all that much, but meeting Lucy reminded me that I had a life of my own as well. I mentioned it to Miranda at lunch the next day.

'Of course you can have a day off, Anwyn. But it's the season and there's so much going on ... and if I don't attend events, father's spies will tell him they haven't seen me and he'll think I've run off somewhere

161

with an Arab and he'll come back from the land of the midnight sun or wherever he is and there'll be a scene.'

'I understand, don't worry about it.'

And she didn't.

Royal Ascot was one of the clearest manifestations of the English class system in the social calendar, and ladies' maids were obliged to take a measuring tape to every aspect of their mistresses' outfits, from headgear to hemline. I was spellbound by the outlandish hats and the extravagant dresses, and there was a ban on exposed midriffs and straps of less than an inch in thickness. Entrance to the Royal Enclosure was a privilege earned only by invitation from established members, and the event was all about selectiveness and exclusivity and nothing at all to do with the nouveaux riches. There were unbending strictures on elegance and I had to make sure Miranda was properly attired to meet the exacting standards of Ascot and I was hoping she didn't drink too much and have herself politely expelled. That would certainly have brought further disgrace down upon her family. But Miranda's drinking was no worse than that of the other aristocratic ladies and I doubted if anyone would have even noticed her in their inebriated states.

The one thing I still wondered about was her family. I knew her mother died when she was very young and she was brought up by governesses. But I hadn't once seen either her father or her brother at any of the events or functions we attended throughout the season. I mentioned this to her one evening in the dining room at dinner.

'They're both travelling this summer, in Scandinavia.'

'Scandinavia?'

'Yes. My father has always been an outdoors type of man and not one for balls or parties, which he refers to as tart gatherings and hasn't been to one since my mother died.'

'And your brother?'

'He follows the old man around, being his blue-eyed, white-haired boy, in case the old bugger changes his mind and leaves everything to me.'

'Is he likely to do that?'

'No.'

We went together to the Summer Exhibition at the Royal Academy of Arts. Many unconventional high-society women like Mrs Bouchard were supporting art movements – modernism and surrealism and other fashionable fads. I liked the old paintings best, where you knew what it was you were looking at, but I learned something about form and perspective and colour and context from being with Miranda and listening to her commentary. On this occasion, she had no other company except for myself and we had a lovely day together. It was as if we were friends and not mistress and maid. We did meet some people she knew at the exhibition and, while she said hello and chatted with them, I stood back and assumed the maid's role again.

The exhibition was held to raise funds to finance the training of young artists in the Royal Academy schools and, as one of its patrons, Miranda was expected to put in an appearance. She chatted to the President and the Keeper and I had time to look round at the paintings – some were strange and a bit sideways for my taste, by artists like Picasso and Dali and Kandinsky and I noticed that there weren't any by women. Afterwards, we went for tea at Fortnum & Mason and laughed and talked and were happy. It was the first time I'd seen Miranda so relaxed while sober.

Through the summer of 1936 we went here and there and everywhere – to West End Theatres to see performances by women playwrights, like *The Happy Hypocrite* by Clemence Dane at His Majesty's Theatre and *Boy Meets Girl* by Bella Spewack at the Shaftesbury and *Bitter Harvest* by Catherine Turvey at the Arts Theatre, and to the Proms at the Royal Albert Hall for *La Bohème*, which Miranda loved. I hadn't heard much classical music before and I must admit, it took me a while to find an ear for it. But I loved Mimi's aria and I could see a tear in Miranda's eye when the soprano was singing it. We also attended a soirée at the Guards' Club in Piccadilly, where I saw Mr Harding again. I don't think he saw me, but he certainly saw Miranda, because he spoke to her for quite a while before leaving. Mrs Harding wasn't with him.

In July, we stayed at Temple Island for the Henley Regatta, just as the Spanish Civil War got under way, and many young working-class men were volunteering for the International Brigades. Miranda's brother was a member of the Leander Club and they used the Temple as a vantage point from which to watch the boats and the races. Because her brother wasn't there, Miranda was invited in his place, which was considered a great privilege for a woman. The island was a fairy-tale place, situated downstream from Henley on a beautiful reach of the Thames, in the midst of rolling water meadows and surrounded by wooded hills. The Temple itself was a folly that was built as a fishing lodge for Fawley Court, the mansion designed by Christopher Wren, and was the first example of the Italian Etruscan style in England – or so Miranda told me. After the boat racing, there was a candlelit dinner and an al fresco party on the riverside lawns. We stayed the night on the island and journeyed back by boat the next day. It was a truly enchanting occasion and one I'll never forget, despite its decadence and its seemingly uncaring attitude towards the tragedy that was tearing Europe apart.

And that wasn't the end of my water adventures. In August, we travelled down to Cowes on the Isle of Wight, where we stayed aboard a magnificent yacht, owned by some Duke or Duchess or other, I can't remember which one. There were champagne parties on board every night and I had to share a berth with two other ladies' maids, but we had a great time and watched the spectacular fireworks display at the end of the wonderful week. At the same time, the Olympics were taking place in Berlin, and all the talk was about a black man called Jesse Owens. Hitler was hoping the German athletes would win everything and show the world what a superior race the Nazis were – better than black people and Jews and Gypsies. But Jesse Owens won four gold medals and it was being said that Hitler was so annoyed he wouldn't shake hands with him afterwards. But Owens was allowed to travel with white athletes and stay in the same hotels as them while he was in Germany, whereas in America he'd have been segregated. I read somewhere, many years later, that Hitler did send Owens a commemorative inscribed photograph, but Franklin D. Roosevelt, president of America, didn't even send him a telegram.

While Europe was starting to burn in a conflagration that would consume the whole world, the summer of 1936 was truly amazing and was one that will be part of my memory till the day I die. It was the most extraordinary time I'd ever had in my young life and it opened my eyes to many things and helped to make me the woman I was to become for the rest of my life. But it was coming to an end, as September arrived and the season ground gradually to a close.

By Friday 25 September, all the arrangements had been made to move up to Warwickshire for the winter. The furniture was covered with dust sheets and the house keys handed over to the caretakers. All the other servants had already taken the train from Marylebone to Royal Leamington Spa, where they would be picked up by horse carriage and taken to Bolde Hall, situated south and west of Stratford-upon-Avon. I wondered why all the servants had to go, but Miranda explained that her father and brother didn't need many servants of their own during the summer, because they were always away adventuring somewhere – and her people came up for the winter to help run the big house. Miranda and myself were the only two left now at Chester Square, apart from Tom the chauffeur, and we waited for him to bring the Bentley round.

It had taken me most of the week to pack Miranda's things properly. Some of the trunks had gone with the others, under the supervision of Mrs Hathaway and Miss Mason, and the rest were being loaded into the car by Tom.

'Did you know that Mary Shelley once lived in this house?'

Miranda offered me this piece of fascinating information as we sipped the last pot of tea for a while at Chester Square and she smoked a cigarette.

'No, I didn't. How amazing.'

'Yes, it was in her later years, after Percy was drowned in the Bay of La Spezia. I thought you'd be interested, with all your book reading.'

'How long did she live here for?'

'I'm not sure. Not more than a year or so. Her only surviving son, Percy Florence, owned the house and she stayed with him and his wife when they weren't travelling abroad.'

'Which room did she sleep in?'

'I don't know, Anwyn, maybe yours. She died here from a brain tumour when she was fifty-three.'

She smiled maliciously when she said that. And I was stunned to think I might have been sleeping in the same room as Mary Shelley. Maybe it was best I hadn't known,

168

the ghost of that unfortunate woman might be still haunting the house – keeping company with her Modern Prometheus.

The journey up to Bolde Hall was long and tiresome. Miranda had drank some wine and napped in the car. I was sad to leave London and had considered leaving the job and looking for something else. I didn't want to go to the country, but the girls in the tea shop said I'd be mad to leave and, anyway, there was nothing in the classifieds that interested me. Besides, I knew Miranda would have persuaded me to stay if I told her I was leaving. And how could I leave her surrounded by spies and snakes-in-the-grass? I'd never met her father or her brother, but I already disliked both of them. They seemed like bullies to me and I didn't like bullies after that dance in Cricklewood when Bart got pushed around. So, I stared out the car window as the country sailed past me – big towns and little towns and villages and hamlets and farms and fields. We drove up through Hertfordshire and Buckinghamshire and on into Northamptonshire.

We stopped for a while at a roadhouse called the Barley Mow, close to Bloxham in north Oxfordshire, and Tom stretched his legs while Miranda and I had tea and toasted crumpets. Eventually, we drove through the big gates and up the long gravel driveway to Bolde Hall. It was a huge place, bigger than anything I'd seen before, except in pictures. It was more like a castle to me than a house and certainly not at all like a hall. As we approached, it grew larger and larger, until it loomed over me like a great gothic mausoleum.

And I knew I'd hate it here.

Chapter Eleven

Bolde Hall was the eighteenth-century residence of the Brandon family, set in five hundred acres of landscaped grounds that were now starting to look a bit overgrown. It had two synchronised wings projecting from either side of the main part of the house and the whole facade was decorated in the gothic style – I was getting to be a bit of a boffin on period architecture, having spent time in a few big houses. But I hadn't seen anything like this before. It only had three storeys, but was spread out and sprawling. God only knew how many rooms were inside – hundreds, I thought, as I emerged from the car and looked up the eight wide stone steps to the front entrance. To me, it was a crime that a building as big as this was used to house two men, and then only occasionally.

The Edwardian days were long gone, so no

servants stood outside to welcome Miranda and me, as Tom drove the car away with what looked like a couple of gamekeepers, to unload the trunks. The front door was open, as if they were expecting us and, when we got inside, Mr Biggs had already arrived, with Miss Mason and Jacob and Heather and Beatrice, and there were three other young female servants who weren't from Chester Square. Mrs Hathaway didn't seem to be there, but I could hear Mrs Jackson and the kitchen girls bustling about to the east of the main entrance hall.

Miranda walked ahead of me and I followed her at a distance, just in case that was another piece of ossified etiquette that couldn't be challenged by a woman – at least not yet. Her father and brother didn't seem to be there either and I heard Mr Biggs remarking to her in a low voice–

'They're out riding.'

The light was already going and it would soon be dinner time. So I imagined Mrs Jackson and her girls would be busy cooking downstairs – even though there was no 'downstairs' as such in Bolde Hall and the kitchen and scullery were on the ground floor. Jacob tapped me on the shoulder and beckoned me to follow him, which I did, leaving Miranda talking, with a serious expression on her face, to Mr Biggs. The rest of the servants were already dispersing to their various duties around the house.

Jacob took me to a room on the first floor of the east wing. It was a big room, much bigger than my bedroom in Chester Square, with an enormous bed and baroque furniture that looked gaudy and extravagant to me, but I was sure even one piece would be worth more than I'd earn in a lifetime. Dressing tables and wardrobes and chests of drawers and upholstered chairs that sneered at me in their shameless grandiosity and dared me to sit on them. The ceiling was high and decorated with swirls and swishes and the windows were long and shuttered on the inside, with floor-length, burgundy velvet curtains. The floor was carpeted in thick burgundy Axminster, and paintings of hounds and horses hung on the flock-papered walls. The whole room had a heavy oppressive feel to it and the only thing that lightened its mood was a child's rocking-chair in one of the corners.

My trunk had already been delivered and stood close to one of the wardrobes. Despite its overbearing aura, the room was chilly, as if it hadn't been used for some time, and I could feel a breeze coming from somewhere. But there was a scuttle of coal and fire-making material by the grate and I soon had a lively blaze going. I was hungry from all the travelling and I'd had nothing to eat since the tea and crumpets that afternoon and it was now 8:00 p.m. I was sure Jacob would call me to come and eat with Miranda in the dining room any minute now – but he didn't. So I unpacked and waited to see what would happen. I was going to go wandering and explore the house, but I'd probably have got lost and, anyway, Miranda might want me to help her dress for dinner.

At 9:00 p.m., Heather came to my room with a tray of food and a pot of tea. I asked her if she'd seen Madam Bouchard, but she hadn't. Mr Biggs told her to bring the food and that was all she knew. I asked if she'd been here to Bolde Hall before and she said once, last year. I tried to find out something more about the two Mr Brandons, but she said she didn't know them at all and hardly ever saw them. Then she hurried away. That night, I slept fretfully and woke early next morning in the cold room with the fire gone out. I had no more fuel to re-light it and didn't know where to go to get any. I washed in the handbasin, using a jug of cold water, both of which were on top of one of the baroque tables. Then I dressed in my warmest clothes and waited. At 8:00 a.m., Heather brought me a breakfast of bacon and black pudding and grilled oatcakes, with two slices of soda bread and a pot of tea. She deposited the tray on a table and collected the one from the night before and was gone before I could ask her any more questions.

I'd hardly finished eating when Jacob knocked on the door.

'Follow me, miss.'

He took me along the cold corridors of Bolde Hall, through the main part of the house and into the west wing. Mrs Bouchard was in a bedroom that was even bigger and colder than mine, with the same ornate furniture crowding every corner. She had a shawl round her shoulders and was sitting up in bed eating a breakfast that looked similar to the one I just ate. Her eyes were puffy and she looked as if she'd been crying.

'Anwyn.'

'Miranda ... are you all right?'

'Yes, of course. Have you settled in?'

Her voice was formal, matter-of-fact. It seemed to me she was making the point that, no matter how much we appeared to be friends in London, the fact of the matter was, she was the mistress and I was the maid. Now we were here in Warwickshire, in the bosom of her family, the correct protocol would have to be observed.

'There's a shoot today. You'll have to find my outdoor togs and air them, I didn't need them in London.'

'Where shall I find them?'

'How should I know? Ask Mason.'

With that, she went back to eating her breakfast. I was dismissed and was about to leave the room.

'Oh, Anwyn, could you light the fire? It's freezing in here.'

'Of course.'

There was a scuttle of coal and some kindling by the fireplace and I lit her a nice fire. By then she'd finished her breakfast. 'Help me into these, will you?'

She pulled out a pair of brown corduroy Oxford bags and a buttoned-up blouse and an off-white Aran cardigan. She discarded the shawl and her underwear and washed quickly with a basin and jug as I did. There were no en-suite bathrooms in Bolde Hall. I helped her into the clothes and dabbed her puffy eyes and made her face up as best I could, under the circumstances.

'Things will be different while we're here, Anwyn. Not like London.'

'I know. It's fine.'

Then I left her to find Miss Mason and the 'outdoor togs'.

I wandered round the west wing of the house for fifteen minutes without seeing anyone and I realised I was lost. Then I bumped into a young man of about twenty or twenty-one as he strode quickly round a corner. He was tall and athletic-looking, with handsome features and tanned skin. He looked a little like Miranda, except that his hair was blond and his eyes were a steely blue.

'Who are you?'

'Anwyn Moyle, Sir.'

'And what are you?'

'Mrs Bouchard's lady's maid.'

'Ah, Peacock's girl.'

He started to walk away.

'Do you know where I can find Miss Mason?'

He stopped in his tracks and turned round.

'Don't you know?'

'Know what, Sir?'

'All the servants' quarters are in the east wing. This side of the house is for family members and guests only'

'No, Sir, I didn't know. Sorry.'

He sighed. It was an exasperated sound, coming from someone who was easily irritated.

'Get Biggs to give you the rundown.'

He stalked away, with me following at a safe distance. He led me back to the main part of the house and from there I found my way to the east wing. Beatrice the parlour-maid was going about her duties and she directed me to Miss Mason's room. I expected the head housekeeper to be her buttoned-up, stony self and I was surprised when she appeared almost affable, as if the country suited her more than the city, and she seemed to be in her element out here in the middle of gentryland.

'Madam Bouchard's shooting clothes are all stored in the master boudoir. Come with me and I'll show you.'

She took me back the way I came and up a flight of stairs and into a room where rows and rows of clothing were hung on wooden rails and covered with linen sheets.

'You'll have to familiarise yourself with what's in here. But I'll find the appropriate outfit for now.'

While she was searching, she told me that both Mr Brandons liked to shoot pheasant and partridge reared on the estate by the gamekeepers and that's what they'd be doing today. They also liked to shoot grouse, which flew faster than the other game birds and were more of a challenge, but they couldn't be reared intensively and they had to travel up to the heather moorlands of Scotland for that sport. Today would be a beaten shoot and beaters from the village would walk through the woods and drive the game towards the line of standing guns in the butts. Pickers-up with dogs would make sure all the killed and wounded game was collected.

'Ah, here we are.'

She pulled out a set of tweeds – jacket, waistcoat and full-length skirt.

'The boots will be in the boot room.'

By the time I'd aired and pressed Miranda's shooting outfit and went back and tidied her room, the guests for the shoot were arriving. There was about twenty of them altogether. Mostly men, but with about half-a-dozen women as well. They didn't have any servants with them and it fell to myself and Miss Mason and the house-maids, Beatrice and Heather and the other three girls, whose names were Betty and Cynthia and Sheila, to sort out their clothes and light fires after they were installed in the guest rooms. They came in deco-print full skirts and pencil wriggle dresses and chiffon maxis and watered taffeta, and the rest of their clothes came in trunks that were carried from the cars and carriages. Cook and her girls were sending over a midmorning brunch from the kitchen – asparagus soufflé and cinnamon toast and colcannon cakes and German crêpes, along with several bowls of brandy punch, brought in by Mr Biggs and Jacob. Everybody assembled in the main dining hall to eat and drink and chat and laugh and catch up with all the gossip from the London season.

Miranda mingled with the guests and I saw the tall blond man again, whom I assumed to be her brother. Miss Mason pointed out their father to me – he was also a tall man, in his mid-fifties. He had reddish-brown hair and sported a wide moustache. He was a commanding figure and the epicentre of the gathering. I waited with the rest of the servants, in case anyone required anything they didn't already have. Miranda approached me.

'I want you to organise the refreshments, Anwyn.'

'In what way, Madam?'

I started calling her Madam again after we arrived at Bolde Hall, as our relationship had clearly changed from what it was in London.

'Cook has prepared hampers. Pick two of the housemaids to come with you.'

I assumed she meant for me to attend the shoot and serve food and drink to the guests. I picked Heather and Sheila and told them to get their coats.

The head gamekeeper arrived and told Mr Brandon that the beaters were in position. The hampers were loaded onto a horse-drawn shooting brake and the guests climbed aboard as well. They were driven off at a slow gait across the estate, with me and the two housemaids walking behind with the gun handlers. I had no boots and neither did the maids and soon our shoes were clogged heavy with mud. It was half a mile to the edge of the woodland and the butts, which were a line of sunken hides, some thirty yards apart and screened by rough stone walls. The guns took up their positions, each one partnered by a loader, while the women perched themselves on shooting sticks some distance away. A signal was sent to the beaters at the other side of the trees, and soon I could hear their calls and the barking of the dogs being carried on the early afternoon air.

Today was a short, afternoon shoot, I was told – often they went on all day. But because

179

of the earliness in the season – it went on from September to February – only about three hundred birds would be flushed, to preserve stocks, as there could be as many as a dozen shoots in the season. The beaters drove the birds to the flushing point where they flushed up about a dozen pheasants at a time. The drives were in fifties, which meant when fifty birds were flushed and shot, they'd take a break. Suddenly, the birds began to break cover, flying out of the woods in all directions. The air was full of the smell of cordite and the crack of shotguns and the sight of the birds falling from the skies in a flurry of feathers and the excited squawks of the women.

'Oh, good shot!'

Between the drives, myself and the maids served up pork and pigeon terrine, roast partridge drumsticks, sandwiches, currant and candied peel cake and plums soaked in whisky - all washed down with port and brandy and flasks of hot sweet tea.

When it was all over and the three hundred unfortunate birds were killed and collected by the spaniels, the guests retired to the nearby hunting lodge, where Cook and the kitchen girls had prepared a supper of hot onion soup, lamb and apricot pie topped with colcannon and crème brûlée for pudding. The wine flowed easily and everyone was getting rather merry by now. I returned to the house with the guests, while the maids cleared away after the meal. I changed my shoes and helped Miranda to bathe in the family's private bathroom and then dress in a black drop-waist evening gown with embroidered front. She asked me to go and see how the other ladies were faring and I helped Miss Mason to get them all ready for dinner. After that, I helped the housemaids to clean and tidy the rooms and to take the shooting clothes away for washing and the boots for cleaning and polishing. Dinner was served at 9:00 p.m. and I ate with Miss Mason and the late-arriving Mrs Hathaway in a small dining room in the east wing, while the Brandons and their guests dined in the main hall. Afterwards, I waited for Miranda and put her to bed in an inebriated state at 2:00 a.m. I gave her room a quick tidy and collapsed into my own bed at 2:30 a.m.

The next day was Sunday and everybody was up and ready for the 11:00 a.m. church service in the village. They returned for lunch and, by then, their trunks had been packed and loaded into their cars and carriages and the guests all drove away in the mid-afternoon. That evening, Miranda had dinner with her father and brother and I ate again with Miss Mason and Mrs Hathaway, both of whom had come to accept me as a competent lady's maid and weren't as snotty and sarcastic to me as they had been in the beginning. They showed me where the ladies' bathroom was in the east wing and I had my first hot bath in several days, lying back and luxuriating in the amniotic warmth of the water. When I dressed again, I went to find Miranda to see what she would be requiring of me for the rest of the evening. She wasn't in her bedroom, so I went along to the main part of the house. As I approached the library, I heard shouting. Jacob was standing outside the door and then Mr Biggs emerged. I hid in the shadows and heard them as they went past me.

'Best leave them to it.'

'I'll clear away in the dining hall.'

When they disappeared from view, being anxious about Miranda, I tiptoed up to the library for a listen. She may have been an uncaring aristocrat, but I felt something for the woman – and her heavy heart. The door wasn't quite closed and I could see inside – and I could hear Mr Brandon's raised voice.

'Everybody is having to compromise, Miranda. Things have changed since the war.'

'Why does it have to be me, father? What about you and James?'

'We're tightening our belts ... you saw the size of the shoot.'

Miranda was sobbing – softly, almost inaudibly, like a young girl who'd lost her true love. I knew I shouldn't be listening and, if I got caught, I'd probably be sacked. But I couldn't just walk away and leave them to it, like Jacob and Biggs. James, the brother, spoke.

'Come on, Miranda, be a sport.'

'Why don't you marry for money, James? Why does it have to be me?'

'You know that's impossible.'

Mr Brandon senior spoke again. This time his voice was softer, more conciliatory.

'At least agree to see him. He'll be here for the foxhunting in November.'

Miranda didn't reply, but came rushing from the library, and I had to move quickly so she wouldn't see me. A few minutes later, I went to her room.

She was quiet when I entered and I just went about my duties cleaning and tidying without saying anything much. I could tell she was distressed but was trying hard to disguise it. But the effort was too much in the end and she broke down.

'Oh, Anwyn...'

'What's wrong, Madam?'

'You don't need to call me Madam when we're alone.'

I went and sat beside her on the bed. She told me her father and brother wanted her to marry some rich earl because they were broke and needed his money to keep them afloat. Since the Great War, and especially with the depression in America, many of Britain's aristocratic families were feeling the cold breath of bankruptcy on the backs of their noble necks. Those who didn't want to sell their estates, like the Brandons, were finding it a struggle to keep up the old appearances. I was picking up bits and pieces of information from Miss Mason and Mrs Hathaway when I ate with them and, apparently, old man Brandon wasn't a very shrewd businessman and he'd neglected the family's fortunes while he'd been gallivanting round the world on his adventures. James Brandon was an even worse entrepreneur than his father and their finances needed a shot in the arm from an outside source. The Earl had money from family investments in India, through the East India Company, which had exported opium to China in the 1800s, resulting in the opium wars and the seizure of Hong Kong by the British. He'd long been an admirer of Miranda, but gave up on her when she married Emile Bouchard. Since she'd become a widow, his amour had been rekindled.

The Earl promised to sort out the Brandons' financial problems just as soon as Miranda hopped into his marital bed.

'What's wrong with him?'

'Nothing.'

'Is he ugly ... old ... smelly?'

'None of those things. He's quite charming, really.'

If the Earl was really a Prince Charming

with loads of money, then I couldn't understand why Miranda didn't want him.

'It's because I love somebody else.'

'Who?'

She hesitated before answering and turned her face away from me.

'You know who, Anwyn.'

'Do I?'

'Yes.'

Chapter Twelve

One afternoon, when I wasn't too busy and Mrs Bouchard had gone out for the day with Mrs Hathaway, into Stratford-on-Avon to see a solicitor or some such thing, I got out of the fossilised containment of Bolde Hall for a breath of fresh air. I asked Miranda what time she'd be getting back, but she wasn't able to tell me. I said I'd probably go out for a walk, as it was such a nice day, and she told me not to hurry back. I decided to go and pick some autumn flowers for my room – dahlias or cyclamen or begonias or maybe some wild crocuses if I could find any. I rambled away on my own from the big house and down past the gardens and the grounds to the fields beyond. It was a pleasant day, with an early October sun slanting across the Warwickshire countryside and shining low into my eyes. I didn't want to pick any of the flowers from the gardens around the house, in case I got into trouble with the groundsmen, so I was searching out some feral spot that was uncultivated and untended and unlikely to cause any furore if I took a few blooms from it.

After walking for a while, I could see a copse or an area of woodland about a hundred yards away across an open field. I climbed over the wooden fence and started to make my way across the wide space that sloped up to the crest of a hill where the sun was hovering, and blinding me to any view in that direction. Suddenly, I heard the sound of pounding hooves, but I could see nothing near me in the field – until a herd of big horses came galloping over the ridge of the hill and straight at me. I was frozen with fear. I'd never be able to make it back to the fence in time, nor would I get to the edge of the copse before they were on top of me. I stood there like a petrified statue, as the big hunters came closer. Then, a shrill high-pitched whistle cut through the sound of the hooves and the horses all turned, as one herd, and veered off to the left of me. I watched them neighing and tail-swishing past, not more than ten paces from where I stood. A rider approached me at a canter, after the herd had rushed past, and came to a stop close to me. The rider was silhouetted by the sun, and it wasn't until harsh words were spoken that I realised it was a woman. The irritated voice flew down at me from the back of her horse.

'What the bloody hell are you doing?'

'Picking flowers.'

'This is private property.'

'I know. I work here.'

She dismounted and I could see her better now. She was no more than nineteen or twenty years of age.

'Didn't anyone tell you we run the horses in these fields?'

'No. Sorry.'

'You're lucky you didn't get trampled.'

I explained who I was and that it was my first time at Bolde Hall and I didn't know 'A from a bull's foot' about the estate or what went on on it. She cooled down a bit and introduced herself as Charlie Currant, daughter of the local village farrier. She worked part-time as a stable-girl and groom for the hunt and ran their horses at this time every afternoon to get them fit for the fox-hunting in a few weeks' time. I thought the name Currant was quite amusing for some-one so serious and I smiled when she said it.

'You think my name's funny?'

'Oh, no!'

'Yes, you do!'

'Well, a little.'

The frown on her face disappeared and she smiled with me. She was shorter than me, though obviously a bit older. Her sandy hair was cropped short like a boy's and she wore britches and riding boots and a tweed hacking jacket. She was actually quite friendly when she found out I was the personal maid of Miranda Brandon, as she called her. Apparently, Mrs Bouchard was quite a celebrity in these parts.

'I know Charlie sounds like a boy's name, but it's not. It's short for Charlotte.'

I didn't tell her it wasn't her Christian name that made me smile. And I found out later from one of the people at Bolde Hall that the name Currant originated in Ireland and the Gaelic version was O'Currain– it meant from Curtain or out of Curtain and Curtain was the name for a spear. So, her ancestors were probably Irish spear-throwers, but it was still a big leap of definition to associate such romanticism with Currant which, to me, was something you put in a cake. Although, if her father was a farrier, it was feasible that his people might have been blacksmiths and spear-makers, once-upon-a-time.

Whatever her name, she was a pleasant enough person when she wasn't frowning at me for wandering across her field the way I did, and we talked together and walked over to the herd of horses that had stopped galloping now and were huddled nodding their heads and whickering. She led her mount behind her and I gave up the idea of collecting a bunch of wild flowers to brighten my room. Charlie was an excellent rider, by all accounts, having been on horseback before she could even walk. The horses she ran were field hunters. They were big beasts and had to have stamina and sense and spirit, 'the three esses', as she called them, to do their job. Then she told me she was nineteen and asked me if I came from Wales.

'Yes, I do.'

'I thought so by your lingo. One of my grandmothers was Welsh, you know.'

'Was she?'

'Yes, on my mother's side.'

I made a casual remark about the horses being very big brutes and she explained they were mostly crossed between thoroughbred and some other, hardier breed – maybe three-quarters English thoroughbred and one-quarter Irish draught, she wasn't entirely sure. Apparently they had to have a safe jump so's not to get caught on any of the solid obstacles found in the hunt field and be good, cross-country steeds that could gallop and jump over varied terrain – ditches and walls and coops and up and down banks and even through water. Then, to my surprise, she abruptly changed the subject.

'What d'you think about Wallis Simpson?'

'Who?'

'The King's crumpet.'

I knew very little about the King's crumpets, or his toast, or his cinnamon buns for that matter. Although he'd holidayed with Mrs Simpson on a private yacht that summer, the British newspapers kept a respectful distance. But the rest of the world's press didn't – and Charlie Currant had an opinion.

'She's American. And married.'

'I know a married American woman ... Mrs Reynolds.'

'American women know what they want.'

'Do they?'

'And how to get it!'

We gabbled away like a couple of schoolgirls and I found myself liking this little freckle-faced person. She had a forward way about her – an impertinence that was fresh in its childlike candour, even if she was older than me. Just.

'You must come to the Forge for tea, Anwyn.'

'The Forge?'

'That's what we call our house. Why don't you come now?'

I didn't know what time Miranda would be back and she'd be sure to want me to help her change for dinner, but Charlie wouldn't take no for an answer.

'Surely she can take care of herself for an hour or two?'

I was sure she could and, anyway, she said I didn't need to hurry back. I hadn't had any time off since I started as a lady's maid and there was always Miss Mason if she wanted anything.

'All right, then.'

'Good. You can help me paddock the horses first. Can you ride?'

'No, not really...'

'Nothing to it. You take Firebird here, he's easy to handle. I'll grab one of the others.'

Firebird?

She helped me get a foot into the high stirrup and then shoved me up by the rump into the saddle. My skirt was up round the tops of my thighs and I was an extremely immodest sight for anyone that might happen to be watching. The big horse moved to the side when it felt the extra weight on its back.

'How do I steer it?'

'Use the reins. Pretend they're the handle-bars of a bicycle.'

Then she grabbed the mane of one of the other horses and swung herself expertly up onto its bare back. She let out a long, low whistle and the herd began to move off, back up to the crest of the hill. Charlie rode behind them, but Firebird refused to move for me.

'Kick him!'

So I did. But I must have kicked him too

hard, because he took off and I let go of the reins and grabbed the animal round the neck and clung on for dear life. My feet came out of the stirrups and my skirt was now flying up around my face. Charlie grabbed hold of the horse's bridle when we came level with her and she brought him to a halt, laughing her head off at my awkwardness and embarrassment. I took control of the reins and stirrups again and we set off at a slow trot after the herd.

Once all the horses were paddocked and Firebird was unsaddled and turned out with the others, we started to walk the half mile to the forge. It was still bright, with an unbroken pale-blue sky and a light breeze starting to blow up from the southwest.

Charlie Currant was an only child and it was clear her father wanted a boy when she was born, because he'd brought her up like one. She was a bit of an Annie Oakley, who I'd once seen in some Pathé News feature in the cinema, performing for Queen Victoria when she came over to this country with Buffalo Bill's Wild West show. Charlie's father was a big man – a typical farrier, used to handling horses. His name was Cedric and he wore a thick black beard and guffawed like a bull when he laughed. Her mother was a small, meek kind of woman who said very little and busied herself in the kitchen most of the time I was there. It was obvious Charlie took after her father in spirit and her mother in size.

We had a plain tea of sliced, fried potatoes, fried parsnips and mutton, with an onion gravy. Mr Currant produced a large jug of home-made cider and insisted I have a glass, even though I told him I didn't drink all that much.

'It'll put hairs on your chest, lass.'

Then he guffawed. I didn't particularly want hairs on my chest and the cider was cloudy and had bits floating in it that could have been toenail clippings for all I knew. But Charlie had some and so did Mrs Currant, so I felt obliged to drink it. When I did, Mr Currant filled the glass again.

'So, Miss Moyle...'

'Please call me Anwyn.'

'So, Anwyn, you work for Miranda Brandon, eh?'

'Mrs Bouchard.'

'Oh aye, Mrs *Boochard*.'

He said he remembered her growing up round these parts. She was a bit of a handful even then, always getting into scrapes and the bane of her poor mother's life.

The Currants gave me a brief history of the Brandons while I was there – how Miranda's mother died of pleurisy when she was only ten. She had a series of governesses after that, but none of them could control her, so her father sent her away to a private school for

193

girls in France, so she could learn how to be a lady. I didn't want to talk about Miranda, as that would have been a betrayal of her trust in me – so I just listened. Mr Currant seemed to know a lot about the Brandons and I supposed he heard all the gossip while he was shoeing the horses. He knew Mr Brandon senior had lost a lot of money through naive investments in the American stock market and now he needed one of his two children to marry well. Otherwise, Bolde Hall would go the way of many other aristocratic country houses.

'Why can't James Brandon marry for money?'

'Him?'

Mr Currant guffawed again, as if I'd said something very funny.

'He can't marry no woman.'

'Why not?'

The Currants looked at each other and shook their heads and my question went unanswered. I decided not to pursue it and Cedric changed the subject.

'What's all this nonsense going on down in London?'

'What nonsense?'

He told me there'd been a battle in Cable Street, which was just across the river from where Lucy lived, and I hoped she and her family were all right.

According to Cedric Currant, the Fascist

Blackshirts organised a march through the area, which was predominantly Jewish. The government refused to ban the march, even though they knew there'd be trouble. People built barricades in an attempt to stop it – a hundred thousand anti-fascist demonstrators turned out, along with six thousand police, who tried to clear the street to let the three thousand Fascists march through. Then it all escalated, with sticks and stones and rubbish and rotten vegetables being thrown at the police. Women in the houses emptied chamber pots onto the head of the coppers and there were skirmishes and running battles up and down the street. Oswald Mosley, the leader of the Fascists, took his Blackshirts away to Hyde Park and left the anti-fascists to fight it out with the police. Hundreds of people were hurt and others arrested and the leaders of the demonstrators were sentenced to three months hard labour while the Fascists walked free. I knew nothing about this because I hadn't seen a newspaper or heard the radio since I arrived at Bolde Hall. And I wished I'd been down there where history was happening, instead of stuck out here with the nobles and the nobs.

By the time I left the Forge, the cider jug was empty and I was feeling a bit tipsy. Charlie said she'd walk me back to Bolde Hall and she pumped up a Tilley lamp to light our way, as it had grown dark by then. The night-time sounds of the countryside surrounded us as we walked – foxes barking and owls hooting and badgers churring and all sorts of insects clicking and clacking. I was glad Charlie was with me. She slipped her arm into mine and we linked each other along.

'What's it like down in London, Anwyn?'

'It's great. I love London.'

'I suppose you get to go to all sorts of parties?'

'I've been all over the place with Mrs Bouchard during the season.'

'It must be a bit boring for you way out here?'

'A bit.'

I told her about the balls I'd been to with Miranda and the dancehalls I'd been to with Lucy and she said she'd love to live in London, if only for a few weeks.

'Wouldn't you miss the horses?'

'Probably.'

Charlie told me she was going back to college in Leicester once the new term started. She was studying to be a vet so she could help the animals she loved so much. I told her I would have loved to go to college, but I had to start work as soon as I was fourteen to help my family. She was sympathetic.

'Have you got a boyfriend, Anwyn?'

'No. I can't be bothered with boys.'

'Why not?'

'More trouble than they're worth. Except as dancing partners.'

She laughed.

'What about you, Charlie?'

'Not likely!'

I was quite tired by the time we got back to Bolde Hall and I hoped Miranda wouldn't want to have a late night. The rough cider had taken its toll on me and I just wanted to flop into bed. Charlie stopped at the edge of the grounds. I could see the lights from the big house illuminating the rest of the way.

'You'll be all right from here, Anwyn.'

'Thank you for walking with me, Charlie.'

I went to kiss her on the cheek, but she turned her head as I did so and our lips touched. She didn't pull away – and neither did I. The moment lingered for a lifetime, and was over in an instant.

'Goodbye, Anwyn.'

She turned and walked away into the night. I stood there watching her go. I could still see the light from the lamp swinging to and fro, long after Charlie Currant had disappeared from view, into the gloaming.

When I got inside the house, Miss Mason told me Mrs Bouchard was looking for me. Miranda was in the dining room and I went straight to her. She was with Mrs Hathaway.

'Ah, Anwyn...'

'I'm sorry I'm late, Madam.'

197

'That's all right, Anwyn, I've not been long back myself.'

She told me she was tired after her day and was going to have an early night. She wouldn't need me for anything else that evening. I was so thankful.

'Have you had dinner?'

'I had tea at the Forge.'

'With the Currants?'

'Yes.'

The hint of a smile broke across Miranda Bouchard's lips. 'You must have met Charlotte?'

'Yes.'

'And how did you find her?'

'Very ... affectionate.'

'Quite.'

I never saw Charlie Currant again.

But I thought of her – often.

Chapter Thirteen

The weeks passed at Bolde Hall and the fox-hunting season arrived – and with it the rich Earl and his entourage. This time the lady guests brought their own maids and it was less lonely for me having these other women to chat to. They brought all the gossip with them, which was mostly about the King and

Mrs Simpson, but some had come up from London and they were gushing on about this thing called television and how the BBC had made the world's first transmission of pictures to a little screen. Some said these little television boxes would be in every household eventually and would do away with the wireless and the picture house – but I didn't believe them. It was great to hear Belgravia mentioned as well, and I wished I was back there with Lucy and Hannah and the girls in the tea shop.

The Earl was, indeed, a charming man – tall and handsome and about thirty-five years old. He looked a bit like an English Gary Cooper and he had a habit of slapping his thigh when he laughed. Maybe that's what put Miranda off him. He was courteous to the servants, unlike the Brandon men, and he had a happy and extrovert demeanour. He was a man any mature women could easily fall for, I thought, and I wondered what the untitled William Harding had to compare with this man's appeal. But then, I knew, I felt it that day in the library – before we were interrupted. I didn't tell Miranda about that encounter, it would only have hurt her and probably got me dismissed, even though I'd done nothing wrong. But it seemed to me that William Harding, despite his appeal, was not a man to be trusted. In the first place, he was married and, secondly, he was a philanderer. Miranda said he'd promised to leave his wife for her when the children were a little older, but I didn't believe he ever would.

The opening meet was held on Wednesday 4 November and over a hundred people gathered at Bolde Hall. I was surprised not to see Charlie Currant there, or her father. But I knew some people were against fox-hunting and maybe the Currants were that way inclined. Or maybe Charlie had already gone back to college. Mr Brandon senior was Master of the Vale of Evesham hunt and James was the Huntsman and carried the horn. The men who had hunt buttons wore their pinks, with white breeches and black boots with tan tops. The ladies, including Miranda, wore navy with buff breeches and black dress boots with patent leather tops. The women who rode side-saddle had long coats and top hats and the others wore half coats and bowlers. The Master and Hunts-man and Whippers-in all wore their ribbons down, while everyone else wore them up. Children under sixteen wore ratcatchers, which were tweed jackets and tan breeches with laced-up field boots. They all wore black stock ties and carried hunting whips with horn handles and long leather lashes. It was truly a sight to see for a young Welsh girl like me, and here was I now, a part of this dubious pageant and not on my hands and knees scrubbing some floor. What a totally disarming thing life was – it had that way of changing all the time.

The Field was divided into two groups. The First Field took the more demanding route with jumps like wide ditches and high fences and stone walls, while the Hill-toppers took a longer route with gates and other types of access on the flat. Myself and some others who were inclined to go out were invited to follow in a four-wheeled dray drawn by two horses. Foot-followers from the village roamed the grounds and the atmosphere was one of excitement and celebration, with everyone saying good morning to everyone else. The local vicar blessed the hounds and the Field drank their stirrup cups, served by all the servants, including myself and Mrs Hathaway and Miss Mason. We served port to the men and sherry to the ladies and many of the gathering had their own hip-flasks of whisky and brandy and sloe-gin and other, more dubious concoctions too, I was sure.

When all the pleasantries were over, the whole hunt moved off to the covert, where the Huntsman drew the hounds to find the line. The dogs were casting round and giving tongue for a few minutes and then they were off. The Huntsman followed first and then the Master and the Whippers-in, whose job was to keep the hounds from rioting, and the rest of the Field followed. We came after them in our dray, passing many of the foot-followers and listening to the distant calls of the Field as they shouted 'tally ho' and 'hounds, please' and 'beware' and 'hold hard'. The Master guided the riders across countryside and farmland, making best use of tramlines and headlands, and jumping the obstacles. Sometimes we could see them and then they'd disappear, only to become visible again somewhere else, as the quarry led them a dance as it tried to find foils and check the hounds.

I lost count of the hours in the strange excitement of it all, but eventually the fox went to ground and the terriers were sent in after it. Then some kennelmen dug down and killed the animal. We'd caught up by then and the fox's blood was smeared on the faces and foreheads of the hunt's two youngest initiates by the Huntsman. The brush and pads and mask were cut off for trophies and the carcass was then thrown to the hounds to be torn to pieces.

On the way back, a young rider came alongside the dray. He was about eighteen and had dark hair and brown eyes. He was on a chestnut hunter that loomed huge beside me and he looked so regal and stately. He didn't say anything at first, just smiled at me and the other ladies' maids in the dray. It was as if he was sizing us all up, seeing who was the prettiest. The perkiest. The others were pretending they didn't see him, but I smiled back.

'What's your name?'

'What's yours?'

He laughed. One of the other maids flashed a disapproving look at me.

'Henry Rivers.'

'I'm Anwyn Moyle.'

'A very pretty name.'

'Thank you, Sir.'

'Henry ... please.'

The disapproving lady's maid looked like she'd swallowed a wasp. But I didn't care, she was no better than me now – none of them were. The days of them looking down their nose at scullery-maid Moyle were gone. Henry Rivers was still smiling at me.

'I like your accent.'

'It's Welsh.'

'I know.'

'Will you be at the ball tonight, Anwyn?'

'I'm sure I will.'

With that he rode off and I watched as he galloped away. My heart was beating a bit faster than normal and I wondered why – maybe it was love at first sight? I'd heard about such things happening. Then I laughed to myself at such a stupid, girlish thought – I loved my family and I loved Lucy and I loved Miranda, in a way, but I certainly didn't love Henry Rivers. I didn't even know who he was. Yet I felt something and it was like nothing I'd known before. The cranky lady's maid looked at me.

'You'll be sorry.'

'Will I?'

'Wait and see.'

When we got back to Bolde Hall, I ran a bath for Miranda and helped her to change, then I took her hunting clothes away to be cleaned, and tidied up the bathroom and bedroom after her. As the other ladies had their own maids, I wasn't required to assist them as I was after the pheasant shoot. By the time my work was done, it was getting on for seven o'clock and I went and had dinner with Mrs Hathaway and Miss Mason. They weren't as cheerful or as chatty as they were before.

'Well, Anwyn, did you enjoy your first hunt?'

'It was an eye-opener, Mrs Hathaway.'

'Rumour has it you were talking to a young man.'

Gossip moves fast in this place, I thought to myself.

'His name is Henry Rivers, Mrs Hathaway'

'*Lord* Henry Rivers, or he will be when he inherits the title.'

Mrs Hathaway went on to tell me that Henry Rivers' family line went all the way back to the tenth century, when they were known as de Revers. They were a blue-blooded family and there would certainly be

no place in it for a girl like me. Mrs Hathaway and Miss Mason both warned me to
steer clear of Henry Rivers, because aristocratic boys like him were known to take
advantage of 'common' girls like me, leaving
some of them with child, before going on to
marry whatever woman their family would
have had arranged for them. That's what
Mrs Hathaway and Miss Mason told me –
but this was the twentieth century, not the
nineteenth or the eighteenth, and my teenage heart was telling me something else.

After dinner, I went back to Miranda and
helped her get ready for the hunt ball. She
wore a stunning black evening dress with
frou-frou bodice and corsage, along with a
pair of stiletto slippers that looked like they
were made of glass. I put her hair up in a
high style that exposed her elegant neck and
she wore a discreet diamond tiara in it with
a matching necklace and bracelet. She
looked truly beautiful and I thought maybe
she'd taken a fancy to the Earl after all. She
told me to join the other ladies' maids at the
back of the ballroom in case she needed me
for anything during the night. I then went to
my own room and washed and dressed as
prettily as I could and slapped on some
extra make-up and went down to the great
hall, from which the house took its name.

I stood at the back and watched the dancing and partying. The Earl was paying a lot

of attention to Miranda, but she didn't seem to be reciprocating, much to the annoyance of her father. Her brother James seemed more interested in talking and drinking with the young hunt boys than dancing with any of the ladies. And I wondered if Miranda had some kind of agenda for tonight – maybe William Harding would arrive and carry her away from the Earl and she'd drop one of her glass slippers on the stone steps outside and the Earl would pick it up and shed a tear into it. And maybe I was reading too many books.

Somebody touched my arm and I looked round to see Henry Rivers.

'Would you care to dance?'

'Oh no ... I'm not allowed.'

'I insist.'

'No ... it wouldn't be right.'

He leaned over and whispered into my ear.

'If you turn me down, I'm going to look a fool in front of all these people around us ... even the servants. Would you want me to look a fool?'

Of course I wouldn't. So I let him lead me onto the dance-floor for a version of Debussy's 'Clair de Lune' which the small chamber orchestra was playing. He was wearing an evening suit with a long tailcoat and a scarlet bow-tie and his dark hair had fallen over his brown eyes. He moved me delicately round the floor and I responded well to his touch. We danced slower and slower and moved closer and closer. I could smell his cologne, feel the pressure of his chest against my breasts. His lips touched the top of my head and my hand moved under the back of his jacket and onto his spine. I could feel the heat of him. Smell the scent of him. I knew something was stirring in him and I leaned in closer against his body. We weren't dancing any more, we were being sexually delinquent.

The music stopped and I opened my eyes. The other guests were no longer dancing they were watching me and Henry Rivers as we moved slowly from one foot to the other in a sensual rhythm. Before he could disengage from me, a middle-aged woman wearing a black lace evening gown strode onto the dance floor and grabbed him by the arm and dragged him away to the safety of her party. I stood alone on the floor, with all eyes upon me. So I curtsied like I saw the debutantes doing in the general direction of Henry's abrupt departure and said, in a hoarse whisper–

'Thank you.'

The crowd stirred from their mesmerisation and the orchestra began to play Handel's 'See the Conquering Hero Comes'. A hum of conversation resumed as Miranda Bouchard appeared miraculously by my side and escorted me to the back of the room where the other ladies' maids stood sniggering.

It was very late when the ball ended with the National Anthem and I accompanied a very inebriated Miranda to her bedroom. She fell on the bed and I undressed her where she lay and hung her clothes up and was about to leave the room.

'Anwyn...'

I turned to see that she'd managed to sit up in the bed.

'Yes?'

'Quite a stunt you pulled tonight.'

'Stunt?'

'With the Rivers boy.'

I didn't know what she meant. Was what I did in having one dance any worse than what she was doing with Mr Harding? I was convinced she was expecting him to turn up tonight and that's why she'd made a special effort to look extra beautiful. But he didn't, so she got drunk. I decided to ignore her remark and, anyway, she'd already lain back down in the bed.

I tried to sleep but my head was full of Henry Rivers and then, at about 3:30 a.m., I heard a gentle knock on my door.

'Who is it?'

'It's me ... Henry.'

I opened the door and let him in and he kissed me and held me in his arms for a long time. When our lips finally parted so we could breathe again, he spoke in a whisper.

'I had to wait for everybody to fall asleep.'

'You shouldn't be here, Henry.'

'Why not?'

'I don't know.'

'Neither do I.'

He kissed me again and moved me backwards towards the bed. We pulled at each other's clothes, even though I knew it was wrong and I might, like Mrs Hathaway and Miss Mason said, be left with a child. But I didn't care. Right then, in that moment, there was no future, just a passionate and overpowering present.

But Henry Rivers proved to be no Don Juan, no Romeo to my Juliet, no Lancelot and no Tristan and no Mr Darcy. He was a boy, even though he thought he was a man, and just as nervous as me. That nervousness, combined with the alcohol he'd imbibed to give him Dutch courage, foiled his futile attempts to send me into an ecstasy of erotic pleasure – and, after exhausting himself trying, he fell asleep. I was so tired I fell asleep too and didn't hear Jacob's tapping on my door in the morning. I was woken by the rough hands of Mrs Hathaway shaking me by the shoulders. Henry Rivers woke too and rushed red-faced from my room, almost knocking over the many servants who'd congregated in the corridor outside.

'You're in trouble, young lady!'

I was allowed to dress, then frogmarched to the library where Mr Brandon senior was waiting, along with Miranda, who'd obviously managed to dress herself, or had been helped by one of the other ladies' maids or Miss Mason. Mrs Hathaway pushed me inside and closed the door.

'Miss Moyle, I'm afraid your conduct has been...'

Miranda put up her hand to silence him.

'Father, please, let me deal with this.'

He threw his arms into the air in an exasperated fashion, while she took me to one side.

'I'm sorry, Anwyn.'

'Nothing happened, Miranda.'

'That doesn't matter.'

'Why not?'

'You don't understand...'

And that's all she said. It was clear that I'd challenged one of the ridiculous rules that couldn't be challenged – by a woman. Mr Brandon asked if I wanted to go back to London or home to Wales. As there was nowhere for me to go to in London and Wales was closer and I hadn't seen my family in nearly three years, I decided on Llangynwyd. He paid me my wages up to that day and a week in lieu of notice and Miranda said I could keep the clothes she'd given me. I packed a trunk and Tom the chauffeur drove me up to Birmingham railway station, where a ticket was waiting for me, paid for by Mr Brandon.

The train journey to Maesteg was a sad and lonely one – down through Herefordshire and into Wales and across the Brecon Beacons. It took hours and hours and I had plenty of time to think. I was disappointed that Mrs Bouchard hadn't stood up for me more, after I'd been loyal to her and kept her secret and stood by her when she wanted me to cover for her. But that was the way of life, you never knew who your friends were until you needed them. I'd learned another valuable lesson.

I didn't know how my family would take my coming home. I had plenty of money, because there was nowhere to spend my wages in Warwickshire and, even in London, I rarely got to go anywhere. So, all told, I had six pounds and fifteen shillings in my purse after buying myself a cup of tea and a sandwich while I was waiting for the train. That was a lot of money and I resolved to give most of it to my mother for my keep, until I could get myself another job.

It was 4:30 p.m. when I arrived at Maesteg station. The November late afternoon was already dark and I had a big trunk to carry. I didn't know how I was going to get it the two-and-a-half miles to Llangynwyd. My family didn't have a phone and nobody knew I was coming and there were no taxis or anything like that – so I was stuck. There was only one thing for it, I asked a porter at the station if I could leave my trunk there overnight and come back for it in the morning. He asked what was in it and I told him nothing but ladies' clothes.

'No dead bodies?'

He laughed and I gave him a sixpenny tip and he took the trunk away. I set out to walk to Llangynwyd. It was starting to rain, as it does in Wales in November, and I had no umbrella. By the time I reached the door of our house I was soaked through and my mother didn't even recognise me.

'What can I do for you?'

'It's me, Mam … Winny.'

She looked closer, then turned back into the house.

'Father, look, it's our Winny!'

'Winny?'

Mam hugged me when I finally got through the door and so did my sister Gwyneth, who was nearly fifteen now, and Bronwyn, who was over twelve. Walter was going on seventeen and had left school and was already working in one of the mines that were still operating, so he wasn't home yet. My father stood me at arm's length.

'Let me look at you.'

'I'm like a drowned rat.'

'No you're not. You're a fine-looking lady now.'

Then he kissed me on the forehead and Mam got a towel to dry my hair and the girls fussed about my fine clothes that were ruined by the rain.

'Have you no suitcase?'

'I left it at the station.'

'I'll go get it.'

'No, Dad, they'll keep it till tomorrow.'

That night, after Walter got home and had his tea, we gathered round the fire and I gave Mam five pounds of my money. She didn't want to take it, but I made her. Then I told them all about London and Warwickshire, leaving out why I had to leave Hampstead and how I got fired from Bolde Hall.

'And are you going back there, Winny?'

'Not to Warwickshire. I may go back to London, when the new season starts.'

'When will that be?'

'Maybe February or March.'

They asked what I was going to do until then and I said I'd get a job here in Wales to tide me over. My father shook his head and my mother clucked her tongue and they both said there wasn't much doing at the moment. But, I thought, with my experience, I was bound to find something. For now, I was glad to be home and they were glad to have me and I slept soundly in my little Welsh bed that night.

After saying a thankful prayer.

Dear Earth, dear Sun,
By you I live.
My loving thanks
To you I give.

Chapter Fourteen

Next morning, I went with my sisters and a handcart and collected my trunk from Maesteg station. The girls were star-struck by all the fine clothes and shoes and stoles and camisoles that Miranda gave me when we were friends, and I shared with them whatever fitted or whatever could be altered to fit. As the days and weeks went by, I searched the surrounding area for a job – going as far as Bryn and Pontycymer and Aberkenfig and even Port Talbot and Bridgend, but I could find nothing but grimaces and shaking heads. In the meantime, King Edward VIII abdicated to be with Mrs Simpson on 10 December, but us poor people in Wales were too busy trying to survive without any work to be very much concerned. I supposed the Brandons and their social peers might be buzzing with the drama of it all, but not us here in the redundant hills.

One day I was in Maesteg looking through notices in a shop window when I heard a voice behind me.

'I recognise that hat.'

I turned round.

'Mrs Reynolds.'

'Where have you been, Anwyn Moyle?'

We went into the Caffi Ambr and had a pot of tea and a plate of cakes and I told her where I'd been. But now I was back home and couldn't find a job because there was no work anywhere in Wales and I was running out of options very fast.

'D'you wanna stay in service, Anwyn?'

'If I can't get anything else.'

She said she might be able to help me. There was a Christmas party being held at Llanyrafon Manor in Cwmbran and she'd been invited and could bring a guest. She said there'd be loads of landed gentry types there and she asked if I wanted to go with her.

'Keep me company.'

'What about Mr Reynolds?'

'He'll be in New York.'

So I said certainly!

On Saturday 19 December, we set off in Mrs Reynolds's Wolseley Hornet car and drove the thirty miles or so to Cwmbran. It was about 6:00 p.m. when we arrived and there were already many fancy motor cars parked around the white exterior of the old historic manor. Mrs Reynolds was dressed in a sheer crimson evening dress with a mink stole wrapped round her shoulders to keep out the deep December cold and I wore a burgundy silk cocktail dress that Miranda gave me, under my overcoat. There were lots of perky people milling about inside, drinking champagne and cocktails and talking with *beau monde* accents, and I wondered where they got all their money from, with the rest of Wales steeped in petrifying poverty, Mrs Reynolds told me to mingle, so I did. I went from room to room and listened for a while to the five-piece combo playing a selection of Christmas jingles and tried to edge into conversations. But nobody knew me and nobody spoke to me. I found a little library and read a brochure about the history of the manor – how it had hugged the banks of the Afon Llwyd river for nearly four hundred years and how it belonged to the Griffiths family until the last one of them died in 1886.

The house had a colourful past of disputes and feuds between the Griffiths and the Morgans of Tredegar, with stories of love and hate that would have rivalled any historical novel. And I lost myself in the retrospective evocation and forgot about the party – until my reverie was rudely interrupted.

'There you are, Anwyn.'

I turned away from the books and

brochures as Mrs Reynolds came into the room with another woman in her mid-forties wearing a full-length mesh lace Chanel gown.

'This is Gwendolyn Morgan.'

'I see you're reading about my ancestors.'

The woman was heavily made-up and tried in vain to look imperious through the layers of foundation and powder on her face. I bowed to her and offered my hand. She didn't take it.

'Pleased to meet you, Madam.'

'You are a Welsh girl, aren't you?'

'From Llangynwyd, Madam.'

'Cook prefers Welsh girls.'

She wasn't looking for a lady's maid and neither was anyone else at the party, but they had a vacancy for a kitchen maid at Tredegar House near Newport, which was no further from Llangynwyd than Cwmbran. It would be a backward step for me, but beggars couldn't choose to turn down job offers in austere times like these.

'It's three shillings and sixpence a week, with every second Sunday off.'

She turned to Mrs Reynolds.

'And you'll vouch for her, Monica?'

'Of course.'

Then back to me.

'Can you start straight away? Cook needs someone for Christmas.'

'I think so, Madam.'

'You think so?'

'I mean, yes ... I can.'

'Good.'

With that, she turned and left the room. Mrs Reynolds made an apologetic gesture towards me before following her. On the way home, Mrs Reynolds apologised again.

'She just said she needed someone. I didn't know the job was a kitchen maid, Anwyn.'

'It's fine. I've worked in a kitchen before.'

'You don't have to take it.'

'I do.'

The following Monday, I packed my suitcase and took the train from Maesteg to Newport, where I was picked up by a silver Daimler driven by a chauffeur in full livery.

'Anwyn Moyle?'

'That's me.'

He held the door open for me to climb in onto the back seat. It was warm in the big car, warmer than the cold wind blowing down the station platform, promising to make it a white Christmas.

Tredegar House was a seventeenth-century country mansion which was once described as 'the grandest and most exuberant country house in Monmouthshire'. It was surrounded by a hundred acres of parkland and was the ancestral seat of the Morgans, who were descended from Cadifor the Great [an eleventh century knight]. The red-brick facade blended into its surroundings and four big windows flanked either side of the arched doorway. The first floor had a row of nine windows, equally as large as those on the ground floor and five smaller, attic windows looked in onto the top floor from the front of the house. Away to the east, a stable block was used for parking the cars, and other outhouses and cottages were dotted round the parkland. It stood well back in its own ambience – aloof and circumspect.

The chauffeur, whose name was David, drove me round to a side entrance and escorted me down a flight of steps to the kitchen and introduced me to the cook, whose name was Mrs Bowen. She was a big, imposing lump of a woman of about fifty, with coal-black hair and the hint of a moustache across her top lip. There were two other kitchen maids, Brenda and Sarah, who were probably about my age, and a young scullery maid called May. Once the introductions were made, David took me upstairs and handed me over to a footman called Cecil wearing the same livery as the chauffeur. Cecil was about twenty-two and looked pale and sickly, his hair was already thinning and he walked like he hadn't long to live. There was another footman called Floyd, who was tall and handsome and about twenty, and the head butler was Mr Evans. He was in his fifties, like the cook, and looked like an undertaker, dressed all in black like Miss Mason used to be at Chester Square. The housekeeper was Miss Maddox and there were three parlourmaids – Nerys and Rhiain and Marged. There was a nanny called Miss Pritchard and a lady's maid called Miss Yates.

All this I learned from Cecil while he took me up the back stairs to the top of the house and showed me to my room. It was small with two single beds and I'd be sharing with May the scullery maid. We shared a small bathroom with all the other female servants on the same floor. Once I deposited my case and my coat, I was taken back down to Mrs Bowen.

'You have experience, I'm told.'

'A year in London.'

'As a kitchen maid?'

'Yes.'

I lied. The kitchen was huge and ventilated by windows high up in the wall at ground level. Milk was delivered daily from a neighbouring farm, along with meat and vegetables, and everything was always fresh. Fruit from the earlier autumn crop was stored in lofts or made into jams and preserves of all sorts. There was a big range in the kitchen and a huge fireplace with hobs either side where a raging fire was burning. A boiler in the scullery heated water and it reminded me of my skivvying days in Hampstead. May, the scullery maid, was covered in ash and soot and I felt so sorry for her – she was only fourteen and fresh out of school and I resolved to help her whenever I could.

The floor was flagstoned all the way through and coal came down a chute and the dust drifted into the kitchen and mingled with the steam and the smells of cooking. And it seemed to me that I'd stepped back in time, away from the coming year of 1937 and into the bad old days of servility. Tredegar House was nothing like the modern and progressive Hampstead, nor the glamorous Chester Square, nor even like the harsh Bolde Hall. It was a rough, rural place where the present was being kept at bay by the past.

'You'll have to feed the dogs, Anwyn. May doesn't have the time.'

That was my first job. The Morgans' deer-hounds were fed a diet of raw meat and cooked vegetables, mixed with broken biscuits and a few tablespoons of honey thrown in for glossy coats. They knew what was coming when I approached the kennels and they were barking and bounding all over the place. The kennelmen took the food from me and said it wouldn't be safe for me to go in on my own – because I was such a tasty morsel the dogs might eat me. Then they laughed and I blushed and tripped my way awkwardly back to the kitchen with them watching me all the way.

Mrs Bowen was preparing beef casserole for lunch and, once it was ready, it was my job to clean up after her, while she and the other kitchen maids immediately started preparing the dinner for that evening. The starter course was hare soup and I had to skin and gut the hares, freshly caught that morning. It was a job I didn't like doing, but my genteel days as a lady's maid were over now, thanks to Henry Rivers, so it was back to the grindstone again. The hare meat was chopped into small pieces and left to simmer with Cook's own concoction of vegetables and herbs. When the meat was tender, it was sieved out and pounded with a mortar until it was unrecognisable as meat, then it was returned to the pot and red wine was poured in after it. The hare soup was followed by a main course of roast pheasant and thinly sliced potatoes that were sautéed, and I was told that was the only way to serve potatoes with game, along with a watercress garnish.

From what I'd learned watching and listening to the Beadle of Hampstead and now Mrs Moustache of Tredegar, I could fit in well to the role of kitchen maid. I was a fast learner and knew how to improvise. I learned it all, filleting fish and marinating meat and garnishing goulashes and à la cartes and entrées and all kinds of entremets and plat du jours and pièces de résistance. And, before I knew it, Christmas was upon us. We had a small festive tree downstairs that was decorated with holly and mistletoe and ivy and belladonna, and the whole house had a joyous and jingly mood running through it for a few days now.

The Morgan family consisted of Mrs Morgan, or Gwendolyn, as Monica Reynolds called her, Mr Morgan who was an earl or a baron or something and was a tall, bald man of about fifty. He had a haughty look about him and rarely spoke to any of the servants. His nickname was Hoppy, because his gait was characterised by involuntary little skips at irregular intervals. They had twin daughters called Isobel and Angeline who were in their early twenties and who were tended to by the lady's maid, Miss Yates, and a young ten-year-old son called Christopher who was the apple of his father's eye. Isobel, the elder twin by fifteen minutes, was married with a baby boy called John and she lived at Tredegar House with her husband, Maurice Smyth, who was a solicitor. The twins were plain-looking women with mousy-coloured hair and they wore clothes that were last year's fashions and didn't have anything of any importance to say. Their brother was a lively young lad, always outside and up to something, like boys of that age should be. The whole family lived in the twilight of their time and seemed unable or unwilling to move into modernity.

Myself and May the scullery maid were the first two up on Christmas morning and I helped her light the fires and get the range and the boiler going.

'You don't have to do this, Anwyn.'

'It's no bother.'

'Merry Christmas to you.'

'Merry Christmas to you too, May.'

Mrs Bowen was in a grumpy mood, despite the occasion, knowing there'd be lots of work to do because the Morgans were having guests for Christmas dinner, which was one of the reasons I got the job in the first place. May made her a cup of tea, like I used to do for the Beadle, while I started on the vegetables. Brenda and Sarah arrived a few minutes later, with Cook shouting at them to shake a leg and saying why couldn't they be more like Anwyn, lazy lumps – which didn't endear me to them one little bit. When breakfast was over, we all had to line up in order of rank, with Mr Evans the head butler at the top and May, next to me, at the bottom. Then Mr Morgan came down and gave us all a present of money, along with a handshake and a merry Christmas wish. May and I got a shilling apiece, but I'm sure the others got more. The gifts were in little red bags tied with tinsel, so nobody knew who got what. A gift from the gentry ... a condescending tradition that was still alive here in Tredegar House, despite the Great War and all the social and political upheaval that followed it. Still, better than a poke in the eye with a sharp stick. Just!

Lunch that day was light and consisted of savouries and sweet pastry and avocados and segmented salmon. It was as if everyone was just nibbling at bits and pieces and waiting for the Christmas dinner without ruining their appetites. In the meantime, I had to feed the dogs and run the gauntlet of the frisky kennelmen who were holding sprigs of mistletoe over their heads and puckering their lips like randy perch peeping out of a river. The guests began arriving in the afternoon, along with the snow. Cars and carriages pulled up and people came hand-blowing into the house, where they were greeted with hot toddies of whisky, boiling water and honey, cloves and cinnamon. Those of a teetotal persuasion were given tea or soup or ginger ale imported from Canada. Altogether, about forty guests arrived and it was our job to wine and dine them. There was goose and turkey on the menu, fresh from the farm. The turkey stuffing was dark and smoky, with shallots and chestnuts and mushrooms and garlic and raisins and parsley and rosemary and imported wild rice. The goose was stuffed with prunes in Armagnac and apples and cloves and mace and a good deal of seasoning. The birds were served with traditional roast potatoes and parsnips and sprouts and a variety of sauces and gravies. A selection of other seasonal vegetables was also served in case anybody fancied a change from convention. Christmas cake and lighted pudding and cream and segmented fruit followed, and it was all washed down with a selection of superior wines.

Later, those upstairs amused themselves with piano-playing and party games and smoking cigars and drinking brandy and, when they were merry enough, singing Christmas carols. Some left that night in their chauffeur-driven limousines, no doubt to be ready for their respective traditional Boxing Day foxhunts, but a few stayed over to join the Morgans in their own particular pursuit of the uneatable. I was glad I didn't have to wait up for the ladies until the small hours, and May and I were tucked up safely in our own little yuletide beds before 11:00 p.m., oblivious to the falling snow outside our freezing window.

Next day was the local Hollybush Hunt and the whole Morgan family attended, including the baby. They were driven to covert and mounted their horses in the snow, while little John looked on from the arms of his nanny, Miss Pritchard. I didn't see any of this, of course, because, unlike at

Bolde Hall, as a lowly kitchen maid I wasn't invited to follow the hunt and had to stay at Tredegar to help Cook with the Boxing Day fare. That consisted of crusted ham with mashed potato and fresh vegetables, kedgeree, turkey sandwiches with the crusts cut off, Stilton and walnut salad, fried duck eggs, English trifle, Christmas cherry soufflé and orange and cranberry pancakes.

And so time moved on. My education as a cook's assistant continued into 1937, with partridge pies and rabbit quenelles and stuffed quail, and I learned how to cook all kinds of game and stews and sauces and stuff that most people of my class had never even heard of. But I longed for London. I missed the city and the life I'd had there. I missed Lucy and even Miranda Bouchard and it was no longer at arm's length, but distant and blended into the larger background of my mistakes.

The snows of late December and January thawed in February, but it was still cold. Working in a country house was different to working in a city house. There were rural duties to perform as well as the household ones end, as the second lowest servant in the house, I was expected to do work outside as well as inside. Besides feeding the dogs on a daily basis, I had to bring in the milk that was left at the gate by the farmer. I had to load the chums onto a four-wheeled bogey and pull it over the gravel driveway, and the wheels sometimes sunk into the stones. I'd be lucky if one of the groundsmen came and gave me a hand, but this didn't always happen, and my hands would almost stick to the cold metal handle of the trolley. I had to run errands to the farm and, in winter, my boots would get covered in mud and cow dung and I'd have to clean them outside in the cold when I got back.

I also had to tend the winter herb garden, and once I was sent to top and tail swedes for fodder, and help May clear the snow from the vicinity of the kitchen steps so the trades and delivery men didn't drag it all in on their boots. I was usually exhausted at the end of each long, hard-working day. So tired that I mostly slept on my second Sunday off and never went anywhere for any kind of fun.

But then, one of the young kennelmen asked me to go into Newport with him for a dance at a little local hall in the Craig area of the town. Although he was younger than me, I thought it'd do me good to get away from everything for a while. His name was Brynn. He wasn't bad-looking and, if he thought he was going out with me, he might keep the others from pestering me every time I went to feed the dogs. So, on Sunday 23 February, we set off on his bicycle, with me on the crossbar, to ride the two miles to the dance. It was very cold after the sickly sun went down and, by the time we got there, I was frozen to the bone and sorry I'd ventured out at all. The room I shared with May wasn't all that warm, but it was positively tropical compared to the crossbar of Brynn's bicycle. I cheered up once we got inside, though, and Brynn bought me a port and brandy and that warmed me up on the inside, while he put his arms round me and tried to warm me up on the outside.

'How old are you Brynn?'

'Seventeen.'

'Really? You don't look it.'

'How old are you, Anwyn?'

'Nineteen ... nearly.'

'Really? You look older.'

I didn't know whether to take that as an insult or a compliment, but I let it go and we danced the night away till 10:00 p.m. and I had a good enough time.

Brynn was drinking strong ale and, on the way back, he was a bit unsteady on the bicycle. We were coming to a sharp bend in the narrow road when a car came round it out of nowhere and the headlights blinded him. He wobbled about trying to control the bike, then steered it through a hedge and into a ploughed field. The bicycle came to an abrupt halt in the deep drilled earth and I went flying over the handlebars and landed face down in the cold filthy mud. It was black as pitch. I couldn't see a thing and my shoes were sinking into the softness of the ploughed earth after the rain of earlier in the day.

'Brynn! Where are you?'

He struck a match and I could see his stupid face grinning at me. I took a swing at him with my handbag and the light went out. He lit another match.

'Help me with the bike, Anwyn. I think it's broke.'

We got back out onto the road with a lot of difficulty and hair-snagging and skin-scratching through the hedge. The front wheel of the bicycle was buckled and the chain was broken. We had to walk the final mile to Tredegar House.

By the time we got back it was getting on for midnight and I was cold and tired and, even though he apologised every step of the way and sniggered a bit when he looked at the state of me, I never wanted to set eyes on Brynn again. He only went and told his friends about the incident and that made them worse than ever. They were unmerciful in their teasing when I went out with the dog food, with comments like, 'Did you enjoy your flying lesson, Anwyn?' and 'Find any truffles when you were rooting in the dirt?' and singing that song, 'A Bicycle Built for Two'. Brynn kept pestering me to go out with him again and I was reaching the very limit of my patience when the London season opened up again and I was glad to leave Tredegar House.

Chapter Fifteen

The Morgan family had a town house in Egerton Crescent, in the Royal Borough of Kensington and Chelsea, which wasn't far from Belgravia, and I travelled down there with some of the other servants at the beginning of April, after Cheltenham. But I was sick of being in service and wanted to do something else with my life. So, one day when I was sent out on an errand, I sneaked round to the tea shop to see how Lucy was. Hannah was behind the counter.

'Lucy doesn't work here no more, Anwyn.'

'Oh no, what happened?'

'Nothing. She got a job working in a pub, the pay was better and she needed it to help her family.'

The pub was called the Duke's Head and it was located in Tooley Street, near London Bridge. It was close to Bermondsey where Lucy's family lived and easier and cheaper for her to travel to and fro. I had to get back to Egerton Crescent that day but, as soon as I got my first second Sunday off, I ventured down there.

The pub was a spit-and-sawdust establishment, full of rough-looking dockers on that Sunday lunchtime when I walked in in my best frock and faithful green hat. There wasn't another woman in the big circular bar and everyone stopped what they were doing and turned to look at me. I couldn't see Lucy anywhere, but there was a big-bosomed lady very busy behind the bar with her peroxide-blonde hair falling into her eyes from rushing about like a redshank.

'Lookin' for someone, love?'

'Yes ... Lucy.'

'Lucy's on this evening. Seven o'clock.'

'Oh, thank you.'

I was about to leave when she called after me.

'Wait!'

I turned round.

'You want to earn a couple of shillings, love?'

'I don't mind.'

'Then get behind this bar with me.'

Her name was Pearl and she managed the pub for the Ind Coope Brewery. She was short-staffed that Sunday because her regular barmaid hadn't turned up and, even though I knew nothing about barwork, I was happy to try anything once. I collected and washed the glasses and tankards and jugs for her in a big steel sink, like I used to do when I had my first part-time job, and I saw to the few ladies who were hidden away in the little snug bar. I carried beer over to tables and swept up spillages and broken glass and opened bottles and even pulled a pint or two. The Sunday lunchtime shift was only from 12:00 noon till 2:30 p.m. and it was soon over. When Pearl called time and rang the bell, I helped her clear the pub by coaxing those who didn't want to go instead of being belligerent. It worked with the men and, once the doors were locked, we cleared up and washed and dried the glasses. Then we sat at a table together and had a couple of glasses of sweet sherry.

I told her I was in service as a kitchen maid, but wanted to get out and be more independent.

'A kitchen maid ... can you cook?'

'As good as anyone.'

Now, very few pubs in London sold hot food back in 1937. Most of them only did a few biscuits or a packet of Smith's potato crisps with a pinch of salt in a twist of blue paper. Otherwise, the cockle-and-mussel man came round with his wicker basket on Sundays and that was your lot. But there were places in the West End that were originally coaching inns and taverns and they still served hot, gamey food to their customers. Trade was slow in the 1930s and Pearl wanted the Duke's Head to imitate some of the posh places up West, to give her an edge over the competition. But she didn't want to serve game pie or loin of venison; she thought more working-class grub like mashed spuds and mutton casserole would go down better in Bermondsey.

'What d'you think about that idea, Anwyn?'

'Will people have the money to spend on food?'

'We'd do it cheap, cheaper than they could do it themselves. And we get a lot of tourists round here, being so close to Tower Bridge. Might as well take a bit of their money.'

'We could advertise it outside ... Traditional English Food.'

'Good girl! You got the idea.'

She offered me a job as a kitchen/barmaid, which meant I'd have to cook the food at peak times and help out behind the bar if I wasn't busy. The pay was six shillings a week, which wasn't as much as I had got as a lady's maid, but it was better than the three shillings and sixpence I was getting in the kitchen.

'I'd like to take the job, but I have nowhere to live.'

Pearl looked me up and down for a few moments, probably sizing me up to see if I'd be trouble or not.

'We have rooms upstairs that we rent out. You can have one of them and I'll take a shilling a week from your wages for it.'

That sounded fair to me. And Lucy worked here, so I'd have a friend to show me all the ropes and rituals and regulations. 'When can you start, Anwyn?'

'I'll have to give a week's notice.'

And so it was arranged that I'd leave my life in service and enter the new world of barwork. Mrs Bowen was sad to see me go because she said I was a good worker and I'd be hard to replace. But on Monday 19 April 1937, I left Egerton Crescent with my suitcase and travelled east on the number 38 tram to London Bridge, then walked the rest of the way to the Duke's Head in Tooley Street.

Opening hours were 12:00 till 2:30 p.m. and then from 6:30 p.m. till 10:00 p.m. But I had to start preparing lunchtime food at 10:00 a.m. for it to be ready when the doors opened at noon. In the evening, not many of the local workers could afford to eat in the pub and I only had to cook if something was especially requested – otherwise, I served behind the bar with Lucy. Pearl preferred barmaids to barmen, because she said the mostly male customers were more amenable to them and they could calm a drunken argument without antagonising the antagonists. But she employed a big Irish cellarman called Kevin who could lay into them with a cudgel if things got too far out of hand.

Lucy was delighted to see me again on that first Monday, and even more so when I told her I'd be working there and living upstairs.

'We'll have a right old time together, Anwyn.'

The best thing about working in a pub was that I didn't start till mid-morning and I got to have a lie-in every day, which was a luxury I'd never known before in my time-regulated life. The room upstairs was cosy enough and there was a small communal bathroom that was used by all the paying, staying guests, whether male or female, and I had to be careful and make sure the door was locked when doing my ablutions in the morning, for fear some man might walk in and catch me in the nippy nude. The other drawback of a shared bathroom was getting in there after some heavy drinker who'd had sixteen pints of Guinness the night before – you'd need to wear a gas mask after some of them and I was often convinced that something nasty had crawled up their bums and died inside their stomachs.

Apart from that, it was a good enough life. The cooking side wasn't much because none of the working-class patrons could afford pub-grub, as Pearl called it, and we sold mainly to tourists who saw our sign and wandered in off the streets after visiting the Tower of London and thought Fagin and the

Artful Dodger still frequented the cobbled streets south of the river. We sold traditional fare that was quick to prepare and didn't take much cooking. Things like scalloped oysters from the Thames estuary and five-minute cabbage and boiled bacon and mashed potatoes and roast mutton and shepherd's pie.

We also tried to compete with the pie'n' mash shops, offering eel pie, with eels from the Thames baked in a pastry crust, or minced beef and cold water pastry pie. Both served with cheap mashed potato spread round one side of the plate and eel liquor on the other, which was made from parsley and the water off the stewed eel. The parsley gave it its green colour and everybody loved it – especially the way I made it, with a sprinkle of cornflour for thickness – one of the little tricks I picked up in the big houses. We sold pickled beets and Campbell's tinned soups and corned beef hash and sardines and sandwiches. For the ladies we had Macfarlane Lang rich tea biscuits and Granola digestives and the thinly sliced sautéed potato chips that I'd learned to cook at Tredegar, a bowl of which were quite a hit with a glass of Dubonnet and a Walters Medium Navy Cut cigarette.

Behind the bar, we sold Martell brandy and Haig Scotch and Jameson Irish and Wood's Old Navy Rum that looked and smelled like tar, and Beefeater London Dry Gin from the nearby Lambeth distillery. The beers included Manns Brown Ale and Bass Stout and Double Allbright Barley Wine and Courage Old English and Watney's Pale and Guinness and Oatmeal Stout for the ladies and Rose's Nut Brown and Brandon's Rustic and Hammerton's India Pale Ale. Some were on the pumps and others in bottles, depending on preference, and Kevin looked after the cellar and ran the pipes through and kept the lines clean and the ruffians in check with his cudgel. Part of my job as last girl in was to light the fires and keep them tended, which I was well used to. I had to clean the taps and the bar areas – both the big bar and the snug – wipe down the tables and polish the mirrors and the windows and keep everything spick and span. A cleaning woman came in every day to scrub the toilets and sweep and spread sawdust in the big bar and wash out the salt-slimy spittoons in a trough in the cobbled yard.

The décor in the Duke's Head was uncompromisingly Victorian, with grained woodwork and bareboard floors and ornamental mirrors behind the bar and tables covered in green linoleum. Coarse voices and columns of cigarette smoke mixed with the fumes of the beer and the chinking of the glasses and the rattle of the cash register. In the evenings, the men played bar billiards and darts and shove ha'penny and pitch penny. On a

Sunday lunchtime there'd be the buzz of earnest conversation about things like the situation in Europe and the chances of another war, how the whole system needed a revolution to make it right and, on a Saturday night, there'd be singsongs and knees-ups and Pearl kept a piano in one of the corners for anyone who had the inclination to play it.

Pearl was the perfect landlady – she welcomed each and every customer in the same big-busted way. She was quick-witted and flirty with the more frisky fellows and opinionated and knowledgeable with those who might want a debate. She could throw a dart as straight as any man and could sink six pints of best bitter in under an hour. She was good with the women too, able to handle all their moods and humours, from the poorest dockworker's wife to the streetwalking strumpet or the airs-and-graces tourist with her department store furs and artificial pearls. She served an honest measure and, under the counter, she kept jugs of rough cider that came in from Essex, which she sold at thruppence a pint. A saucepan always stood by one of the fires for the old-timers to mull their ale, and there was always a wink and an extra measure for the visiting policeman or campaigning politician.

Spring turned to summer and Lucy and I became the most inseparable of friends. On our days off, we'd go sightseeing round

London – to the National Gallery and Madame Tussaud's and the Serpentine and Oxford Street and Battersea Park. Whenever we could get the time off from the pub in the evenings, we went dancing at the Palais or the Astoria or the Bag o' Nails in Soho. I sent my mother half-a-crown from the five shillings I had left every week after paying the rent and I was loving life as an approaching twenty-year-old. I got on well with Pearl and Kevin and the other barmaids I crossed paths with from time to time. The customers liked me and I liked them. They were plain people, not rarefied and rude like the toffs in their big houses and country estates – honest working people who came in the pub to take a little break from their hard and heavy lives. And I thought to myself, if the rich would only accept a little bit less, a bit they wouldn't even miss, then these people could have a little bit more – a bit that would mean the difference between life and death to some of them. But I was young back then, and still full of naive vitality and joie de vivre.

As 1937 went on, the mood in the pub became more sombre. Now *all* the talk was about Europe and what Germany was doing. The Civil War was still raging in Spain and more and more people were convinced there was going to be another Great War as well. And I thought, oh no, not so soon after the last one! Scarcely twenty years later and the country still hadn't recovered, and now they were rattling the bayonets again. As well read as I was, I didn't really understand everything that was going on. I listened to the talk about the terrible hardship that was caused by the first Great War, and the Wall Street crash had rippled itself across the Atlantic and every country in Europe was feeling the effects – though not so severely here in Britain, because we didn't experience the full belt of the roaring twenties boom that went before it. I heard the men talking in the pub, saying how democracy was being undermined by dictators who promised the people a better way of life, and Germany, Italy and Russia had gone in for systems of government that violently put down all opposition. Some were communists who supported Stalin, but others said Russian peasants were dying in the streets, and the arguments could get heated, until Kevin came with his cudgel and calmed them down. Germany, worst hit by the depression because of the reparations it had to pay for the Great War, fell into the hands of the Nazis and Adolf Hitler. Italy was being run by the Fascists, led by Mussolini and, along with Germany, re-arming in a big way and many people were afraid that war would be inevitable. But others said it was all blather and the Bosche wouldn't start up again for fear they'd get another pasting like the last time.

241

This was the kind of conversation I'd hear every day in the Duke's Head and, although I listened to that talk, which swung from brooding despondency to careless self-deception, life in London was still gay for a girl like me. I went dancing with Lucy and exploring the sights and sounds of the city and kept myself at arm's length from the men who came mooching round, looking for what they could get.

It was September when the fight happened – a Saturday night. The pub was crowded when a group of Oswald Mosley's men came in. Like I said, many of the dockers were Communists and a heated argument started about Spain and what was going to happen here when the Fascists took over. It wasn't long before the first punch was thrown and it all quickly descended into chaos and violent confusion after that. Kevin wasn't able to control things with his cudgel and bottles and glasses soon started flying in all directions. I was out collecting empties at the time and Lucy screamed at me to get back behind the bar. I tripped as I ran towards the hatch and lost my left shoe in the confusion. After I got back on my feet, I stepped on a broken glass that had landed base down with a long shard sticking up, and it sliced open my foot.

The police came and cleared the pub, but I was losing a lot of blood and they allowed someone to drive me to one of the hospitals in south-east London. Nobody was able to come with me because Lucy and Pearl and all the others had to stay behind to give statements to the police. I can't remember who drove me, but it was in the cab of a lorry and the blood was coming through the rag tied round my foot. They left me just inside the hospital door and drove away. The health service before the NHS was ramshackle and chaotic and everybody was afraid of falling ill, unless you could afford it. A nurse came and found me a wheelchair and tried to stop the bleeding so she could see what damage had been done. I was getting weak and thought I was going to faint, but the nurse kept shaking me and telling me to stay awake. I finally lapsed into unconsciousness, despite the nurse shaking me and slapping my face.

When I woke up again, it was a day and a half later and I was in a room with a lot of other injured people. My left foot was heavily bandaged and set in a pointed position, but at least the bleeding had stopped. After a few hours, a nurse came to see me.

'You're a lucky girl, the doctor managed to stop the bleeding.'

'Can I go home?'

'Can you pay?'

'I don't think so.'

'Then you'll have to go home. But you

243

mustn't stand on that foot.'

'I have to work.'

'Out of the question!'

Then she walked away and left me in the room full of baleful moans and the sickly smell of anaesthetic.

Lucy turned up in the afternoon and I asked her to try and find out what the extent of the damage was. She went away and came back with a young doctor sporting an aloof and superior manner.

'Your name is Anwyn Moyle?'

'Yes.'

'I understand you have no means?'

'No means?'

'To pay for your treatment.'

'I'm a barmaid. I earn five shillings a week.'

His undisguised contempt smiled down at my naivety. Then he told me the glass had pivoted up through the back of my heel and badly damaged the Achilles tendon and opened my ankle to the bone. I went into shock from loss of blood. I would have to keep my foot tightly bandaged for four months, initially in a pointed position to keep the ends of the tendon together, and gradually the foot should be brought upwards before re-bandaging. I would be unable to walk without a stick, even when the injury healed.

They gave me a makeshift crutch and Lucy helped me into a car sent down by Pearl. I went back to the Duke's Head and lay on the bed in my room for two days, with only the crutch to help me go back and forth to the bathroom. Pearl and Lucy were good to me, taking turns to bring me food and cups of tea and to sit with me and keep me company. But they both had to work and I knew Pearl would need the room for a new girl, even though she didn't say so.

There was nothing else for it – I'd have to go home to Wales. In those days, very few people were entitled to free medical aid. Under the 1911 National Insurance Act, access to a doctor was only given free to male workers who earned less than £2 a week – and that didn't cover their wives or children. Hospitals charged for services, which most people couldn't afford, so they didn't go there, and many people, especially children, died through lack of simple care. Everybody tried to heal things themselves and they all had a folk remedy for something – turpentine for lice, and tomatoes for hair loss, and onions for colic, and urine for chilblains, and cloves for toothache, and dock leaves for stings, and enemas and Epsom salts and poultices. Doctors were aggressive and snappy with the poor, believing that it would be better for most of them to die than to waste resources on being treated.

So, there was no way I could stay lying on my back in London for four months, and then hobble about on a crutch for the rest of my life after that. I had to go home – at least I'd be with my family who loved me and would take care of me. I wrote to my mother and explained what had happened. She wrote back and said coming home was the right thing to do. My brother Walter would come down to London on the following weekend and collect me and take me back to Llangynwyd – probably for the last time in my life.

On Sunday 26 September 1937, Walter arrived at the Duke's Head. I was dressed and packed and waiting for him with the makeshift crutch the hospital gave me. Lucy cried and hugged me and even Pearl had a tear in her eye. She gave me a bag with £5 in it that the customers had collected between them to see me on my way – and I was deeply touched. People who could barely afford to feed their children had contributed to this gentle gift, while those who could afford the obscenity of indecent extravagance thought hard over giving their workers a shilling for Christmas.

Pearl provided a car to take us to Paddington station and Walter helped me to board the train for the journey home. We sat in silence for most of the way, except when he unpacked some food and a bottle of milk, and we ate and talked about the family and how my father's lungs were getting worse and my mother was tired from working and looked older than her years. But Gwyneth had already left school and Bronwyn would be leaving next year and they'd both be able to get jobs and help out with the family finances. And I resolved there and then to get the better of this injury. I would *not* be a cripple and a burden on my family for the rest of my life.

I would *not!*

Chapter Sixteen

My mother and sisters were so glad to see me and fussed about me and made me sit and put my foot up out of harm's way. But my father's broncho-pneumonia had turned into emphysema. His condition was worsening all the time and he could hardly breathe without coughing up blood and bile. The little house was like an infirmary, with me laid up and bandaged and my father choking and my mother tired from the hardship of her whole life.

The local doctor came round and re-bandaged my foot to stop it getting infected and, although my father got the free medical aid, it didn't cover me and I had to pay him 2s/6d each time. I gave my mother the five pounds the customers collected for me in the Duke's Head and I had a few shillings from my wages – though not much because I spent it as I earned it, dancing and dawdling round London with Lucy.

The autumn of 1937 was setting in and it was wild and wet and windy in South Wales. It was difficult for me to go anywhere with the crutch, in case I got the bandages damp or dirty with coal dust and had to have them changed again for another 2s/6d. After a few weeks, my mother started changing the bandages herself. She'd wash and dry one lot, then alternate them with the dressing that was already on my foot when that got dirty. I was in a lot of pain, but I didn't like to complain because everyone was doing their best, and I didn't want to be any more of a burden than I already was. My sisters rigged up a makeshift wheelchair for me with a wooden seat and the handle and wheels off an old pram, and they pushed me around in it when the weather was kind enough and Gwyneth wasn't working and Bronwyn wasn't at school. Gwyneth was coming up to sixteen and she was doing what I was doing at that age, working at whatever part-time job she could get to help ease the burden on my mother and brother – and Bronwyn was too young to be puffing and pushing a lump like me around on her own.

The snow came early to the village that year and then I couldn't get out at all. By late November I'd read every book I could lay my hands on twice over and it was still only two months since the accident. Then, one day, I was sitting looking out the top window at the people trudging past in the black and white street when this Wolseley car pulled up outside our house. I drew back quickly from the window when I saw Mrs Reynolds get out. I thought she must be angry because I'd left the Morgan family after she was good enough to get me the job. I kept peeping from my secluded position as she approached the door and knocked on it vigorously. My mother answered.

'Is this the Moyle residence?'

'It is.'

'Is Anwyn at home?'

'She is.'

I went and lay on the bed, then I heard footsteps on the stairs.

'Anwyn, you have a visitor.'

Mrs Reynolds was shown into the room by my mother, who asked her if she'd like some tea and some Prince-of-Wales cake.

'That would be very nice, thank you.'

Monica Reynolds sat on the bed beside me, with a stern look on her face. I was afraid she was going to scold me and I pulled the blankets as high as I could without covering my face.

'I'm not pleased with you, Anwyn Moyle.'

'Aren't you, Mrs Reynolds?'

'No, I'm not.'

'Why?'

'Because you didn't tell me about your accident. I had to find out by chance.'

'I'm sorry.'

Someone who frequented the hat shop in Maesteg had seen me being pushed around in the pram by my sisters and they were all having a good laugh about it and she overheard. She asked me what the doctor's diagnosis was. When I told her, she said I should get a second opinion. But I couldn't possibly afford anything like that.

'I know a good man. And don't worry about the cost, honey.'

'Oh no, I couldn't.'

'Don't start that again!'

'All right.'

My mother brought the tea and cake and Mrs Reynolds stayed for half an hour and we had a chat and a laugh and it was like being back with Miranda Bouchard again – when she was my friend.

Next day, a Doctor Mulhearn from the Welsh National School of Medicine arrived and removed the bandaging from my foot. There was a lot of tightness and pain and it hurt when he tried to move my toes up and down. He told me the tightness was caused by the restrictive bandaging – although it was necessary in the beginning to keep the Achilles tendon together and allow it to heal, it was now necessary to work the lower leg to flex the tendon and enable the entire foot structure to perform better. The pain was caused, so he said, by excess chemicals floating round in the sponge that was my foot tissue. He told me I must open up the tissue of the lower leg and that would help the tendon to heal quicker.

'And how should I do that, doctor?'

'Massage ... and lots of it.'

'The bandages...'

'The external wound has healed. Leave the bandages off and start moving the foot. This will prevent muscle atrophy and joint stiffness.'

I was worried about walking too much, in case I caused more damage to the injury than I was curing. He explained that the Achilles tendon bore a lot of weight with each step and I'd be in danger of re-tearing it by putting too much load on it too quickly. But it also needed strengthening and this could only be achieved by exercise.

'Use the crutch at first and don't overdo it.'

He showed me some motion and strengthening exercises.

'A little bit more every day. It's a matter of common sense, young lady. I'll come back and see you in a fortnight.'

'Doctor...'

'Yes?'

'Will I be able to walk without the crutch?'

'Eventually, I don't see why not.'

'But when?'

'That will be up to you.'

He left and, for the next two weeks, I massaged my foot and did the exercises and walked a little further every day, putting my foot to the floor but using the crutch to support some of the weight – a little more the next day – a little more the day after. Monica Reynolds came again and we had tea and cake again and I told her I was walking again – and she smiled. It was almost Christmas when Doctor Mulhearn came back and he was more than pleased with my progress. He said I was a plucky young lady and my lower leg and Achilles tendon were strong enough now for me to walk without the crutch. A little at first, just a few steps – then a little more and a little more. He'd come back in the new year to see how I was getting on. I was unsteady at first without the crutch and needed a shoulder to lean on. But gradually I got used to balancing again and could walk on my own.

But I had a bad limp.

Christmas came and it was the first one I'd spent with my family in four years. We had a small goose for dinner that Walter bought with his hard-earned wages, along with herb stuffing and mashed swede and roast potatoes from mother's patch. Afterwards, father sat in front of the fire and loosened his trouser buttons and slept. Mother drank a glass or two of nettle wine and my sisters cleared away and washed up. Walter smoked a cigarette in the homely afternoon with the snow descending outside the smiling windows of our little house. I did my walking to and fro for a while, until I got tired, and then I sat with Walter and drank a glass of mother's green and winsome wine. The sky outside was unbroken and the snowflakes prevented any view of more than a few feet – and it was quiet on that Christmas afternoon. It was as if we were alone in the world, us Moyles, and everybody else had disappeared into the strange, bleak whiteness beyond our windows.

Father woke in time for tea and mother laid a hot bread pudding and a plate of homemade griddle scones on the table. Ghosts tapped silently on the dark windowpanes, wanting to come in. But we didn't see or hear them in our secluded womb-world. Wild animals howled on the black and barren hills – we knew they were out there, but we paid no heed. The fire was warm and the tea was strong and the food was sweet and we sang a carol together.

Sleep my child and peace attend thee
All through the night.
Guardian angels God will send thee

All through the night.
Soft the drowsy hours are creeping
Hill and vale in slumber sleeping
I my loving vigil keeping
All through the night

And then we went to bed and I took a long look out the bedroom window at the smoke-coloured snow, half expecting to see the Mari Lwyd come trotting through the blizzard, followed by its band of rowdy revellers.

I got into bed and said a short prayer in the long and dream-laden darkness.

Day comes to end
The sun descends
Moon enters sky
And so do I.

And then I slept.

Doctor Mulhearn came back in the new year and said my foot had healed, but I'd always have the limp. Now that I was able-bodied again, I had to find work because I'd been wallowing in the hospitality of my family for long enough. But there was no work in the village, or anywhere else in Wales in the deep, depressing days of 1938. In desperation, I wrote to Miranda Bouchard at Chester Square and asked if she had anything in her household. Maybe she'd feel some sense of obligation for the fidelity and unconditional friendship I'd given her. I got a letter back from Mr Peacock saying there was nothing at Chester Square, but he enclosed a letter of recommendation for a kitchen maid's job in a house near Regent's Park, if I was interested. I was. He suggested I should write to a Mr Morecambe of the household, which I did, enclosing Mr Peacock's letter of recommendation. Within a week, I received a letter back, asking me to come down for interview, along with an open train ticket to Paddington.

War clouds were gathering in Europe in 1938 but, in the early part of that year, no one was panicking yet and life in London seemed to be going on as usual. I arrived in Paddington like I had before and made my way to Devonshire Place, close to Regent's Park. I was used to London now and was easily able to negotiate my way around. It was a large, five-storey house, four main storeys and an attic. The exterior of the ground floor was white, with an arched door and two large arched windows to the right as I looked at it from the street. Each of the floors above had three windows, surrounded by pale beige brickwork. There were steps down to a basement and, again, I didn't know whether I should knock on the front door or try to conceal my limp as I climbed down the steps. I decided to go to the front door. A man whom I assumed to be Mr

Morecambe answered and introduced himself as the major-domo, whatever that meant. Unlike most butlers I'd come across, he was a jolly sort and not snooty at all. He wasn't dressed formally in livery, but had on a shirt and breeches, with the sleeves of the shirt rolled up. He had a mop of uncombed fair hair and a rather large chin that made him look a bit like Tommy Trinder. He could have been a gardener, not a butler, as he held the door open for me to walk through. I tried in vain not to limp as I followed him down the hall.

We went into a small anteroom and he asked me to sit down.

'Welcome to Devonshire Place, Anwyn. May I call you Anwyn?'

'Most butlers call me Moyle.'

He smiled.

'You'll find we're a little different here. And I'm not a butler, I'm a major-domo.'

I felt at ease in the house. It seemed a comfortable place, unpretentious, confident in its homeliness and not feeling the need to assume airs and graces. He told me the owners were a Mr Fletcher and a Mr Jennings. There were no ladies and no children, but the Misters Fletcher and Jennings frequently entertained.

'You understand the nature of the job, don't you, Anwyn?'

'Kitchen maid, Sir.'

'Well … kitchen maid-cum-waitress-cum-parlourmaid-cum-a-kind-of *Jill de tous les métiers,* if you will.'

He sounded quite pleased with his French, although I'd never heard of such a thing, but I needed the job. And it must have been all right if Mr Peacock had offered a letter of recommendation. In any case, I was here now and I wasn't traipsing all the way back to Wales empty-handed.

'It's ten shillings a week, with Sundays off. And I think you'll find we are fairly flexible in this house, Anwyn.'

'I'll take it.'

'You will?'

'Yes, Sir.'

'Capital!'

Mr Morecambe showed me to my room, which I thought strange, as it was normally a footman or a maid who did this. He huffed and puffed as he climbed the stairs to the attic and had to lean against the wall to get his breath back. The room was bigger than I was used to, with only one bed, so I knew I wouldn't be sharing. There was a small table and chair, a sofa, a wardrobe and a dressing table with a mirror, and a washbasin with hot and cold running water. There was linoleum on the floor and patterned curtains on the window that looked out over Devonshire Place.

'There's a bathroom on the floor below,

and you are free to use it, Anwyn.'

'Thank you, Sir.'

'Call me Aldous.'

'Oh no, Sir ... I couldn't.'

'As you wish.'

He told me the Misters Fletcher and Jennings used the private bathroom on the ground floor, so I wouldn't be disturbed – apart from when they had house guests, then all the bathrooms on all the floors were on a first come, first served basis.

'But you, being a young lady, should have nothing to fear.'

I didn't know what he meant by that, but I didn't ask. Mr Morecambe was a queer sort of cove, I thought. But it took all sorts to make a world and I wasn't a one for casting cynical aspersions.

On the way back down to the kitchen, he noticed my limp for the first time.

'Your foot...?

'An accident.'

'I see.'

And that's all he said. Never passed another remark on it. And neither did I. When we got to the kitchen, I nearly fainted. I was used to kitchens being spick and span, with everything in its place and a place for everything. This kitchen was a complete mess. Skillets and strainers and cutlery and colanders and porringers and jorums and ramekins were strewn about everywhere. There were potato peelings on the floor that could've been there for a year by the look of them. The range was stained with gravy and grease and the sink was piled with unwashed pots and plates. There were bits of bread and vegetables and fruit and meat and fish-heads and other things I couldn't identify that were starting to rot, and the smell reminded me of the toilets in the Duke's Head after a rough night on the rum. Mr Morecambe shook his head disapprovingly.

'You can see why we need a woman's touch round here.'

'Where's Cook?'

'Cook?'

'Yes, Cook.'

He laughed. Then he stopped laughing and looked at me. Then he laughed again. When he finally stopped chuckling and wiped his eyes with a white handkerchief, he spoke again.

'Didn't Mr Peacock tell you?'

'Tell me what?'

'The Misters Fletcher and Jennings do all their own catering, my dear.'

I was amazed. I'd never heard of any such thing. Gentlemen doing their own cooking? It couldn't be right; he must be having a laugh at my expense.

'But they're not very good at cleaning up, as you can see.'

He realised I was bemused and confused,

so he explained that the Misters Fletcher and Jennings owned the L'Astrance gourmet restaurant on Shaftesbury Avenue. They were both award-winning Cordon Bleu chefs and always ate out, except when they threw parties, and that was quite frequently. Otherwise they spent most of their time at the Buck's Club, where they were members, or at Claridge's, where they had investments, or at the Marquis of Granby public house, where they had many 'friends'.

'What about the other servants?'

'There are no other servants, Anwyn.'

He began to walk away, leaving me standing in the midst of the carnage.

'What should I do now, Sir?'

He turned and looked at me with an expression of puzzlement.

'Whatever you think needs doing, my dear.'

With that, he was gone, and I was left to my own completely disorientated devices. For the next few days I cleaned and cleaned and cleaned, until my hands and knees were raw and my foot was swollen and aching like a ground-level gumboil. I cooked for myself and Mr Morecambe and never saw another soul or caught sight of the Misters Fletcher or Jennings. Mr Morecambe was delighted with my progress in the kitchen and commented that he'd never seen it sparkling so magnificently. They'd had other kitchen-cum-scullery-cum-parlourmaids before me – a parade of *Jills de tous les métiers* – but none stayed for more than a month. And I wondered why.

I was a week and a half into the job and life was gradually getting easier at Devonshire Place. Mister Morecambe wasn't a demanding major-domo and I'd cleaned up most of the mess both downstairs and upstairs. It was a Saturday morning when the pseudo-butler came down and had a cup of tea and some toasted crumpets with me. He was dressed more formally than usual and I knew something was different. He drank the tea and ate the crumpets and small-talked for about ten minutes. Then he stood up and walked towards the door, but turned before leaving.

'Oh, by the way, Anwyn, the Misters are back today and will be hosting a dinner party for ten tonight.'

He hummed his way through the door and was gone before I could tell him I wasn't prepared for a dinner party.

I didn't know what to do. There was food in the house, but certainly not enough for any kind of entertaining. I didn't know what should be on the menu or who was going to help prepare it, and I was just about to follow Mr Morecambe upstairs to find out when the basement doorbell rang. It was a delivery man in the charcoal-grey livery of

Claridge's. He began to bring in boxes of food from a flat-nose van parked up on the street. Canapés and salad stuffs came first, then salmon and chicken and lamb and duck, followed by an assortment of fruit and vegetables and puddings and pastries and cheeses. I stored everything as best I could and placed the perishables carefully in the refrigerator. Then I made sure the big range was fully operational. Mr Morecambe was busy lighting fires in all the rooms upstairs and I was peeling the potatoes when the Misters arrived. I could hear them upstairs, conversing loudly and extravagantly with Mr Morecambe.

Then they came down to the kitchen. They were both men in their late thirties, of slight build and ostentatiously dressed in suits the like of which I'd never seen before, but came to know some years later as zoot suits – with tramos trousers and carlango coats and wide lapels and padded shoulders. They wore silk shirts and pointy-toed French shoes and wide-brimmed felt hats and they both sported twirly moustaches and smiled at each other extravagantly. Fletcher spoke to me.

'Ah, you must be Annette.'

'Anwyn, Sir.'

'I'm Donald and he's Peter.'

They took off their coats and hats and donned a couple of aprons from the cupboard.

'Right, Annette, let's get to it.'

For the next five hours, the Misters whizzed round the kitchen like a couple of dervishes, poaching salmon and lyonaissing chicken and glazing duck and boiling vegetables and wilting cress and painting éclairs. I was trying to keep up with washing and replacing the utensils like I'd been taught, and clearing away and peeling and chopping, and my foot was on fire from running about. Then it was all done. They took off their aprons and threw them on the floor.

'Well done, Annette.'

The guests started arriving at 7:00 p.m. and Mr Morecambe came down with a parlourmaid's outfit for me to wear. He himself was still dressed formally and it was now our job to serve at table. We had to carry all the food for each course up first and plate it in an annexe to the main dining room. Then we served it to the Misters and their ten guests. It was a five-course meal and I noticed the guests were all men – not a single woman in sight. Except me. Fletcher and Jennings sat either end of a long table, with five guests on each side. It was while serving up the first course of canapés á l'Amiral and cream of barley soup that I noticed Mr Peacock. He noticed me too and nodded. The main course was poached salmon with mousseline sauce, along with chicken lyonnaise and Calvados-glazed roast ducking in applesauce, served with château potatoes and minted green pea timbales and creamed carrots.

The third course was punch romaine, with asparagus salad and saffron vinaigrette and pâté de foie gras. Then came chocolate-painted eclairs with peaches in chartreuse jelly and French ice cream. All finished off with a fifth course of assorted fruits and cheeses, accompanied by coffee and liqueur.

All through dinner, Mr Morecambe kept up with the demand for a variety of drinks, including aperitifs and wines and ports and brandies, leaning against the wall every now and then to catch his breath. When it was all over, the men retired to the smoking room for cigars and Mr Morecambe brought in decanters of drinks. The doors were then closed and I was not allowed to enter.

Mr Morecambe helped me clear away and then I returned to the kitchen, which looked now as bad, if not worse, than it did when I first arrived. Mr Morecambe said I should leave the washing-up until morning, but I couldn't countenance such a thing. After he left to go back upstairs, I got stuck in and was finished after a couple of hours. It was approaching midnight and I was completely exhausted. I trudged upstairs and went to use the bathroom on the fourth floor as usual, before going to bed. The door wasn't locked so I walked in and, to my shock and horror, there was one of the gentlemen I'd served at dinner. He was combing his hair in the mirror and was completely naked from head to toe. I ran back out of the bathroom and was trying to catch my startled breath and compose myself when he walked out past me, still naked, and never batted a brazen eyelid.

'Goodnight.'

With that, he walked away down the corridor, the cheeks of his bum swivelling like an oversized peach in a hammock.

I didn't go back into the bathroom, in case there were more like him in there, but ran to my room and bolted the door. All through that night there were sounds of laughter and music and banging and bustling and it was like someone had let in a load of prankster schoolboys. There were footsteps up and down the stairs and calling and clapping and other strange noises that I couldn't put a name to. I eventually fell asleep and it was all quiet when I woke on the Sunday morning at 6:00 a.m.

I went downstairs and got the range going and made myself some tea. I had a leftover breakfast from the night before and it was only then I realised how hungry I was. I'd been so busy I hadn't had anything to eat since the previous morning. I thought I'd better prepare something for the gentlemen who'd stopped over in the guest rooms, although nobody told me to. I put on a traditional English breakfast of bacon and sausage and black pudding and fried bread in dripping. Then I scrambled some eggs and fried some mushrooms and I was about to peel the tomatoes when Mr Morecambe appeared. He poured himself a cup of tea and helped himself to a sausage.

'Well done for last night, Anwyn.'

'Thank you, Sir.'

He looked like he wanted to say something else, but was unsure how to phrase the words.

'Any ... problems during the night?'

'Problems, Sir?'

'Any ... interruptions?'

'I'm sure I don't know what you mean. I was asleep before my head even hit the pillow.'

'Good! I mean good ... I'm glad you had a peaceful night.'

He helped me bring the breakfast food up to the dining room and put it on covered chafing dishes, along with percolated coffee and pots of tea in cosies to keep them warm.

The gentlemen guests came down to eat at irregular times and I noticed several others who hadn't been there at dinner – younger men with white teeth and lovely skin. Then they all drifted off into the drizzling day. I asked Mr Morecambe what to do about lunch and he said not to bother. The Misters came down to the kitchen at about 4:00 p.m., long after I'd cleared away and washed the breakfast things. They were wearing matching blue blazers with white baggy trousers and two-tone shoes and straw boaters – and I wondered if they always wore the same clothes. Like twins.

'Ah, Annette, thank you for breakfast. It was sublime.'

'So ... traditional.'

'You're very welcome, Sirs.'

'How did you find it last night?'

'Fine, Sir.'

'Not too much for you?'

'No, Sir.'

I lied. My foot was still hurting and I was trying not to limp even more than normal. They gave me half-a-crown and a pat on the shoulder and then they were gone – back to their restaurant or their club or their hotel or the fraternity of their friends.

Chapter Seventeen

On one of my Sundays off I decided to pay a visit to the Duke's Head to see all my old friends – Lucy and Pearl and all the customers who were so good to me when I had the accident. It was just after opening time when I got down to London Bridge and I tried not to look like I was limping when I walked into the pub. Nothing much had changed; it was still the same spit-and-saw-dust pothouse, full of hardy-looking dock labourers, only this time they all recognised me.

'Anwyn? Hey, lads, look ... it's Anwyn!'

Well, I was hoisted up on their shoulders and carried round the bar and I was afraid of my life lest they'd let me drop on my spinning head.

'Put her down this minute!'

Pearl's warning voice came loud and clear from behind the counter.

'Put her down, you bunch of blockheads!'

Her scowl was enough to subdue the boldest of them and they gently placed me feet first back on the floor.

Pearl came out from behind the bar and clasped me in a bone-bending hug.

'It is you, Anwyn. They said you wouldn't walk again.'

'They were wrong, Pearl.'

'I can see that.'

She had a couple of girls on with her that lunchtime, so we went and sat at a table and she brought over a bottle of sweet sherry. I told her all about what happened in Wales and how I got my foot healed and how I'd always walk with a limp from now on.

'I'm sorry about that, Anwyn.'

'Better than not being able to walk at all.'

'What are you doing in London?'

'I'm working in Devonshire Place.'

'Oh, very la-de-da, I'm sure.'

'I'm just a kitchen maid.'

Pearl laughed when I told her about the Misters Fletcher and Jennings and the strange dinner parties and the naked man. She laughed and laughed and I thought she was going to burst a blood vessel.

'Oh, Anwyn, you're a bit green, ain't you?'

I didn't think I was green at all. I'd read more than she ever would and I'd been a lady's maid and seen the hunts and the balls and been the object of several men's desires. Pearl poured two more glasses of sherry, still trying to suppress her urge to continue laughing.

'It's a ginger house.'

'A what?'

'Ginger beer.'

I still didn't understand and Pearl was on the verge of exploding from trying to keep in the chuckles and chortles.

By now, some of the men round the bar had overheard our conversation and they were all laughing too and passing silly remarks.

'Plenty of fruits in your kitchen, Anwyn?'

'Does the tooth fairy leave anything under your pillow?'

I felt they were laughing at me and I grew quite indignant. I stood up sharply.

'Anyway, I just came here to see Lucy. I forgot she doesn't do the afternoon shift.'

All the laughter stopped abruptly. The men turned their faces away and Pearl touched my arm.

'Sit back down, Anwyn.'

I did, and she poured more sherry. She reached across the table and took my hand and I felt an icy chill on the back of my bare neck.

'Anywyn ... Lucy's dead.'

The glass fell from my hand and the sherry spilled across the table like blood. My mouth opened to gasp out the air that was choking me. No! This couldn't be true! No words would come for a long time. Then, finally–

'When? How?'

'Tuberculosis. She died during the winter.'

I could taste the salt in my mouth long before I realised I was crying. Tears streamed down my face and I felt like I was going to faint. I stood up again and rushed out into the thick Tooley Street air. Pearl followed to make sure I was all right, but she stood back, giving me space to grieve. A loud bawling sound broke from my heart and people passing by stared and some came across, but were turned back by Pearl. I leaned against the wall for support. Lucy – dead? No! I couldn't believe it.

I had to see for myself. I had to get over to her family. I wouldn't wait for a bus or tram or for Pearl to call me a cab so I stumbled as fast as I could along the length of Tooley Street and into Jamaica Road. I was almost in a state of collapse by the time Lucy's mother opened the door to find me on the step. As soon as she saw my tear-stained face, she started crying too – and I knew it was true. We hugged each other tightly for comfort and Lucy's sisters came out and soon all five of us were crying in the doorway. The father came and brought us all in and made a pot of strong tea and we sat round the table and sobbed. They told me Lucy got TB shortly after my accident, but she didn't tell anyone until she was coughing up blood and it was too late.

'She didn't want to lose her job.'

Once the disease was diagnosed, they moved her straight to a sanatorium in case she infected the rest of the family.

'They put her bed outside in the snow...'

'For hours...'

'And strapped a sandbag to her chest...'

'And collapsed one of her lungs...'

But she still died. She wasn't strong enough to fight the disease – or endure the treatment.

Lucy died in February 1938, just a few weeks before I came back to London. She was buried in Bow Cemetery and I went along there with one of her sisters that afternoon. I bought a bunch of flowers from a street vendor on the way. The cemetery was like a little piece of the country that had been taken up and dropped right into one of the dirtiest parts of the city. There were trees and flowers and early spring birds and bats and beetles. People strolled through it like it was a park and children played and I knew the sound of their little voices would make Lucy happy here. We placed the flowers on her grave and I knelt and said a simple prayer.

May she walk on the earth again
Again beneath the same blue sky
And may our lives again entwine
When we remember, you and I.

Then we left and I kissed her sister and said I'd come back down every chance I got.

Mr Morecambe was nowhere to be seen when I got back to the house in Devonshire Place – which was just as well, because I didn't want to talk to anyone. I went to the bathroom on the fourth floor and washed the dried-in tears from my face. Then I went to bed and cried again and it was a long time before the salve of sleep came stealing.

The politicians were telling everyone that war was going to be avoided and there were a lot of opinions flying about regarding Germany and what Adolf Hitler was going to do next, but I barely took any notice, because all my time was taken up being a skivvy and a cook and a parlourmaid and a cleaner and a

Jill de tous les métiers for Mr Morecambe and Fletcher and Jennings. The shenanigans at the house grew louder and more boisterous as time went on and the dinner parties grew more frequent, despite the darkening war clouds. And I wondered if these people really didn't know what was going on in the world around them, or if they chose to ignore it simply because to accept the reality of it would have been too horrendous to contemplate. I was kept busy morning, noon and night and I kept my bedroom door safely locked tight when the naked and the naughty were roaming round.

I found out from visits to the Duke's Head that the area known as Fitzrovia round Marylebone was very bohemian and the pubs and clubs were often frequented by actors and artists and soldiers and sailors and kilted musicians and queer men and women. Now, when they said queer men and women, I thought they meant those people were a bit eccentric, just like the Misters Fletcher and Jennings, and I could understand why the two of them lived and socialised in that area.

But Pearl explained to me that there were certain types of men who rouged their lips and pencilled their eyebrows and scented their clothes and spoke with high-pitched voices. She showed me a report in the newspaper about 'painted and perfumed travesties of men, who lounged around Fitzrovia, leering at passers-by' – although I'd never come across anyone like that. The Misters dressed extravagantly, it had to be said, but certainly not to that degree. Pearl said these men attended private dances called 'drags'. They went as 'kings' and 'queens' and the kings wore lounge suits and the queens wore evening dresses. I couldn't imagine what a man might look like in an evening dress – it made me laugh to myself. But I'd always been a one to live and let live and I minded my own business and got on with my work. As long as they didn't interfere with me, it was their own business what they got up to.

One day in July 1938, Mr Morecambe came to me and said there would be a fancy dress party on the Saturday evening. As usual, Fletcher and Jennings zoomed round the kitchen and prepared everything and then left me to clean up the awful mess they'd made. At 7:00 p.m., I expected to have to dress in my parlourmaid's uniform and help Mr Morecambe to serve.

'It's a buffet tonight, Anwyn, so you won't be needed.'

He told me I could take the rest of the night off if I liked. But I was too tired and it was too late to go out anywhere, so I just went to my room. Music was coming up from downstairs and a tumult of loud laughter and, later on, squeals and shouts and other strange sounds. I couldn't sleep for the din of it all, so I decided to take a look. I crept downstairs in my chemise and peeped in through the half-open door of the main dining room.

'Oh, my good God!'

There were men dressed in lounge suits and others in evening dresses. I knew they were men and not women because they were big and brawny and some of them had moustaches. It was a drag dance, just like Pearl had told me about. There was a group of musicians in one corner playing jazz, and everyone was dancing and cavorting around like lunatics. Mr Morecambe was in the middle of it, serving drinks as fast as his feet could shuffle. Then the lights went out and there was a terrible commotion of screeching and whistling and howling like a pack of wolves and caterwauling like cats. When the lights came back on again, half the clothes were on the floor and the naked stuff was starting. Time for me to get back to my bedroom and lock the door! Tight. But before I could, the front door came crashing in and about twenty policemen swarmed into the house. I didn't know if they were real coppers or more guests in fancy dress – until they grabbed me and handcuffed me.

'This one actually is a woman, Sarge.'

I was hauled into the dining room, which had become more chaotic than it was a few minutes ago. Policemen were running round the room trying to catch the guests, who were jumping over chairs and tables and trying to get to the door, blowing kisses back at their pursuers as they went. The Misters Fletcher and Jennings, dressed as a king and queen, tried to reason with the police, saying it was a private party and they were way outside their jurisdiction. But the sergeant wasn't listening, even when he was threatened with being reported to the Home Secretary. The guests were eventually rounded up and continued to, what I can only describe as, spoon over the policemen.

'What's the matter, dear?'

'Don't call me dear!'

'Are you a real policeman?'

'Of course.'

'You look far too nice.'

Mr Morecambe was being questioned by the sergeant, while the gaudily dressed guests were led out, still flirting with the constables, and shoved into a police van.

'Why are these men dressed as women?'

'They're queens tonight. They take it in turns.'

'Take what in turns?'

'To be kings or queens.'

It all seemed very natural to Mr Morecambe and he assured the sergeant that he was merely a servant and not a participant in the impious party. The police believed him, but not me. I was taken to Harrow Road police station.

'Are you a lesbian?'

'A what?'

'You know, a woman who likes other women.'

'I like some other women.'

Apparently, it wasn't illegal to be a lesbian, so they had to let me go and they told me I'd have to make my own way back to Devonshire Place. I said I had no money because they'd arrested me in my nightshift, but that made no difference to them. Luckily, Mr Morecambe was in the reception room when I came out. He drove me home.

I wanted to ask him about the drag dance but I decided not to say anything. He said nothing either until we got back to the house. He let me in and told me he had to go back to the police station because he'd left a solicitor there who would sort out the misunderstanding and the Misters Fletcher and Jennings would want to be taken somewhere to settle their nerves. I was glad it was all a misunderstanding, as I didn't like the thought of them having to spend the night in a police cell.

Mr Morecambe said I should go to bed and leave everything until the morning. But I wouldn't have been able to sleep, knowing that the dining hall was in such a state, so I cleared it all up and it took me two hours. It was 3:00 a.m. when I finally got to bed. I locked the door in case there was a naked man still lurking – one the police had failed to find. Mr Morecambe didn't come back that night. I was up and in the kitchen when I heard him coming in at about 9:00 a.m.

News of the raid on Devonshire Place got round, even though it was never in the newspapers and no charges were ever brought against anyone. But some policeman must have leaked the story because everyone in the Duke's Head knew about it the next time I went down there and they all had a hearty laugh at my expense. Shortly after, the house was put up for sale. Mr Morecambe said he was very sorry, but he wouldn't be needing my services any more. He gave me a very good letter of reference and a month's wages and said I could stay on in the house until I found somewhere else to live or it was sold – whichever came first. He himself would be around because he had some matters to see to, but the Misters wouldn't be back. I never saw them again.

I asked Pearl for my old job as a barmaid-cum-cook back, but she said she couldn't just sack one of her girls to make a place for me. That wouldn't be fair. However, she knew they were looking for someone at the White Lion on Commercial Road in Aldgate. She gave me a letter to show them and told me to ask for Albert.

The White Lion was even rougher and more working-class than the Duke's Head.

The clientele seemed to be a mixture of Spitalfields market men, part-time labourers, street-sellers, loafers, criminals and characters who looked like they'd just stepped out of a Charles Dickens novel. It was Monday lunchtime when I got over there and the bar was full of men drinking strong ale out of pewter tankards. At least if a fight started here, there'd be no broken glass. As usual, the conversation stopped and all heads turned towards the door as I entered. Unlike the Duke's Head, there was a big burly man behind the bar.

'Is Albert here?'

'Who's asking?'

'Pearl sent me.'

'Pearl who?'

'From the Duke's Head.'

I limped towards the bar and handed him the letter. He pretended to read it, but I could see he was holding it upside down. Then he shouted.

'Boss!'

A grumpy-looking man wearing a gaudy waistcoat came up from the cellar with a dripping wet cloth slung over his shoulder.

'What?'

The burly man handed him the letter and pointed at me. The boss read Pearl's note.

'Annywinny?'

'Anywyn.'

He tried to say my name, but he couldn't

get his tongue round it.

'I'll call you Annie.'

He took the wet cloth off his shoulder and threw it to me, then beckoned for me to follow him through the bar and down some steps into the cellar. I could see he noticed my limp.

'What happened?'

'An accident.'

'Long as it don't hamper your work.'

'It won't.'

Albert was a gruff man with a heart of gold. He looked like a criminal of some kind, with long sideburns down his face and a wide wool cap perched on the side of his head. There was devilment in his eyes and his nose had been flattened more than once in fist fights. The floor of the cellar was covered in beer and Albert had been trying to clean it all up. He explained that one of the barrels had sprung a leak and the girl who would normally have been doing this had walked out last week.

'Why did she walk out?'

'Caught her with her hand in the till.'

'Didn't you call the police?'

'Nah ... I'd have been doing the same if I was her.'

He said she was a poor girl from a big family and what was the point of putting her in jail? It wouldn't get him his money back. But he couldn't have her working there after that, so he had to give her her marching orders. I helped him to clean up the spillage and he asked me what I did at the Duke's Head.

'Cook, barmaid.'

'Cook?'

I explained to him about Pearl doing the food and how it had caught on and brought in the passing trade. He was interested. 'You think that might catch on here?'

'It might.'

'What kind of food?'

I told him it was just basic, traditional stuff at the Duke's Head – pig's feet and pie 'n' mash and bacon 'n' cabbage and sandwiches and stuff. He said he'd look into it. Otherwise, the job at the White Lion was similar. But there was no cleaning woman coming in, so I'd have to take care of the toilets and clean the floors and sprinkle the sawdust, as well as washing the tankards and serving behind the bar. The pay was a pound a week to start with, rising to twenty-five shillings if I was seen to be suitable – which was more than I'd ever earned in my life, and I had alternate Saturdays and Sundays off. There was a room upstairs for me to live-in and Albert didn't want any rent for it.

'When can you start?'

I threw the wet cloth back at him.

'Looks like I already have.'

He grinned at me and I knew we'd get along.

Chapter Eighteen

The White Lion was an old pub with an infamous history of crime and conspiracy and murderous carnage. Albert didn't mind much about my limp, because it didn't interfere with my work and he said it gave the pub a bit of atmosphere, whatever that meant. I think he told people I was the Strange Limping Lady from Tom Norman's Circus or something like that. I don't know if they believed him or not. After they got to know me, the men who drank there were friendly, just like they were at the Duke's Head, and they were just as frisky after they'd had a few pints of Dutch courage.

The big burly man was called George and he ran the pub during the day, with me helping out behind the bar if I wasn't busy cleaning and clearing up. There were two other barmaids, May and Lizzie, who worked the evenings with me, and Albert was usually around then too. The room upstairs was fairly basic, but it was comfortable enough once I tidied it up and made it my own. There was a bathroom that I shared with Lizzie, who also lived above the bar, and I had use of a small kitchen for cooking whenever I wanted. But there were no paying guests like at the Duke's Head and there was a separate side door to the rooms upstairs. So privacy was an added perk of this job.

The area round Spitalfields had a long reputation for being the worst criminal rookery in London and the haunt of robbers and prostitutes back in the late nineteenth century. Flower and Dean Street was known as the most dangerous street in the city and nearby Dorset Street was the site of the brutal killing and mutilation of Mary Kelly by Jack the Ripper. Some of the worst wynds had been demolished by the time I got there, but it was still a dodgy place and homeless vagrants still slept in Itchy Park, in the shadow of Christ Church. Albert told me never to go wandering down the side alleys on my own at night, but I liked dancing on my evenings off, despite my limp, and I sometimes took shortcuts. Luckily enough, no nasty mishap ever befell me.

Probably next in notoriety to Jack the Ripper was Ikey Solomon, who plied his trade round Houndsditch and Petticoat Lane. He was said to have frequented the White Lion to do his dealings and Albert had several pictures of him hanging on the walls. Ikey was a receiver of stolen goods, otherwise known as a 'fence'. He dealt mainly in jewellery, but also in valentia cloth and lace and bobbinet and all sorts of other articles that he sold in a pawn shop in Bell Lane. He ran a whole tribe of boys who he trained to steal and pick pockets, and it was said he was the inspiration for Fagin in Dickens's *Oliver Twist*. He was once caught stealing from a large crowd at a meeting outside Westminster Hall and he got rid of the evidence by eating the banknotes.

He was eventually convicted and sentenced to penal transportation, but he escaped from the prison ship *Zetland*. He was recaptured and taken by hackney coach to Newgate Prison. But the coach was being driven by his father-in-law, who took a detour through Petticoat Lane, where Ikey's friends overpowered the guards, and he got away again. He fled to New York, but his wife and children were arrested and transported to Tasmania. When he found out about this, he followed his family out there and that was the end of his reign around this area of London. But some said his ghost stalked the streets around Houndsditch and Whitechapel, and Albert was sure he'd seen the man's silhouette sitting at a back table in the pub one moonlit night. It didn't bother me. I'd seen worse things than Ikey Solomon's ghost wandering around in the dead of night.

I had every alternate Saturday off, and Sunday the following week, and I went out dancing on those nights with either May or

Lizzie, or on my own if they were working. Most of the big dance halls were in the West End, but there was the Sackville Club in Fenchurch Street, which wasn't far away, and Quaglino's near The Tower and the Victoria Danse Salon in Holborn and the Moulin Rouge in Brixton. Local church halls also ran dances on a Saturday night and there was always somewhere to go. I liked to dance and my limp got a lot of funny looks when I was doing the Lindy Hop. The bigger venues had orchestras and the smaller ones usually had a three-piece combo and some just a piano. The floors in the West End were sprung or highly polished and the others were just plank or stuck-down sheets of linoleum. Most of the people could dance after a fashion, at least enough to get round the room without crippling their partner for life – if you'll pardon the pun. The music was a mixture of all sorts – traditional waltzes and quicksteps and jazz and swing, and it took people's minds off the drudgery of their working lives and the doomsday predictions of global warfare.

And so life went on. I stayed at the White Lion all through the rest of 1938 and into 1939. Then the war came, despite what the politicians had told us. The war started on 1 September 1939, with the German invasion of Poland. Britain and France declared war on Germany two days later. It didn't affect us all that much in the beginning. We thought the brave boys of the expeditionary force would go over there and mop it all up in a matter of months and we were more affected by the cold winter in January 1940, when the Thames froze over and everyone went out to skate on it. But the mop-up didn't happen. The Germans surrounded our troops, along with the French and Belgians, and in June 1940 they had to swim for the boats at Dunkirk to make it back. After that, the Luftwaffe tried to destroy our air defences so the Germans could invade. They attacked Portsmouth and the RAF airfields and aircraft factories, and the Battle of Britain started and was fought out during the summer of 1940. But Hitler failed to gain air superiority and chose not to invade. Instead, he decided to blitz London.

They'd been evacuating people from the south of England from late 1939 – then the London Blitz started in September 1940 and loads of cockney kids began to get sent away to the country. Everything had to be blacked out. The windows of the White Lion were painted black to stop the light from getting through during the hours of drinking, and the lamps were dimmed inside. We never knew if it was day or night and, during that winter, it was black as the hob of hell outside at night-time. The street lights were either switched off or dimmed by being taped up, so only a pin-point of illumination was visible. All vehicles and traffic lights had slotted shutters fitted which aimed the beams downwards, and the edges of the kerbs were painted white so people would know where they were. The bases of trees were also ringed with white paint and men were told to leave their shirt tails hanging out so they could be seen. Signposts and train station names were removed in case the Germans invaded, and loads of people got lost as a result. Deaths doubled on the blacked-out roads and thousands of people were killed from accidentally walking into trees and falling off the kerbs and getting run over.

East London was hardest hit during the Blitz, because the Germans wanted to destroy the factories and the docks – it went on for hour after hour, night after night, and we had to run to the air-raid shelters until the sirens went for the all-clear. I considered going back to Wales at this time, but there would be no work for me there and it felt like I'd be a rat deserting a sinking ship. No, if May and Lizzie and George and Albert had to put up with it – so would I. A lot of pubs in the Aldgate area were bombed during the Blitz and the White Lion was one of the few that escaped. We held events to raise money for the war effort and sometimes the cellar was used as a bomb shelter when we didn't have time to get to the Tube station. Pubs were seen as the beating hearts of their community, a place where people could meet and gain strength from comradeship in a very British way. As more and more pubs were destroyed, the busier we became, so the war did well for Albert and the breweries that didn't get blown up.

Albert had started selling hot food like I suggested by then. It didn't catch on at first, but now it was proving to be a wise investment for him, catering for police and soldiers and air-raid wardens working long shifts and for bachelors who'd rather pay for a meal than have to make it themselves. A lot of the East End cafes and pie 'n' mash shops were blown up during the Blitz, or their owners just shut up shop and left town till the bombing was over. Albert saw this as an opportunity and it was true what the old saying said – it's an ill wind that blows nobody any good. Meat and butter and sugar and tea were all rationed and the already basic fare we served became more and more like Mother Hubbard's menu. But there were always dodgy geezers coming in with stuff for sale, and Albert made good use of the black market in the area to get food the ordinary person wouldn't be able to lay hands on. But, even then, a lot of the essentials were hard to come by.

Aldgate East Tube station was the nearest and safest place to go when the bombs began to fall but, one Saturday night at the end of February 1941, I was out at a local dance when the air-raid sirens went off. The closest shelter was the basement of the London Fruit Exchange at Spitalfields Market – it was called Mickey's Shelter after Mickey Davies, who was a marshal there. The place was crowded, as it would be on a Saturday night, and we were packed in like sardines. I was standing and the man next to me was sitting on a packing case. He stood up and offered it to me and I accepted, as it was difficult for me to stand still in one place for a long time, with my foot. He was quite a good-looking man and his clothes were expensive and fashionable. He was short in stature, about my height maybe, and slight of build. He sported a thin Clark Gable moustache and his teeth were pearly-white when he smiled.

I was getting on for twenty-three and he looked a good eight or nine years older than me, but not really middle-aged, as some of the men in their late twenties looked then. He offered me a cigarette, but I told him I didn't smoke. Then he held out his hand for me to shake.

'Alan Lane.'

'Anwyn Moyle.'

'Welsh?'

'Yes.'

'*Sut wyt ti?*' ['How are you?']

It took me by surprise that he asked how I was in Welsh. So I answered him back in Welsh.

'*Yr wyf yn.*' ['I am well.']

He laughed, and his teeth shone in the shelter lamplight.

'I'm sorry, I only know that one phrase. It was taught to me by a colleague.'

'A Welsh colleague?'

'He was a Dylan Thomas enthusiast.'

We got talking about literature as the bombs fell on the burning city above us and I found him to be intelligent and charming and very good company in such a crisis. I hardly knew I'd been down there when the all-clear siren went and we were able to emerge into the smoke and flying sparks. He noticed my limp and offered me his arm for support.

'Where do you live?'

'Commercial Road. It's not far.'

'I'll walk with you.'

'Oh no, that's all right.'

'I insist.'

So he walked with me to The White Lion and, on the way, I told him I was cook/barmaid there and he said he'd pop in for a pint and a pie some night when there was no madness falling from the screaming skies. He doffed his hat and bowed slightly to me, like gentlemen did, and I rushed upstairs to my room and watched from the window as he disappeared round the corner into White-chapel.

The following Wednesday night myself and May were working and it was quietish by comparison to the weekends, with just a steady crowd in. Then the door opened and I saw Alan Lane standing there. He looked round first, then walked slowly towards the bar. I ran into the kitchen to fix my hair and put on some lipstick and, when I came back out, May had served him a whisky and water and they were chatting together and laughing. My eyes went green.

'Ah, Anwyn, *sut wyt ti?*'

'I'm very well, thank you.'

I elbowed May out of the way and she flounced off, pouting, to serve some of the other customers. We chatted when I wasn't busy and he told me he worked as a dealer, though he didn't say what in. He lived in a big house in Clerkenwell and I didn't see a wedding ring on his finger, so I assumed he was single. He asked me what I did on my nights off and I said I liked dancing. This seemed to surprise him and I knew he was thinking about my limp.

'You don't notice it so much when I'm on the dance floor.'

'What?'

'The limp.'

He laughed, and his face smiled, even if his eyes didn't.

May came over and tried to butt in, but my expression warned her away again.

'You ever been to the Palais de Danse in Hammersmith?'

'Yes, I used to go there with a friend.'

The mention of the Palais reminded me of the times with Lucy and I felt guilty as I hadn't been down to her grave for a while. I made a mental note to go there and see her family on my next Sunday off.

'Do you still go there with him?'

'Who?'

'Your friend.'

'Her ... it was a girlfriend. No, we don't go there any more.'

He had another whisky and water and lit a cigarette. He offered me one, which I declined.

'Why don't you let me take you? We can have dinner as well.'

'Really? I'd love that.'

'When's your next Saturday off?'

'Week after this one.'

'I'll pick you up here at six, then.'

I went to serve someone else and, when I came back, he was gone. May wanted to know who the handsome man of mystery was and I played it down and told her he was just someone I met in an air-raid shelter.

'Well. If you don't want him, Annie, I'll have him.'

I couldn't wait for my next Saturday night off. But I had a free Sunday before that, so I went over to Bermondsey to visit Lucy's family. The war was making things even harder for them than before, and I felt really sorry for the working-class people of London who seemed to bear the full brunt of everything, while the rich could swan off to their country estates or some other safe haven. If it wasn't poverty, it was disease, and if it wasn't disease, it was bombs and bullets. I went again with Lucy's sister down to her grave in Bow Cemetery and I laid some fresh flowers and said another little old ways prayer.

Emptiness engulfs me.
Loss languishes me
In grief, as my guide
To the essence of the shadow,
Recorded forever in the dream.

There was an air raid on the way back and I was a long way from any shelter. I saw a group of people run towards Tower Bridge when the sirens began to squeal and I followed them. They ran down onto the pebbles near the water's edge and took shelter underneath the bridge on the south side. I ran with them and we had to crouch down to get into the tight space underneath the bridge span. Next thing I knew the air was alive with noise and fire and bits of shrapnel were flying everywhere. We covered our heads with our arms, but it wouldn't have done any good if we'd got hit. I could hear the deadly drone of the planes overhead and the sound of the anti-aircraft guns trying to shoot them down. The acrid smell of burning was everywhere and the thick smoke nearly choked me. Some of the people under the bridge were crying and others were praying and I just hoped I lived long enough to see Alan Lane again. The raid only lasted about twenty minutes, but it seemed like a lifetime to me. We stayed under the bridge until the sirens sounded the all-clear.

Then we came out to the aftermath.

I made my way back up off the bank of the Thames onto the walkway and across Tower Bridge. The view from the parapet, looking east, was like a view of the end of the world. Fire and smoke spread throughout the East End and buildings crumbled and minor secondary explosions rang out. I stumbled along past the Tower and East Smithfield and the Royal Mint and into Mansell Street. Fire engines were spraying water everywhere and soldiers and air-raid wardens were trying to cover the dead bodies with black sheets and tarpaulins. Ambulances and military medics were ferrying the wounded to hospitals and the whole place was dark and hell-like, apart from the searchlight beams piercing the sky like giant lighthouse lanterns. It took me over an hour to pick my way the mile and a half home and I had to have a brandy off Albert to steady my nerves when I got in.

The White Lion continued miraculously to escape the bombs and life went on behind the bar and in the kitchen. But I had more than the London Blitz on my mind. I was looking forward to dinner and dancing with Alan Lane.

He came for me in a black Morris Oxford car at 6:00 p.m. precisely on the Saturday evening. He drove us to the Black Gardenia restaurant near Tottenham Court Road and we had a three-course dinner of carrot soup with brown bread, followed by roast chicken with parsnips and potatoes and then home-made chocolate cake for pudding. It was lovely. I don't think I ever tasted anything so nice in my life. We went on from there to the Palais and we danced the evening away to the music of the Lou Preager Orchestra. Alan was a good dancer and he made allowances for my limp. We had a wonderful time. He was very knowledgeable and talked about many things and I felt so scintillating and sophisticated in his company. We left before midnight and I thought he was going to drive me home. Instead, he took me to a place called Crockfords in Curzon Street, Mayfair. The man on the door obviously knew Alan because we were ushered inside with a well-practised smile while others were being turned away.

I don't know what I was expecting, but it was a private gambling club for members only and there were green baize tables with people playing cards and roulette and dice and all sorts of other betting paraphernalia. A waiter came and gave us two cocktails off a tray and didn't ask for any payment. The drink tasted wonderful, like nothing I'd ever drunk before. I thought this Alan Lane must be very well-to-do to be getting us treated like this. He took me through the club and asked me to sit on a chair in a corner for a few minutes till he 'did some business'. Everyone was staring at me, as if I had two heads, and I thought it must be something to do with my limp. Alan joined a table where six men were playing poker. I knew it was poker because I'd seen them playing it in the Duke's Head for pennies. But there was no money on this table, just coloured counters. There were other women in the club besides me – two kinds of women. Ones that came in with a man, like I did, and others scantily dressed, who hung round the tables watching the winners.

Alan didn't come back after a few minutes, but the cocktails kept coming and I felt a bit tipsy after an hour or so. I was never a big drinker and I wasn't used to this kind of liquor either. The waiter came over again with another glass.

'What do you call this drink?'

'A manhattan, Madam.'

'What's in it?'

'Whisky, sweet vermouth and a maraschino cherry!

'How very erotic.'

'Don't you mean exotic, Madam?'

'That too.'

We left the club at about 3:00 a.m. and I didn't know my own name. Alan poured me into the back of the car and I didn't remember much more, apart from him being very happy and lively and whistling on the way. He saw me to the side door of the White Lion, then got me up the stairs and into bed fully clothed, although he did take my shoes off. He kissed me on the forehead before leaving and I fell into a room-swirling sleep.

Next morning, there was a hammer in my head, beating an anvil. I threw up in the toilet and swore I'd never drink manhattans again – or any other alcoholic beverage for that matter. I didn't remember saying goodnight to Alan Lane or whether I'd made a spectacle of myself in the club or not. And I wondered if I'd ever see him again.

Chapter Nineteen

I needn't have worried. He was back in the pub the following Wednesday, with his pearly teeth and Clark Gable moustache, drinking his whisky and water and buying a round for the whole bar – which made him very popular. Lizzie was on with me that night and, just like May, hanging on his every well-considered word. We were quite busy due to the lack of other pubs in the area – most of which had been bombed or had run out of drink. But Albert and his black market connections made sure we were able to keep going. I didn't get to talk much to Alan that night because I had to keep serving the customers, but before he left he slipped me a note.

Dearest Anwyn,
I hope I didn't offend you by leaving you so long on your own last Saturday. Please allow me to make it up to you. I know you get every second Saturday off, so next week I'll come pick you up at the same time.
Yours adoringly,
Alan

What could I say? My heart skipped a beat – *yours adoringly*. Now, I was no pushover for the passionate phrase. I'd heard it all before, from William Harding and Henry Rivers and Brynn the bicycle boy and others as well. But there was something about Alan Lane – he seemed to have that aura of hazard about him that some men have; men a woman knows she should stay away from, but is drawn to like a moth to a flame. It was an ideal – an image, a fiction – something I expected him to be from the books I'd read, but which didn't actually exist. I showed the letter to the other girls and they were green with envy.

The days passed greyly until my next Saturday off, then he was there, just as before with his Morris Oxford, at 6:00 p.m. precisely. This time we went to a secluded little brasserie in Soho for a fish supper and he was very quiet to begin with, not saying much at all. When we'd eaten, he ordered a bottle of champagne. It wasn't real champagne because that would have been impossible to get, even for him. But it was the gesture that impressed me and I wondered why a handsome, sophisticated man-of-the-world like Alan Lane would want to spend so much time with a Welsh village woman like me and tell me he was mine *adoringly*.

He leaned across the table.

'This will probably seem impetuous, An-wyn...'

'What will?'

He took a little box from his pocket and opened it. Inside was what looked like a diamond ring. My hands went to my mouth.

'Would you consider marrying me?'

I didn't know how to answer. My jaw dropped down to my chest and my mouth stayed open to catch the startled flies. A moment or two passed before I realised he was waiting for an answer.

'Marry you?'

'I know this is sudden, but let me ex-plain...'

He told me he was going to be called up for military service soon and he might be killed on active duty in North Africa. So he wanted to marry me now, because later might never come.

'I ... I don't know what to say.'

'Will you at least think about it?'

'Yes ... yes, I will.'

'Very well, we can consider ourselves en-gaged.'

And he slipped the ring onto my finger.

It was a whirlwind engagement. Alan Lane swept me off my feet and showed me all the sights of wartime London. We went to places off the beaten track that few ordinary people would know about and he seemed to be able to get anything he wanted, despite shortages and rationing. We set a date for the end of April to get married, as he was expecting to be called up in May. I was busy working in the White Lion and he said his mother and sister would take care of all the arrangements, but I'd have to give up the bar job when we tied the knot, because no wife of his would need to work. I didn't object, I'd been at the White Lion for nearly three years and that was the longest I'd ever spent in a job. It was time to pack in the slogging for a living and give married life a go.

When he said his family would make all the arrangements, I believed it would be a big wedding, with the church swollen with guests and all the trimmings. I dreamed of walking down the aisle to the sound of Mendelssohn and an entourage of little bridesmaids throwing flowers behind me – a choir singing somewhere in the chancel and the people dressed like they were at the May Ball I went to with Miranda Bouchard. But it turned out to be a small ceremony in a register office in Waltham Forest. None of my family could afford to come down from Wales, so Albert and Pearl came on my side and Alan's mother and sister were there for him. That was it. Afterwards, we went for tea and buttermilk scones at the Bull's Head Hotel & Tea Rooms in Barkingside. Then Albert and Pearl had to get back to their respective pubs and I travelled to a house in

Clerkenwell I'd never seen before. It was a four-bedroom terraced house in Woodbridge Street and he lived there with his mother and sister. I had about twenty pounds in savings from Devonshire Place and the White Lion and he told me he'd put it in the strongbox at the house for safekeeping.

It turned out Alan was actually fifteen years older than me, though he didn't look it, and the mother and sister doted on him like he was Little Lord Fauntleroy. Alan's father was dead, but nobody told me how he met his end and the man's name was rarely mentioned. His mother was small and slight, like him. Her name was Clare and she was a pinched little woman of about sixty with a frugal face and grey hair. His sister was bigger, almost my size, with spectacles and a permanent wave. Her name was Geraldine and she was about thirty and heading down the road to spinsterhood. They waited on Alan hand and foot and he never did a thing for himself. As I'd never actually met them before, I expected that they were in favour of us getting married, but I soon found out that wasn't the case.

We didn't honeymoon anywhere 'because of the war', but spent our wedding night in the house on Woodbridge Street with the other two women just a couple of partition walls away. Despite my close encounters with a number of men, I was still a virgin on my wedding night and I was a little nervous when we went to bed. It was cold in the room even though it was late April and I got between the sheets first, wearing a floral cotton nightdress. Alan slipped in beside me wearing a white string vest and knee-length drawers and his arm went round me. It wasn't long before he manoeuvred himself into position and, after a few grunts and pushes, it was all over and he rolled off me and lit a cigarette. Maybe it was because they were Catholics, but Alan wasn't the most imaginative man in bed, despite his playboy persona, and I couldn't help remembering Mr Harding and the way I felt in the library with him all those young years ago. We did it again in the missionary position that night and then the honeymoon was over.

The Blitz ended in May 1941 and things got a bit quieter in London, while the Germans were designing their doodlebugs and buzz-bombs. I waited for Alan to get called up and sent to North Africa, but he never was, and he kept saying it would probably be tomorrow, then the next day, or the day after that. Apart from in the bedroom, he was quite attentive to me, but his mother and sister were cool and I was more or less left to my own devices for the first week or so. They continued to look after Alan as they'd always done and I looked after myself. I think they believed me to be beneath them because I was once a servant and then a barmaid, and they thought they were on a higher level because they came from a professional family. As the days went by, I was increasingly given little jobs to do, like lighting the fires in the morning and cleaning up the kitchen after meals and making the beds and washing the floors. It felt as if I was being treated like their private maid and I'd gone back to being a skivvy again, only this time I wasn't being paid. Alan came and went at odd hours. He didn't seem to have a job like most men that took him out in the morning and back home in the evening. But he was kind and considerate to me, and his mother and sister kept their superiority complexes under control when he was around.

Alan never did get called up for military service. I found out, from accidentally overhearing a conversation, that his family had paid a doctor to diagnose flat feet for him and he was exempt. So there was no chance of him being killed in action. I wondered why he was in such a hurry to marry me. Then I found out. After about a month of married life, he insisted I come with him to another gambling club, even though I didn't want to because he'd only leave me on my own again and I'd drink too many cocktails. But he wouldn't take no for an answer.

The club was down a dark alley round the

back of Regent Street. There was just a plain black door set into the wall and you'd have walked past it if you didn't know it was there. Alan knocked slowly twice, then three times in quick succession. A viewing slot opened and a pair of eyes looked out. The man inside knew Alan because he opened the door and let us in. It was obvious to me that this was an illegal gambling den and the clients looked like a rum lot. I'd say most of them were villains of some sort and there were others who looked foreign – maybe Spanish or North African or even Indian – soldiers and sailors and pirates and pickpockets.

They all stared at me and scowled as I limped across the room, and I wondered why – hadn't they never seen a woman with a hobble before? Maybe not. Alan kept me closer to him this time, as he went from table to table and won money at all of them. I wasn't offered a single drink and Alan had to give me money to go to the bar. When I spoke to the barman in my Welsh accent, I thought the man wasn't going to serve me. He gave me a look like I had the plague, but another man in a tuxedo nodded to him and he, gave me the drinks. I was nervous in this place. They were openly hostile to me and they watched Alan like hawks. He was delighted with himself after winning and we left at 3:00 a.m., to the great relief of the 'management'.

The next day I asked Alan why they were

all giving me the evil eye in the club and he laughed.

'Don't you know the old saying?'

'What old saying?'

He told me there was an old Gypsy superstition that had been bandied about for centuries in gaming circles – that a limping woman who spoke softly in the Celtic tongue would bring luck to anyone she was with. There was a rhyme associated with the superstition that he couldn't quite remember the words of. He tried to say it.

'It goes, "the girl who limps ... speaks with a mysterious voice" ... something like that.'

I knew exactly what it was–

> *The nymph who limps*
> *With mystique speaks*
> *In Celt clan teang*
> *And moonstruck luck*
> *Will stalk who walks*
> *With she in chroí.*

That was a rough translation that I'd read and I also knew that *teang* meant tongue and *chroí* meant heart or love in old Celtic. Alan laughed again.

'It's some kind of old folklore thing. I never took any notice of it before, until I met you. I thought it was a load of old cobblers, but it's working for me.'

'What about the others in the clubs?'

'What about them?'

'Do they believe it?'

'Gamblers are the most superstitious breed of people in the world!'

They all had their individual rituals and lucky charms and would wear odd socks or a certain tie or recite words backwards or turn round three times – anything to give them that edge – that elusive piece of good fortune. I told Alan he ought to be careful, but he said what could they do, report him to the police? Some of the clubs were illegal and he wasn't doing anything against the rules. Alan's attitude was, they'd been happily taking money off him for years, and now it was his turn to take some of that money back.

Alan made me come to the clubs with him over a period of several months in the summer of 1942 and I came to the conclusion that he married me because he wanted a good luck charm on his arm. I was more of a mascot than a wife. Word was spreading that there was some kind of sibyl in town and each time we went out it got more frightening, with the management and even the other clients gathering round to see if the 'lucky fetish' would work one more time. And it did – until one night at an illegal gaming club off the King's Road, Chelsea, that was later to become the Kray Twins' Esmeralda's Barn, when a couple of big bruisers came threateningly over to us.

'Take your witch out of here, Lane!'

'She's not a witch.'

'What is she then?'

'She's my wife.'

Alan wasn't a fighter and we should have left there and then. But he was winning again and didn't want to go. I grabbed him by the arm and tried to get him away from the table, but he pulled out of my grip and accidentally punched one of the heavies in the stomach.

That was it!

I went to the hospital with Alan. He had concussion and a broken nose and several cracked ribs. While I was there, I started throwing up violently and I thought it was the trauma of the fight in the gambling den. I looked very pale and washed-out and one of the doctors decided to examine me for injuries, even though I told him I didn't have any. Alan's mother and sister arrived on the sordid little scene and they glared at me as if it was all my fault and then went and lay across him in the bed crying, even though he was only half-conscious and I don't think he even knew who they were. The doctor who examined me came back and called me into a room.

'You seem to be all right, Mrs Lane.'

'I told you I was.'

'Apart from being pregnant.'

'What?'

He told me I was about three months gone, which I should have known myself as I hadn't had a period since April. But I didn't put two and two together. I was naive for my age in matters of female bodily functions because nobody ever told me anything and I never read about it in any of my books. I left home to be a skivvy when I was barely sixteen and neither my mother nor anyone else had ever explained anything. The girls I met in service and in the pubs probably assumed I knew everything, because we never discussed pregnancy or babies – and I'd kept out of the lascivious arms of the young lads in the dance-halls. It meant I probably got pregnant on my wedding night, and that could be considered either lucky or unlucky, depending on what your definition of luck was.

Alan was allowed out of hospital after a few days. I told him I was pregnant and refused to go back into the gambling dens with him. What if I got hit and something happened to the baby? He pleaded with me, but my mind was made up – I was adamant. It was far too dangerous. It didn't matter anyway because we were both barred from all the gaming joints in London, including the private clubs. News travelled fast in that fraternity and the legacy from his father's will that he lived off was suspended, under some clause or other in the codicil. Apparently, old man Lane knew about his son's gambling addiction and knew he'd blow the whole inheritance if it was left to him in a lump sum. So Alan was given an allowance on condition he didn't gamble with it. Now he had to get a proper job as an accountant, which he was trained to be, at the firm of Douglas & Philips, where his father had been a director before his death – and he didn't like it one little bit. His attitude towards me changed. I wasn't his lucky charm any more – his talisman – his tau. He was no longer kind and considerate and he blamed me for getting him such a bad name in the gambling world.

His mother and sister firmly believed I got myself deliberately pregnant out of wedlock and trapped him into marrying me. They were Catholics, so he was stuck with me now and they started calling me the Welsh Whore whenever they thought I was within earshot. Alan never gave me any of the money he earned, which mostly went on the backs of racehorses and greyhounds, and he'd gambled away the savings I gave him for safekeeping. So, I was totally dependent on them in the house on Woodbridge Street.

I was moved into the spare bedroom and treated like a slave and wasn't allowed to go anywhere in case I said bad things about them. As if things weren't bad enough already! I was like Cinderella down in the ashes and the others were like the two ugly sisters standing over me while I did all the work. But there was no glass slipper for me, my prince had already been and gone, and there would be no white doves coming to comfort me. I think they might have been hoping I'd lose the baby with all the hard work, but I thrived and got bigger and they came to accept it as a fact of life. That brought with it a change in attitude; it was Alan's baby after all and a Lane by blood. So they started lightening my load. I was worried about having the child, as I knew nothing about babies being born and didn't understand even the fundamentals of child-birth. I decided to ask my mother-in-law.

'Can I ask you a question, Clare?'

'I suppose so.'

'How does the baby come out?'

'Don't you know?'

'Yes, of course I do, but I just want to make sure.'

She laughed derisively.

'It comes out the way it went in, you stupid girl.'

Then she walked away, still laughing. So much for the Welsh Whore handle! But I was still unsure of the actual physical nature of the process. I asked Alan, but he just snarled and said I should know about these things and it was nothing to do with him. The midwife would explain everything.

At 4:00 a.m. on the morning of 28 January 1942, my daughter Charlotte was born. I named her after Charlie Currant. And the old bat was right: she came out the way she went in. I had the baby at home and the midwife was there, along with Clare and Geraldine. They took the baby away from me as soon as she was born and I wasn't even allowed to hold her. They said they'd taken her to be cleaned up and they'd bring her back, but they never did. I was weak because I'd lost a lot of blood and I wanted to sleep. I woke the next morning about 10:00 a.m. and there was no one in the room with me. I got up and made my way to the bathroom and had a wash and then went downstairs. There, in the sitting room, were the three members of the Lane family with my baby.

'Ah, just in time, Anwyn.'

'In time?'

'For her feed.'

I was allowed to breastfeed my baby, then she was whisked away from me again. I complained to Alan.

'I want my baby.'

'You need to rest.'

'No ... I'm all right.'

'Go back to bed. The baby's being taken care of.'

'She's my baby, Alan!'

312

'No, she's *my* baby.'

And that's how it was – I was allowed to nurse Charlotte and breastfeed her, then she was taken away by the ugly sisters. Alan told me I was Welsh Chapel and would be a bad influence on her as they were obliged to bring her up as a Catholic. They were afraid my Congregationalism would rub off on her – even though she was only a few days old.

'But, I'm not really all that religious...'

'That's even worse!'

I realised Alan had only married me for my limp, which he saw as a device for his gambling scam. Now that he was persona non grata in the gaming dens I was no longer an asset. They wanted to keep the baby and I was useful as a wet nurse, not as a mother. As soon as Charlotte was old enough to go on the solids, I'd be redundant in that department too and I'd be relegated back to the role of domestic slave – or thrown out onto the street.

There was only one thing for it, I had to escape, and take my baby with me. But there was always one of them in the house, watching me. I had no money and nowhere to go, while they had influential friends that could make things difficult for me, to say the least. I decided to do it in the middle of the night, but first I had to get some money. Alan blew all his cash on the horses and dogs, but the old woman looked after the strongbox where he was supposed to have stashed my savings. Clare and Geraldine both had incomes from the father's estate, so they were independent of Alan and let him do as he pleased with his own money. Geraldine always paid the bills. They didn't trust me to do it because they believed I'd be off with the cash. I had to act fast. It was April 1942 and a year since I married Alan. I watched when the old woman went to the strongbox to get the money for Geraldine to go into town and pay the bills. She hid the key behind some books in the study. It was on a Friday and I decided to wait until the following Thursday; that would be the time when there was most cash in the box.

Over the course of the following week I planned everything carefully. The first train out of Paddington was at 5:30 a.m. and I went to the strongbox at 3:30 am. I found the key and opened it. There was a lot of money inside, but I only took the twenty pounds that was mine. Getting the baby would be more difficult. She always slept in a little open nursery area that Alan had built, with Geraldine's bedroom on one side and Clare's on the other. If she woke in the night, they'd call me to come and feed her. I had a carrying bag ready and I took my left breast from my blouse before sneaking into the room as quietly as I could. The baby gurgled when I lifted her gently from her cot and immediately clamped her sucking mouth onto my teat. Then I made my way slowly from the room. Geraldine stirred in the bed when I reached the door and I stood still for moment, not daring to move. She turned over and settled back down and I made my way carefully down the stairs, carrying the baby on my breast in one arm and the bag in the other. I opened the front door and closed it quietly behind me and was away down Woodbridge Street as fast as a frightened fawn.

It was a mild spring early morning and I waited until I got out into Clerkenwell Road before putting Charlotte into the carrying bag. She'd had her fill of mother's milk by then and slipped back into a sound sleep. Clerkenwell Road was a main thoroughfare and I managed to hail a hackney carriage fairly quickly. We arrived at Paddington station just after 5:00 a.m., giving me time to buy a ticket and find the platform for South Wales.

And we were gone!

I arrived at Maesteg with my bag and my baby at 1:00 p.m. and I caught a lift with a lorry driver who was going down to Bridgend. He dropped me close to the village and I walked the rest of the way to our house. My sister Bronwyn answered the door when I knocked and she was so surprised to see me.

'Winny, what a surprise. What are you

doing here?'

'I've come for a visit.'

'Come in. Come in.'

Charlotte started to cry in the carrying bag, it was time for her feed.

'And who's this?'

'My daughter, Charlotte. Say hello to Auntie Bronwyn, Charlotte.'

Inside the house, my father was very ill and bed-ridden. The onset of emphysema had further deteriorated into chronic obstructive pulmonary disease and he didn't have long to live. Mother was trying to be cheerful and smilingly glad to see me, but her face told the true story of her situation. And I felt guilty again. Every time I came home, I brought some trouble with me. And they didn't need any more than they already had. Walter was married now and living with his wife and little son at the other side of the village. And Gwyneth was away at nursing college in Cardiff. Bronwyn was eighteen and working as a trainee teacher in Maesteg. None of them had followed me into service and I was thankful for that at least. I gave my mother most of my money, apart from what I'd spent getting away from London – and Charlotte and I settled into my old room, and I looked out across the hills again and wondered where I was going to go from here.

Chapter Twenty

Alan Lane arrived in Llangynwyd the very next day. He brought with him the sounds of the city and the smell of wrath and a solicitor from London and a police sergeant from Maesteg. My mother let them in and the sergeant took off his hat and smiled when she offered him a cup of tea. I got Bronwyn to take Charlotte out in the old pram we used when we were babies, while the sergeant introduced the other two to my mother. Bronwyn went out the back door so they wouldn't see her. The sergeant was a jolly man by the name of Jones and he settled back in a chair with his cup of tea and a slice of barmbrack.

'Lovely, Mrs Moyle. I haven't tasted barmbrack as good as this for many a year.'

'Would you like another slice, sergeant?'

'If you can spare it.'

The other two had nothing and the expressions on their faces made them look like they were both constipated.

'These men have come over from London with a complaint against your daughter, Anwyn.'

'I'm Anwyn Moyle.'

All the faces turned to look at me as I came through the door into the room. The men all stood up. Alan scowled and glanced at the solicitor. The sergeant smiled at me as he settled back into his chair.

'Good afternoon to you, miss.'

'And what might the complaint be?'

The sergeant took another mouthful of brack and chewed it a few times before washing it down with the tea.

'That you've run off with a baby.'

'*My* baby!'

This seemed to take the sergeant by surprise, as if he hadn't been given the full facts of the matter. He shot a stern look at the other two. Alan piped up.

'My baby too!'

The sergeant put his cup down in a rather dramatic way.

'So, this is a domestic dispute? I was led to believe it was a case of abduction.'

'She also stole twenty pounds.'

'Did you, Miss Moyle?'

'Certainly not. It was my own money.'

Another glare shot the way of Alan and his solicitor, this one even sterner than the first. My mother refilled the sergeant's cup and slipped another slice of brack onto his plate. Alan nudged the solicitor, who looked a little bit embarrassed by now. He spoke up.

'Miss Moyle, I think it's totally unreasonable of you to run off and take Mr Lane's baby with you.'

'And I think it's totally unreasonable of Mr Lane to treat me like a slave and gamble away my money.'

Both the solicitor and the sergeant shot stern looks at Alan, who squirmed in his seat. I tearfully elaborated on the situation at Woodbridge Street and, by the time I was finished, the sergeant was ready to clap Alan Lane in irons and the solicitor was ready to prosecute him for high treason and send him after Ikey Solomon to Van Diemen's Land. But then Alan played what he thought was his trump card.

'The baby would be better off with me.'

This riled the sergeant even more.

'Are you saying, Mr Lane, that we're less able, here in Wales, to take care of our children than you are in London?'

'I'm not saying that at all.'

'Well, that's what you seem to be saying.'

The solicitor kicked Alan in the shin and he shut up.

'There's obviously been a misunderstanding...'

The sergeant growled back at him.

'Obviously.'

'I think Mr Lane and I should return to London and see if we can work out the terms of a reconciliation.'

'Good idea.'

The two of them left with their tails between their legs. The sergeant finished his tea and currant cake, then doffed his hat to my mother before replacing it on his head and following them out into the street.

Three days later my father died.

The curtains were immediately drawn and his body was washed by a *corff golchwr* [body washer] and laid out on a table in the main room of the house. White sheets were draped over the walls and the mirrors were covered for reasons of respect, as was the custom. Sweet-smelling herbs were brought in from the garden and placed on the counterpane that covered him and candles were lit and stood either side of his head. Mourners came to pay their respects right up to the day of the funeral and the whole village brought cake and ale and spice-wine to be offered round. There was a constant flow of visitors, coming in through the front door and out through the back door, stopping to eat and drink on the way. Some sang songs and others said prayers and I'm sure many of them came more than once.

On the burial day, the chief mourner was a man who did it for all the deaths in the village. He came to the house covered in crêpe and hung his head. Black gloves were handed out to me and my family and strips of crêpe were draped round our shoulders. The water and cloth used to wash my father's body were kept in a bowl under the table and only thrown out into the street when the funeral party left the house. The whole village was gathered on the road outside and they sang a hymn before the coffin moved off, carried by Walter and three other men and led by the local preacher.

Fi bererin swael ei wedd,
Na does ynof nerth na bywyd
Fel yn gorwedd yn y bedd:
Hollalluog, hollalluog,
Ydyw'r Un a'm cwyd i'r lan

['Guide Me, O Thou Great Redeemer']

Everybody filed in and walked behind the coffin to the cemetery on the hill, about half a mile away. Gwyneth came up from Cardiff and she walked with me and Mother and Bronwyn at the front of the procession. I wheeled Charlotte in her pram.

The gravediggers stood by with their shovels as we arrived at the graveside. Another hymn was sung while the coffin was lowered down.

Wele'n sefyll rhwng y myrtwydd
Wrthrych teilwng o fy mryd;
Er o'r braidd 'rwy'n Ei adnabod
Ef uwchlaw gwrthrychau'r byd:
Henffych fore! Henffych fore!

Caf ei weled fel y mae
Caf ei weled fel y mae

['Guide Me, O Thou Great Redeemer']

Then the preacher said prayers while the gravediggers filled in the consecrated pit and the coffin disappeared under the clay. The prayer went on and on and Mother cried, so did Gwyneth and Bronwyn. Me and Walter didn't.

When it was over, many of the people came back to the house and the curtains were opened and the covers taken from the walls and mirrors. They ate and drank and sang songs into the late evening.

That night, in bed with Charlotte beside me, I said my own prayer for my dearly beloved father.

Deep peace I breathe into you,
O weariness here:
O ache, here!
Deep peace, a soft white dove to you;
Deep peace, a quiet rain to you;
Deep peace, an ebbing wave to you!
Deep peace, red wind of the east from you;
Deep peace, grey wind of the west to you;
Deep peace, dark wind of the north from you;
Deep peace, blue wind of the south to you!

Alan Lane came back at the end of May.

This time he came alone. He was sorry for what happened in Woodbridge Street, but he'd managed to find a nice flat in Finsbury for us and I wouldn't have to go back there any more. He knew we could be happy together if I'd agree to come back to London. In those days, there were few one-parent families and a woman's place was held to be by her husband's side, no matter how much of a rogue or rascal he was.

A woman on her own with a child was viewed as loose and wanton, even if the opposite was true, and I'd been getting funny looks from the village people since my father died. So I agreed to go back. Gwyneth had already returned to Cardiff and Bronwyn was back teaching in Maesteg and Walter was working and with his new family, so it was only me and mother – and she was still doing whatever bits and pieces she could to make ends meet. Once my savings ran out, she couldn't afford to have me and Charlotte living there and me not bringing anything in. I thought of going to see Monica Reynolds and asking her to find me something local, like she did before. But it would be impossible with a baby and I couldn't leave Charlotte with my mother to mind. So it was the right thing to do, going back with Alan.

At least, I thought it was at the time.

What I didn't know was, Alan was back

323

gambling in the casinos again and he'd given up his accountancy job. His short stint of employment had convinced his father's executors that he was a reformed character, and he'd made amends with the private clubs where he was a member and they'd allowed him back in after his year in the wilderness – on condition that he didn't bring me with him.

The flat was on the top floor of a three-storey town house. There was no lift and I had to hump Charlotte's pram up and down the stairs. Alan was kind and attentive for a couple of weeks and he climbed on top of me and grunted and pushed a few times and I fell pregnant for him again. After that he came and went as he pleased, just like before, and he rarely had any money to give me for food. That didn't bother him, because he was always running round to his mother's when he was hungry. The rent was paid from his father's estate, so there was no danger of being evicted, but he gambled away the rest of the monthly allowance left to him under the reinstated terms of his father's will, and there was never anything left for me and Charlotte.

Things gradually became more desperate and I eventually had no other option but to take on cleaning jobs to feed my child and the one I was expecting. When Alan wasn't around, I went with Charlotte in her pram and cleaned the houses of the authors and artists who lived in the affluent areas of Bloomsbury and Holborn, which were within walking distance of the flat in Finsbury. The work involved washing floors and windows and dusting and polishing and brassing and buffing – cleaning kitchens and bathrooms and dining rooms and it was much the same as skivvying only I could go home when I was finished.

Alan and I didn't have sex any more – he wasn't all that bothered and I didn't want to do it while I was pregnant, in case it harmed the baby I was carrying. He didn't seem to care either if I was in or out when he came and went. I didn't tell him I was working because he'd only have wanted me to give him my money so he could gamble it away along with his own. I think he thought I was just out walking to get away from the boredom of the flat, and I got on with the cleaning for as long as I could.

I had to stop when I was eight months pregnant and, instead, I took in washing and ironing like my mother used to do, right up until I went into labour. My son, Daniel, was born on 8 March 1943. I had him at home with a midwife, just as I did with Charlotte, who was now thirteen months old, and I had two babies to feed. As soon as I could manage it I had to go back out cleaning the houses again. I put both children in the pram that I had to lug up and down the stairs and it hurt my foot every time. It was very hard during that summer of 1943, living on the top floor of the town house with two young children and a war on. Almost everything was being rationed by then and there was no sign of it all coming to an end.

After the Americans joined the war in 1942, London was full of GIs, as they called their soldiers. GI stood for government issue and it was a kind of joke that the soldiers called themselves that. They brought their own culture with them and they seemed to have plenty of free time and money to spend, and they brightened up gloomy old London that had been struggling through austere times for what seemed so long. One day, I was coming back from work when I encountered a small group of these GIs near Gray's Inn Road. They were exploring the area and I must have looked like I was ready to drop, pushing the pram and limping along.

'Are you OK, ma'am?'

'Yes, I'm all right.'

'You sure?'

'Yes, I'm sure.'

They offered me cigarettes, which I declined, and chocolate and stockings, which I accepted. The stockings were called nylons and were made of a new material that was sheerer and more hard-wearing than either silk or rayon. We got chatting about which dancehalls were good and which were bad and they were impressed that I knew so much about the subject. They brought their own dances with them across the Atlantic – like the jitterbug and the balboa and swing and jive and boogie and I longed to be able to go hopping with them, like in the old days, before I got married.

As they were going in my direction, they asked if they could walk with me and I could give them more information about the London dance scene on the way. I found them to be well-mannered and very polite and respectful gentlemen. They even wheeled the pram for me and carried it up the front stairs. Just, then the door opened and Alan stuck his head out to see what all the laughing and joking was about. He said nothing when he saw the American soldiers – until I got inside.

'So that's how you're making your money.'

'What do you mean?'

'Bringing back Yank soldiers.'

'I didn't bring them back.'

'Oh no? Then what were they doing here?'

I tried to explain that they were only being perfect gentlemen and trying to help me, which was more than he ever did. But he wouldn't listen. He flew into a rage when I took the chocolate and nylons they'd given me out of my pocket and he tried to hit me.

I've already said that Alan was no fighter, and he was older and smaller than me. So I avoided his swipe and punched him straight on his previously broken nose.

Blood began to flow and he looked at me in disbelief for a moment, before storming out of the flat and slamming the door behind him. I don't know who was more surprised, me or him. He came back later that night, having been to see his old bat of a mother for some sympathy, no doubt. But it started a period of sustained mental harassment by him. He became insanely jealous and suspicious to the point of being paranoid. He'd leave the flat and pretend to go off somewhere but when I went to do my cleaning he'd follow me at a distance and spy on me. I always knew he was there, but I pretended not to notice and, if I even said hello to someone, he'd start an argument when I got home and accuse me of all sorts and even that the children didn't belong to him.

He knew he couldn't beat me in a fair fight, face to face, so he'd have a brainstorm and sneak up on me from behind and try to strangle me. I'd reach back and grab him by the goolies and we'd both be screaming like Saturday night slatterns, and the neighbours would rush in and separate us. He'd apologise and say he didn't know what came over him – until it came over him again.

The war ended on 8 May 1945. Charlotte

was three by then and Daniel was two. The whole of London celebrated and danced and drank and sang and went wild. More than a million people took to the streets and crowds assembled in Trafalgar Square and along The Mall and outside Buckingham Palace. It was a warm, bright day and the King and Queen and Prime Minister came out onto the balcony and everybody cheered. There were parades and marching bands all over London and street parties up in Finsbury and the pubs stayed open to help christen the celebrations. Flags and bunting flew everywhere and girls kissed soldiers and sailors kissed each other and children ate cakes and drank lemonade. Kings danced with pearly queens, and queens danced with pearly kings, and it was all over at last and everyone was truly thankful.

But the war between me and Alan went on.

He continued to follow me around, even after all the GIs went back to America. He'd hide behind cars and around corners and sometimes he'd come into the house where I was cleaning and kick over a bucket of water or run away with my washing rags. I'd run after him and trip him up or throw some-thing at him and he'd go and tell the old bat and her ugly daughter. They came round the flat to complain once, but I was in no mood to listen to their lectures. I told them they could have him back, because he was no use to me – in anyway, shape or form. They threatened to stop the rent payments and I told them to go ahead, I'd pay it myself and Alan could find somewhere else to live. But he wouldn't leave the flat and the rent continued to be paid.

His antics became more and more bizarre and I often thought about having him committed to a lunatic asylum. I read somewhere that Sigmund Freud's daughter, Anna, was taking the theories of psychoanalysis further than her father and new treatments for sexual aggression were being developed every day. Maybe they'd be able to cure Alan if he went in somewhere for a while. But, when I thought about it, I knew they'd never believe me and might commit me instead. Then he'd take the kids and move them back in with his mother. And I couldn't have that.

He continued to sneak up behind me when I wasn't looking and try to strangle me, and I continued to grab him by the goolies and the neighbours continued to come in and pull us apart. We didn't sleep together any more, but I always kept one eye open, in case he crept into my room in the middle of the night with a carving knife. He never did, but I kept a rolling-pin under my pillow just in case and I'd have clouted him with it across the side of his schizophrenic head if he came anywhere near me.

In 1945, Alan was forty-two and I was only twenty-seven. The fact that I was so much younger than him added to his paranoia that I was seeing someone else – and maybe more than one. But he was enough to put me off men for all time and I didn't need any more of them in my life. In fact, I was getting increasingly fed up with Alan and his antics and I didn't think I should have to put up with this kind of existence. I longed to be free and single again. I loved my two children and wouldn't be without them for the world, but the thought of living a life on my own, without some madman constantly watching my every move, was like a dream that would never come true – until he died. Or I did.

Then I thought, what if I left him?

How much worse off would I be?

Chapter Twenty-one

During the war, women had been doing all the jobs men normally did – working in the factories and on the land and, now the men were coming home, many of them didn't want to be forced back into their traditional roles of housewives and mothers. The Equal

Pay Campaign highlighted inequalities in the treatment of women in the workplace, but old prejudices about women's capabilities were still alive and used by the government to stall reforms. Nevertheless, things would never be the way they were again and attitudes to single mothers were changing, as there were many more young widows than before. I was aware of these developments because I continued to read the newspapers, even after I left service, and I knew it was time to go out on my own. So I found myself a cheap flat near St Pancras and went there to live, Alan-free, in September 1945.

I didn't sneak out in the middle of the night. I told him I was going and I didn't want him coming with me. He kicked up the usual hullabaloo and went off crying to his mother and silly sister. They all came round and threatened me with court action for custody of the children. I told them to go ahead and try it. I was a good mother and earning my own money and well able to look after myself and my children. Alan was a compulsive gambler who lost all his money and never gave me anything and he was violent and unstable, which the neighbours would testify to. They went off with several fleas in their ears, but I knew it wouldn't be the last I'd hear or see of them.

The flat was on the ground floor, and more

accessible for the pram, and there was a little garden out back with grass and a line for the drying of clothes. The rent was reasonable and I was able to take in washing and ironing jobs as well as going out to clean the houses. It was hard work and I didn't get much time to rest, but I had the children with me and they weren't neglected in any way.

Then, in early 1946, I got a summons from the court saying Alan had applied for custody of his two children. I couldn't afford legal representation, but there was a duty solicitor at the court and he agreed to speak for me after a brief interview where I gave him the bare bones of what life was like with Alan Lane. I had no one to look after the children on the day, so I had to bring them along to the court. The clerk let them sit beside me and I listened to Alan's solicitor saying I dragged them with me when I was working and I had men friends back at my flat and he made me out to be a right trollop. The duty solicitor asked him if he had any evidence of men coming back to my flat and, in response, Alan's solicitor related the tale of the GIs helping me to carry the pram upstairs in Finsbury.

'Mr Lane was at home on that occasion, and a good job too!'

I gave my evidence about how Alan gambled all the money away and gave me nothing, so I had no alternative but to go out to work to feed the children. I also had statements from the neighbours saying he was violent and unpredictable. His solicitor asked if there was any medical evidence of his violence. When he was told there wasn't, he tried to turn the tables and insinuate I was the violent one, and he said there was an instance of Mr Lane being admitted to hospital with a broken nose and cracked ribs and concussion.

'I didn't do that!'

'No? Who did?'

'The bouncers.'

'What bouncers?'

'In the gambling club.'

As it was an illegal gambling club, Alan whispered to his solicitor and the matter of his alleged injuries was withdrawn.

The judge did his summing up, after hearing all the evidence and the arguments to and fro. He said it wasn't right the children should be dragged around to clean houses with me. I wanted to say they didn't clean the houses, I cleaned the houses and they played while I was cleaning them. But the duty solicitor told me not to interrupt or be impertinent. The judge also conceded that Alan was wrong to gamble all his money away and force me out to work as a cleaner, but he did have a mother and sister at home who didn't go out to work and could have cared for the children while I was out cleaning. I didn't like the sound of that, and things didn't seem to be going my way. He said it wasn't clear who, if either of us, was violent in the relationship, so he was going to ignore that evidence altogether.

Clearly, according to the judge, Alan could provide the safest and most appropriate environment for the children. My heart sank – they were going to take the kids away from me. Plans already started formulating in my mind to take them back, abduct them, like I did before with Charlotte and run away to Wales with them. And the police sergeant would be on my side again and I'd live there forever in the coaldust and sheep dung and never come back to London again.

But the judge wasn't finished yet. He said he was a traditionalist and he believed children belonged with their mother. Good, it was swinging back my way again. However, a wife and mother also belonged with her husband. The ideal scenario, in his view, was for me and Alan to reconcile our differences and get back together. That would solve all the problems. Alan was under obligation as a husband and father to provide for his wife and children and he should give me enough money to live on, so I didn't have to go out to work and I could stay at home and take care of the children. He recessed the court so we could discuss it with our respective counsels.

We went to a private room in the court, while the children stayed outside with the uglies. Alan wasn't happy about the money side of things and I didn't want him back. Stalemate. My solicitor told me if I didn't agree to the judge's proposal, the court would award custody of the children to Alan and his family. It was either take Alan or lose the children. Alan's solicitor told him if I agreed to the judge's proposal and he didn't, then the court would award custody of the children to me. Neither of us seemed to have any choice. It only left one issue to be resolved.

'I'm not going back to live at Woodbridge Street.'

'I'm not living in St Pancras.'

Both solicitors shook their heads in exasperation. I said if I went back to Clerkenwell, things would continue as they had before – Alan wouldn't give me any money and his mother and sister would monopolise the children. They'd eventually find an excuse to get rid of me altogether. My solicitor said he'd explain that to the court and allow the judge to decide where we should live. Abduction plans resurfaced in my mind.

The court was recalled and the learned friends told the judge we'd agreed to his proposal. He was delighted about that. I think he saw himself as a marriage guidance counsellor as well as an esteemed m'lud. However, the issue of residence still remained. Alan's solicitor argued that Woodbridge Street would provide a more stable family atmosphere for the children and the duty solicitor made my case about being marginalised by the uglies. Luckily for me, the judge was a traditionalist about this as well and believed that a man and wife should live together, independent of the wider family group, if at all possible. As there was an independent residence in St Pancras, then that was clearly the best option. And so it was resolved, Alan and I would live together again for the sake of the children and he would behave like a proper husband and father and support us financially. I didn't believe for a single minute that this would happen.

But the judge did.

I asked the duty solicitor what I should do if Alan didn't keep his side of the bargain.

'He's under a court order to do so.'

'Yes, but what if he doesn't?'

'You'll have to come back to court.'

'Can't I just throw him out?'

He told me I'd have to convince the court that Alan was in breach of its order. They would probably fine him and, if he broke it again, he could risk going to jail. But all that would take forever and a fortnight and, in the meantime, me and the children would starve if I didn't go to work and do the cleaning. But that was the reality of the situation and the legal eagles weren't concerned with reality, only the letter of the law.

Alan moved into the flat in St Pancras in May 1946 and things went well for a while. He gave me enough money to buy food and I didn't have to go out skivvying and he didn't have to follow me to make sure I wasn't going on the game. We even had sex again and I fell pregnant again. My daughter Estelle was born on 17 March 1947. This time I had the baby in hospital and Alan looked after the other two until I got back home after three days. And that's when things changed and he went back to his old ways. He had a run of bad luck on the horses, combined with even worse luck in the casinos, and the money he was giving me dried up. I had three children to feed now. Charlotte was five and Daniel was four and they were both going to nursery school. So I was able to go out cleaning again and only had to bring baby Estelle with me, as long as I was finished in time to collect the other two from school. As soon as I started going back out cleaning, Alan put his jealous head on and all the bother started up again. I just couldn't be having it.

Then I saw a small shop to let down the street from the flat. It had accommodation above it and the rent for both was all-inclusive. I decided there was an easier way for me to make money. I went along to see the letting agent and they said they needed an advance down-payment of fifty pounds. Now, I had about fifteen pounds saved up for emergencies from my cleaning money and from the child benefit allowance I was getting for Daniel and Estelle, after it was introduced in August 1946. But I didn't know where I could get the other thirty-five pounds from. I racked my brains, but there was nowhere I could go and no one I could ask. Then I thought of Alan – and his horses. I didn't want him to know I had fifteen pounds, because he would have searched the flat for it and created and kicked the walls and I didn't need all that melodrama. I had to think of a way to get the information I needed from him.

I knew he kept racing sheets in the house, with lists of horses and meetings. I found one, but it meant nothing to me – just a list of eccentric names and all sorts of abbreviations and hieroglyphics that obviously meant something to racing punters, but nothing to me. I put the sheet in a prominent place where Alan would be sure to see it when he came in. True to form, he picked it up and started to peruse it. I nonchalantly looked over his shoulder.

'What does it all mean?'

'What does what mean?'

'All those letters and squiggles and stuff.'

'Why do you want to know?'

'No reason.'

He gave me a suspicious look, but he liked to think of himself as an expert on all things to do with gambling and he couldn't resist the rare chance to show off his knowledge to me. He explained that the numbers and letters told you the weight the horse would be carrying, the trainer and the jockey and a bit about the horse's racing history and the odds on the horse winning that particular race – which was what I was interested in.

Alan explained that short odds meant the horse was fancied and had a better chance of winning than long odds, which meant the horse was an outsider.

'Say you want to double your money?'

'Then you bet on evens.'

'What about triple it?'

'Then bet on two-to-one against. You double your money and get your stake back.'

I knew what had to be done. To come away with fifty pounds I had to bet my fifteen pounds on a horse with odds of three-to-one, then I'd win forty-five pounds and get my own fifteen back as well. I'd have my fifty pounds with ten pounds to spare.

'But isn't betting illegal?'

'Not on the track.'

'But you don't go to the track.'

'There are horse joints, just like gambling dens ... there's one in Gray's Inn Road.'

After Alan went out the next day and I dropped Charlotte and Daniel off at school, I came back and studied the racing sheets for that day. I only looked for horses that were three-to-one. Then a name caught my eye Mari Lwyd – and I remembered the bony skull and the fiery green eyes and the snapping jaws of that skeleton horse from days gone by. I saw it as a sign – a premonition. It had to be this horse.

I wrote down all the details and put Estelle into her pram and walked down to Gray's Inn Road. I'd been in and out of the illegal casinos with Alan so I knew what to look for – an inconspicuous side door with men coming and going. I stood close by it for a long time. My mind was in turmoil. How could I justify doing this? I was no better than Alan. What if the horse lost? Fifteen pounds was a fortune to throw away and I'd had to work hard to earn it. I should wait, save up some more money. But it would take me ages to get fifty pounds and the shop would be gone by then and I'd never get another chance.

I waited.

I watched the faces of the men going in. Who could I trust to put the bet on? It was a lot of money and they might just run off with it and there would be nothing I could do. No, this was wrong. I couldn't risk it. I was about to turn away and leave when I saw a familiar face across the street, coming out of a bank. It was Mr Harding, from Hampstead and all those years ago.

'Mr Harding! Mr Harding!'

He was the perfect choice. He was well-to-do and no one would bat an eyelid at him placing fifteen pounds on a horse. That's if he'd agree to do it for me. He looked in my direction and hesitated. Then he smiled and came across the street.

'Moyle ... Anwyn ... am I right?'

'Yes, Sir, it's me.'

I could smell that scent of sage and cedar-wood, and feel his breath on the side of my face – like before, in the library. It was intoxicating. I forgot why I'd called him over.

'Would you like a cup of tea?'

'Yes ... yes, I would.'

He took me to a tea-shop called Hepworth's in the Gray's Inn Road. Estelle was asleep in her pram. He noticed my limp. 'What happened to you, Anwyn?'

'An accident.'

'I'm so sorry.'

'It's all right. I'm used to it.'

We sat together in the tea-room and talked for a long time over a pot of Earl Grey and a plate of scones. I told him about my life since leaving Hampstead and how I was married now with three children. He told me he was still living with his wife in the same house. I asked him about Miranda Bouchard and he said she'd remarried – the rich Earl. She gave up the house in Chester Square and went to live in Wiltshire. She rarely visited London because the social season wasn't what it used to be before the war and things were totally different now. He very seldom saw her and I noticed the sadness in his eyes when he said that.

It was obvious there was still something between them – but it was something that could never be allowed to flower in the stiflingly closed society in which they moved and manoeuvred. He was married and she was an aristocrat whose family needed money – and it didn't matter if they were in love. Love had nothing to do with family or tradition and doing the honourable thing – the decent and not the decadent thing. I almost asked him if they were lovers but I didn't need to know.

It felt strange sitting there, talking like two ordinary people – no longer master and maid. The old order was changing and I was no longer a naive teenage girl but a twenty-nine-year-old woman. We seemed to talk forever and I got the feeling he wanted to ask me something but he never did.

'It seemed urgent.'

'What did?'

'You calling to me, as if there was something that needed urgent attention.'

I suddenly remembered the bet and looked at the clock on the tea-room wall.

'Oh, God, it's too late.'

'For what?'

I felt ashamed to tell him what I wanted him for – it seemed so inappropriate now. But he insisted on knowing and eventually I explained that I needed fifty pounds to rent a little shop to start up a washing and ironing business and the only way to get the money was to risk my savings.

'Rather foolhardy, don't you think?'

'I suppose so.'

'Why don't I loan you the money?'

'Oh no, Sir. No!'

'Of course I must. I owe you.'

'You owe me nothing.'

He said he did, as it was his fault I was let go from the scullery maid's job all those years ago. I told him he did me a favour, but he wouldn't take no for an answer. We walked back to the bank and he drew out fifty pounds and gave it to me. He said I could pay him back when my business started making a profit. I knew where to find him. I thanked him profusely. We said goodbye and he held on to my hand for a long moment and smiled and then disappeared into the coalescing crowd on Gray's Inn Road. And I just hoped Alan wasn't stalking me on that day, because he'd really have something to be jealous about this time.

Next day, I went to the letting agency and paid the deposit of fifty pounds and signed the lease for a year. I still had my savings and I used that money to paint the shop after I'd cleaned it all up and washed down the walls and the window. It had a little kitchenette out back and the floor was in good condition, so all I needed was to install some clothes rails and an ironing board. I also bought a second-hand top-loading washing machine on instalments and ran water pipes to and from the sink in the kitchenette. It was all makeshift and I had to take the washing up to the flat and hang it on the line in the garden to dry, then take it back down to the shop to iron and hang on the clothes rails. I put a sign in the window.

WASHING, DRYING & IRONING
REASONABLE RATES

Business was slow and, for a while, I thought it wouldn't take off. I was competing on a small scale with the Chinese laundries in Central London, and St Pancras wasn't exactly an affluent area where people could afford the luxury of having their linen washed and dried and ironed by someone else. Alan wanted to know where the money came from to open the shop, so I lied and told him I won it on a horse. He laughed, then he remembered me asking him all about the racing sheets and he was constantly trying to get me to pick winners for

345

him after that. I picked a few and I don't know whether they won or not, but he seemed happy enough. I never did find out whether Mari Lwyd won that day – and I didn't want to know either.

A few weeks after I opened, a chauffeur-driven Rolls-Royce Silver Wraith pulled up outside and the driver brought in bags full of stuff to be washed, dried and ironed.

'Who's washing is this?'

'From Viscount Huntingdon's house.'

'Really?'

He confirmed that my shop was recommended by a Mr William Harding, so they were giving it a try. I was still skivvying for the upper-class. But I welcomed the business.

'When will it be ready for collection?'

'Tomorrow?'

'That soon? Wonderful. The housekeeper will be pleased.'

The next day, a Bentley pulled up, with washing from the home of the Marquess of Aylesbury. The next day more came from another high-class house. I was struggling to cope with it all in the end. I worked night and day, keeping the children with me in the shop when they weren't in school or with Alan.

But it was my business.

What I did.

Chapter Twenty-two

It wasn't long before I could afford one of the latest Bendix Deluxe front-loading washing machines and an automatic dryer. I had them plumbed in properly and didn't have to have water pipes running all over the place. I installed some chairs and a couple of tables and tarted up the kitchen and sold tea and snacks to anyone who wanted to wait, and the little shop soon became a local meeting place for gossiping and chinwagging and some days there would be queues waiting for their washing. Some didn't bring washing at all, just came in for a cup of tea and some company. But it was getting too much for me, so I had another two front-loaders and another dryer installed and employed a girl to help me out.

I was too busy building up the washing and ironing business to worry much about Alan and, as I wasn't going round other people's houses any more, he was happy that I'd stopped 'soliciting'. And anyway, as long as I kept picking winners for him, I could do whatever I wanted. The 1940s rolled into the 1950s and Estelle grew up enough to go to school with the other two. I had six front-loaders now and four automatic dryers and I expanded the kitchen into a cafe. The latest trend in America was for Laundromats and Wash-A-Terias, as they called them, where the machines were coin-operated and people came in and did their own washing and drying and all you had to do was come round and collect the cash. But they still hadn't invented a machine for doing the ironing. and I didn't think they ever would.

My mother died in 1952. She was only fifty-one, but the hard life she lived finally took its toll on her and she gave up the ghost and followed my father to the Summerlands. I went back up to Llangynwyd for the funeral and I brought the children with me – Charlotte was ten and Daniel was nine and Estelle was five. I was thirty-four. We travelled by car, because Alan had taught me to drive and I bought myself a second-hand Vauxhall Velox saloon. The wake was over by the time we arrived and I didn't want the children to have to walk behind the coffin in the old way. So I drove to the cemetery, behind the mourners, and told them to stay in the car while the gravediggers threw the clay in on top of her.

Take me now, take me now
for to face the Summerlands
By the earth and wind and the fire and rain
I'm on my way, remember me.

We went back to the house afterwards and I stayed overnight with my brother and sisters and Walter's family and my children and the house was full of little voices and laughter like it used to be when we were young. I'm sure my mother would have liked that. Gwyneth was a qualified nurse now and living in Cardiff and Bronwyn was a teacher and the only one left living in the house, now that mother was gone. They were all talking about leaving Wales for the big new world out there, now that our parents were dead. The house was owned by the government after nationalisation of the coal mines in 1947 and was now classed as a council house and would have to be handed back if Bronwyn left. We drank some beer that night and sang some songs and remembered our childhood, and the ghosts of those ragged children stood outside on the dark street and looked in through the warm windows.

The next day I left the kids in Bronwyn's care and drove out to Monica Reynolds's house. I pulled up in the gravelled driveway that I'd trudged along when I was fifteen with the green hat in my hand – nearly twenty years ago. I climbed the six red-brick steps to the front door, which was painted navy-blue now and not green, like the first time I saw it. I knocked and waited, half expecting Monica to come sashaying out, smoking a cigarette in a long black holder and sipping a Martini, wearing a backless Madeleine Vionnet dress and smiling with those big white teeth of hers. 'What's up, honey?' I could hear the words, drifting down the years. But the door was opened by a dour-looking woman about my age with straight black hair and wearing a rather plain land-girl dress.

'Can I help you?'

'I was looking for Monica.'

'Monica?'

'Mrs Reynolds.'

She didn't seem to know who I was talking about.

'She's American, married to Arthur Reynolds, coal exporter?'

'I'm afraid I don't know who you mean.'

'Sorry to trouble you.'

I started to walk back to the car.

'You could ask at the estate agents in Maesteg. We bought this house from Mr Williams. Maybe they could...'

'Thank you.'

What was the point? She wasn't here and I had to get back to London. And, anyway, she'd be sixty now, if she was still alive. I asked my sisters and brother about Monica Reynolds, but they didn't know anything about her – except that she came to our house one snowy night when my foot was in a bad way and she sat on my bed. But they never saw her again after that, or knew where she went – back to America probably.

Probably.

Next morning we said our goodbyes and I drove back to London with the children.

I was really interested in these new coin-operated washing shops. One of them had opened up at Queensway in Bayswater and I went along to take a look. It was called a launderette. It had six coin-operated washing machines and four coin-operated dryers. There was one person manning the place, to provide advice on how to use the machines and change for the customers. They didn't offer an ironing service, just washing and drying, and this was where I had an advantage – the personal touch, which was lacking in this place. I talked to the woman who was manning the Queensway launderette, but she didn't know much about the business side of things. She was just employed by the absent owners. So I set about investigating. There were two ways it could be done. I could lease the machines on a franchise for a five-year period, with a six-month deposit payable in advance – there would also be the expense of refurbishing the shop, installing flues and air vents and new power sockets and an extractor to remove excess water. The owners would be responsible for the maintenance of the machines and I'd get a percentage of the profits for running the place. The other option was to fit out my own launderette, which I preferred to do – but I'd need new premises and the machines were way out of my price range. With renting or a franchise, I'd be going back to working for someone else and I'd had enough of that in my life. If I was going to be a skivvy, I'd be my own skivvy and not someone else's.

But there wasn't any way I could get enough money for new premises and the machines and refurbishment I needed. Alan would be no help; he was still losing all his money, even with the winners I picked out for him. But I knew I'd have to act fast. The launderette business was about to boom and I wanted to get in on the ground floor and not be left behind.

Then Alan was killed in a road accident.

It was January 1953 and he was driving in the Covent Garden area of the city. A double-decker bus driver lost control of his vehicle and rammed into Alan's car, driving him towards the pavement and pinning him against a telegraph pole. He died instantly.

Alan's mother and sister organised a requiem mass for him at Clerkenwell's Catholic Church of St Peter and Paul and he was buried at Bunhill Fields Burial Ground. The funeral was well-attended and there were several shady-looking characters present, who backed away from me and gave me the evil eye. The children came with me and we threw flowers into the grave. Despite his shortcomings in the husband and father department, we were genuinely sorry to see him go, especially in the way he did. He was only fifty.

About a month later, I received a letter from a firm of solicitors in Stephyns Chambers, Chancery Lane, asking me if I could come in for a meeting. I thought it must be something to do with money Alan owed, but how could I be held responsible for that? I went along while the children were at school and was shown into an office where a tall, beak-faced man was sitting behind a large mahogany desk. He stood up and shook my hand.

'Mrs Lane, how good of you to come in. Please, take a seat.'

I sat down, worried about whatever it was he wanted to see me about.

'We are acting solicitors for Mr Lane.'

'My husband?'

'Mr Joshua Lane, your late husband's father.'

He shuffled some papers on his desk and adjusted his spectacles.

'With the sad demise of your husband, the inheritance from his father's last will and testament passes to you.'

'To me?'

'Yes, you.'

'What about his mother and sister?'

'They have independent incomes from the estate. Mr Lane junior's inheritance passes to his next of kin, which is you, Mrs Lane.'

He explained that the terms of the will ensured that Alan could only take his inheritance as a monthly allowance and not as a lump sum. On his death, however, those terms altered and I could either continue to receive the monthly allowance or take the entire amount of the legacy.

'How much?'

'The monthly allowance is, at present, fifty pounds.'

'How much is the lump sum?'

'Twenty-five thousand pounds.'

It was a fortune!

'I'll take it all.'

Thank you.

I skipped out of the solicitor's office in Chancery Lane and did mental somersaults along the street. I was rich! My skivvying days were over. I could get a new premises and kit it all out as a proper launderette and let the people do their own washing and drying and I'd pay someone to do the ironing. I'd be a lady of leisure at last, like Miranda Bouchard and Monica Reynolds and all the others I'd slaved for over the years. I opened a business bank account and employed an accountant to look after all the paperwork. The children and I moved into a three-bedroom house in Holborn, like the ones I used to clean a few years earlier. I opened my first Wash 'n' Dry shop in Ilford Street in July 1953 and I sold my old Vauxhall Velox and bought a brand-new Humber Hawk.

But there was still one other thing I had to do.

I drove along the quiet street in Hampstead until I came to the house. I got out of the car and walked up to the front door. Mr Ayres didn't answer it this time, but another, younger butler. And he wasn't wearing the usual butler's attire, just an informal-looking suit.

'Yes?'

'I'm Mrs Lane. I'd like to see Mr Harding.'

'Do you have an appointment?'

'No, but I'm sure he'll see me. Tell him it's Anwyn.'

I looked down the flight of stone steps behind the black railings that led down to the basement at the side of the house. And I remembered coming here on that first day I arrived in London with all my naive hopes and expectations. The butler came back.

'Follow me.'

I didn't need to follow him. I knew every inch of this house, from top to bottom. He showed me into the library and I ran my fingers across the leather bindings while I waited. They were still there, the books on history and politics and exotic places around the world, the books about philosophy and

gold mining, the memoirs and encyclopaedias and novels and volumes of poetry. I
was still in love with this room. The dark
reddish stain on the bookcase hadn't come
back – or maybe it had and been removed
again several times since I came to clean it.

I turned and he was there.

'Do you remember, Anwyn?'

'Yes, I remember.'

He came closer, until I could feel his
breath on my face, smell the scent of sage
and cedarwood. I took an envelope out of
my pocket.

'I've come to return the money you loaned
me.'

'Can you afford it?'

'Yes.'

He took the envelope and put it into his
pocket, without counting the money, then
he went over to the library door and looked
back at me.

'Should I lock the door, Anwyn?'

'In case someone should come in?'

'Precisely.'

I nodded my head. My legs felt a little
trembly as he turned the key in the lock and
slipped it into his waistcoat pocket. Then he
came back across the room – slowly, deliberately – smiling with the same straight teeth
and seductive scent and the words that were
blown like kisses. And I felt like I was beautiful and glamorous and drinking from a

stemmed glass with a green berry and smoking a cigarette from a long black holder and he was seduced by the situation – entranced by my aura – overcome by my all-pervading presence. Then his hands cupped my face, gently, caressingly. His green eyes looked deep into mine, and mine looked back and into his soul. His lips were as gentle as before, barely touching mine, brushing mine, while his right hand moved slowly down my body to my breast. His left hand moved to the nape of my neck and then down along my spine to my waist. I whispered something he didn't understand and had no need to – words that meant the same thing in any language.

William Harding was in his mid-fifties now, but he still had a powerful presence and I wanted him to know me, who I had become – better than all the others. He made me feel those emotions again that I'd felt for the first time back then in this library. I felt alive – really alive, not just going through the motions. I felt eternal – part of everything, here in the library again with him.

He was less of a man than before – slighter, and without the light that shone from his eyes back then. He seemed to be carrying some sorrow and I knew it was for the loss of Miranda Bouchard. But he was still more of a man than any other I'd met and I was now a real woman. Not a fragile, incomplete avatar of someone I once was, but a woman with a more profound identity; with a soul that any man could float away on. A woman who needed no man to make her complete.

Despite the years, there was still something about him, not just the charisma or style or charm or the scent of sage and cedarwood – something else. I couldn't put my finger on what it was exactly but he had it and I wanted it. Or maybe it was just my fantasy and there really was nothing for him to give – nothing *of* him to give. Just something in my mind, what I wanted him to be. Was he nothing and was I something? What could there be between us, apart from a memory? I tried to tell myself that, not to be stupid, to push him away and remind him he was married. But I couldn't. I wanted to be here with him because there was nowhere else worth being right then. I knew of his erstwhile reputation – the old rumours. But there had to be more to a man than his reputation – maybe he didn't even know what he was himself any more. And that didn't make it any less there. The thing about him.

He moved his left hand inside my blouse and across my bare back. I closed my eyes. He kept speaking all the time as if to reassure me and his voice was like velvet as he lowered me down to the carpeted floor. This time there was no apprehension. I wasn't drowning in expectation and my breath didn't come in short gasps and my voice sounded calm and self-assured.

It was growing dark in the library as the evening closed in and William Harding removed my clothes and I removed his. No sounds came from outside the locked door – it was as if there was nobody else in the whole house except the two of us. His hands retraced the patterns they'd made before and his body seemed to know mine from the first time they'd met. All thoughts of who we once were flowed away on the tide of sensuality that washed over us – embraced us – in its egalitarian grip. And, when it was over, he rose and lit a cigarette and poured two glasses of sherry from a decanter on the table. We sat opposite each other in the high-backed, studded leather chairs and sipped the sherry without speaking for a long while.

Then he asked me how my little shop was doing and I told him about Alan being killed and me inheriting his money and how I'd opened my first launderette.

'First?'

'Yes. I want to own a chain of them.'

'How ambitious.'

'Why shouldn't I be ambitious? It's not the preserve of the rich and titled any more, you know.'

'I'm sorry. I didn't mean–'

He leaned over to pour more sherry, but I placed my hand over my glass.

'I'm driving.'

Then I stood up and we shook hands. He gave me the key and I walked to the door. I turned and took a last look back – at a man who represented so much to me once, but who now looked rather forlorn. Like his world that was fading into the past.

I unlocked the door and stepped out into the future.

I never saw William Harding again.

Epilogue

The Wash 'n' Drys went from strength to strength in the rest of the 1950s and into the 1960s. I opened a chain of eight launderettes all around London and I worked in the business doing service washes and ironing, even though I said I wouldn't and I'd let someone else do the slogging. I suppose I was never cut out to be a lady of leisure. My children grew up and went to college and I found myself alone again. I still limped badly and the girls in the shops called me Limp Along Leslie after the character in the *Wizard* comics who had one leg longer than the other. I didn't mind, they didn't mean it in a nasty way – more a term of endearment. And I had many a nickname for the people I'd come into contact with over the years.

One of the launderettes was next to an Italian restaurant in Islington and, whenever I went up there, the Italian owner would pester me to go out with him. He'd sometimes sneak up behind me and put his arms round my waist – and that was all right until once when I was standing there daydreaming and he did it and, for a split second, I thought I was back in Finsbury and it was Alan. So I reached back and grabbed him by the goolies and he howled his head off. He left me alone after that.

I was what they called a wealthy widow and still only forty-two in 1960 and many's the man who tried his luck with me and got nowhere. I was spoiled for them all by the two men who influenced me most – Alan Lane, who made my life a misery, but who gave me my beautiful children and then left me everything I needed to achieve my goals. Ironic, eh? And William Harding, who introduced me to a deeper passion and knowledge of who I was capable of being – until I realised that it wasn't him at all. He was the catalyst, but ultimately he was an ineffectual man and the true measure of me lay within myself. Both these men contributed in their own very different ways to the woman I had become. Maybe if I'd met another man who was truly genuine, he might have changed me again. But I didn't. They were all just cyphers with no substance. So I stayed on my own.

My sister Gwyneth emigrated to Australia in the 1960s and my brother Walter went to Canada. Bronwyn continued to teach in Maesteg and live in our house in Llangynwyd until she got married to an Irishman and moved to County Cork with him. The house went back to the council and I don't know if it's still there or if it's been demolished to make way for modernity. I never went back to Wales because there was nothing there for me any more. The rest of my life was pretty uneventful. My daughter Charlotte went to university and became a doctor of some ology or other. She lives in America and has grandchildren now.

I went to that estate agents in Maesteg some years later and found out that Monica Reynolds divorced her husband Arthur and went back to America. She lived in New Jersey until she died at the age of eighty. On a visit to Charlotte and her family in 1979, I took a trip down to Philadelphia and found her burial place in a memorial garden. It had a headstone with the simple inscription: *Thank God I wasn't sober when I died.*

And I smiled. It was Monica.

Daniel joined the army in 1961 and he was killed in a helicopter crash three years later. He was buried with full military honours and the army gave me a medal to commemorate him and I always keep it close to me, wherever I go. When I die, I want it to be buried with me. Estelle went into the music business and I hardly knew where she was half the time. She moved to Australia in 1972 and she lives close to my sister Gwyneth out there. They've asked me to come live with them in New South Wales, would you believe? But I don't want to live in old South Wales, so why would I want to live in New South Wales?

Charlotte asked me to go live in America too, but I don't want to.

I'd rather stay here.

During the 1980s, when I was well into my sixties, I read a piece in one of the upmarket magazines I always kept in the launderettes to remind me of my days as a hat-shop girl and the inspiration and education those 1930s fashion magazines gave to me when I was so young and impressionable. Anyway, it was an article about the Earl and how he'd passed away at the good old age of eighty-nine. He died childless, even though he was married for a number of years to a woman who'd died tragically thirty years earlier. The Earl had been heartbroken and never re-married and now there was no heir to the title and it would expire. The woman fell from the top of the family home in Wiltshire. Nobody knew what she was doing up there and there were rumours back then of suicide. But the coroner returned a verdict of death by misadventure, due to the state of disrepair of the balustrade where she was accustomed to walking. She'd had several names during her short life – Miranda Brandon and Miranda Bouchard and Miranda Fitzroy when she married the Earl.

But never Miranda Harding.

I felt so very sad.

I kept going in the launderette business until I retired in 1990, then I sold the shops and moved out of London to Hertfordshire. The people who bought them turned them into coffee shops, I think – so they're not there any more. I bought a nice house with a garden and that's what I do, a bit of gardening. My grandchildren and great-grandchildren come to see me sometimes when they're over on holiday from Australia and America and I enjoy having them. I read a lot because I always loved books.

And now I've written one of my own.

I hope you like it.

Anwyn Moyle died on 1 May 2013. She
was ninety-four.
1 May is the pagan feast day of Belthane –
when the Lord has reunited with his Lady
and joins with her to beget the new Sun.

On the fragrant plain
On the mountain slopes
From sea to sea
And every river mouth
I am there
In the Circle

The publishers hope that this book has given you enjoyable reading. Large Print Books are especially designed to be as easy to see and hold as possible. If you wish a complete list of our books please ask at your local library or write directly to:

Magna Large Print Books
Magna House, Long Preston,
Skipton, North Yorkshire.
BD23 4ND

This Large Print Book, for people
who cannot read normal print,
is published under the auspices of

THE ULVERSCROFT FOUNDATION

... we hope you have enjoyed this book.
Please think for a moment about those
who have worse eyesight than you ...
and are unable to even read or enjoy
Large Print without great difficulty.

You can help them by sending a
donation, large or small, to:

**The Ulverscroft Foundation,
1, The Green, Bradgate Road,
Anstey, Leicestershire, LE7 7FU,
England.**
or request a copy of our brochure for
more details.

The Foundation will use all donations
to assist those people who are visually
impaired and need special attention
with medical research, diagnosis
and treatment.

Thank you very much for your help.